EXODUS
BURMA

EXODUS BURMA

THE BRITISH ESCAPE THROUGH THE JUNGLES OF DEATH 1942

FELICITY GOODALL

For Pat Givan
Godmother, mentor and friend

First published 2011

Spellmount, an imprint of
The History Press
The Mill, Brimscombe Port
Stroud, Gloucestershire, GL5 2QG
www.thehistorypress.co.uk

© Felicity Goodall, 2011

The right of Felicity Goodall to be identified as the Author
of this work has been asserted in accordance with the
Copyrights, Designs and Patents Act 1988.

British Library Cataloguing in Publication Data.
A catalogue record for this book is available from the British Library.

ISBN 978 0 7524 6092 5

Typesetting and origination by The History Press
Printed in EU for The History Press.

Contents

Acknowledgements

My name may be on the cover, but without the people below, this book would not have been possible. Principal among these is my godmother Pat Givan, and for her generosity and kindness I thank her. My husband Alan Denbigh, and sons Thomas and Stephen have supported and encouraged, and put up with long absences. My father Stephen Goodall lent books and shared recollections, and my niece Katie Pearson put up with me during my London research trips.

I am indebted to Roderick Suddaby, Keeper of Documents at The Imperial War Museum, who first pointed me in the direction of material on the trek out of Burma. It is a wonderful place to work thanks to the staff in the Reading Room, in particular Head of Documents and Sound Archives Tony Richards, and archivist Simon Offord. In another excellent institution, the British Library, I would like to thank the staff in the Asian and African Studies Reading Room, in particular Arlene Callender and Jeff Kattenhorn. Barbara Roe, Kevin Greenbank, and Annamaria Motrescu in the archives at the Centre of South Asian Studies at Cambridge University, were similarly helpful and accommodating, and for that I thank them. George Streatfeild and David Read at the Soldiers of Gloucestershire Museum were invaluable and traced references to Gordon Mellalieu. I would also like to thank all those who have given copyright permission, in particular Sterling Seagrave for permission to include extracts from *A Burma Surgeon* by his father Gordon Seagrave; Sir Eric Yarrow who also allowed me to use many of his photographs; Simon Stoker; Anthony Foucar; Anita Mountain; Jean Melville; Alan Scott. While every attempt has been made to contact copyright holders, I would like to extend my apologies if any individual or organisation has been overlooked and welcome any information or further contact (via my publishers) in regard to those responsible.

Many whose families were in Burma have shared photographs, documents and memories. In particular I would like to thank John Bostock who lent me photographs and documents; Les Halpin for giving me his father's account; Elephant Bill's niece Di Clarke who gave me many contacts; Pamela Backhouse for allowing me to quote from her mothers' papers; Yolande Rodda; and Diana Millington who also gave me much advice about the country today. Thanks are also due to the many people with whom I have corresponded via email, among them Patricia Herbert, Ron Findlay, Mark Steevens, Carol Horne, Ian Bootland, Nick Eades, Chris Eldon-Lee, and experts from the Oxford Centre for Refugee Studies for opinions, contacts and memories. I would also like to thank Jerry Quinn, Piers Storie-Pugh, Philippa Crockett of Raleigh International and Andrew Francis from UNHCR. Thanks are also due to my excellent guides in Burma. Finally I would like to thank my commissioning editor Jo de Vries, for sharing my enthusiasm for this story and the Forgotten War in general.

Preface

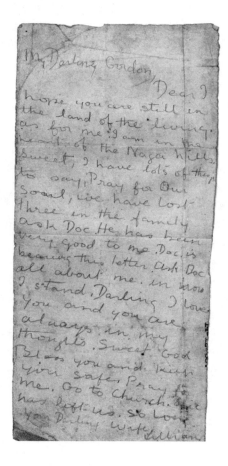

A torn scrap of paper, the size of a shopping list is one of the few relics to survive from an incredible journey made 70 years ago. There are 104 words written on it in pencil. The handwriting slopes down to the right, the address is written on the bottom and folded over, and the paper is slightly stained, but intact. It is a love letter from Lillian Mellalieu to her husband Gordon, a lance corporal in the British Army.

Lillian had walked over 300 miles across some of the harshest terrain in the world to escape from the Imperial Japanese Army. All those caught up in the war in the Far East knew of their fearsome reputation. Women could expect to be raped and disembowelled, soldiers from the 'land of the rising sun' did not believe in taking prisoners. In 1942, as the Japanese swept up through Burma, civilians fled into the jungle while the British Army fought soldiers considered amongst the best in the world, and lost. What the army did achieve, was to delay the enemy until the monsoon arrived. On 12 May the rain turned Burma into a vast paddy field; it forced the Japanese to abandon their pursuit of the army and consolidate their occupation of the land; it turned the escape of both army and civilians into a nightmare. Many of the refugees running from the enemy did not reach the safety of India for months. They clawed their way up steep mountainsides, through mud which sucked at their struggling feet, while they also battled starvation and disease. Lillian Mellalieu was one of those refugees.

Lillian's story began just before Christmas 1941. She and her two sisters, Ethel and Irene, were brought up at No. 2 Dalhousie Street, Moulmein, with their brother Eric. Moulmein lies 120 miles east from Rangoon, across the Gulf of Martaban, and then, as now, was a town famous for painted paper umbrellas. After the invasion of Burma, the entire family fled north with the Japanese Army close behind them. A thousand miles from home, deep in the Naga Hills between Burma and India, exhausted and starving, Lillian rummaged for a scrap of paper among her belongings. She found the remains of a piece of foolscap. On one side was a list of precious possessions: a silver bowl and tray. These treasures may have begun the journey wrapped in her bundle, but by this stage any non-essential items had been discarded. Lillian sat down to write the note to her husband:

My Darling Gordon,

Dear I hope you are still in the land of the living. As for me. I am in the heart of the Naga hills. Sweet I have lots of things to say, Pray for Our Soul, we have lost three in the family ask Doc. He has been very good to me. Doc is bearing this letter. Ask Doc all about me. In how I stand, Darling I love you and you are always in my thoughts. Sweet God Bless you and keep you safe. Pray for me. Go to Church. Eric has left us.

So long your Darling wife Lillian.

Gordon had also made the trek out of Burma. As a lance corporal in the 1st Battalion, The Gloucestershire Regiment (Glosters) he had been fighting the Japanese for 5 bloody months. His battalion was acting as rearguard, holding off the enemy while the rest of the British forces leap-frogged backwards in a staged retreat. Finally at the end of April the Glosters too turned and made for the hills. They had fought across the hot dusty plains of Burma, now they had to travel through the steamy leech-infested jungle to reach safety.

Gordon Mellalieu arrived over the Indian border on 23 April 1942. As a lance corporal in the medical corps he would have accompanied the wounded. Shortly afterwards he was sent to a base hospital in Lucknow. Lillian got as far as a refugee camp at the Naga village of Tarap Ga in the mountains between India and Burma. And there she remained, marooned in the dense jungle, unable to go any further because the rivers were too wide and deep to cross. She died in August 1942 at Tarap Ga, which may well have been where she wrote that last note. Her sister Irene was the only member of the family to survive, but she did not reach India until 20 October. Irene and hundreds of others had remained stranded in the Naga Hills, marooned by the monsoon rains which turned streams to torrents.

Lillian and Gordon's story is but one example of the tragedy of the flight from Burma. In the aftermath of the invasion anxious families wrote to the India Office asking for news. Refugees had poured over the 900-mile long frontier and dispersed all over India. The personal columns of *The Statesman* newspaper, which covered the region, were full of heartrending appeals for news of those who were 'last seen on the road at Shinbwiyang', or some other remote location. Rumour and misinformation sometimes thrust families into mourning, only to be reprieved later. In 1943, a group of volunteers gathered and cross-referenced the names of known casualties in an attempt to make a definitive record. This casualty list is now in the British Library. With it are the registers of those *known* to have arrived in India following the invasion. At the front of each volume is the caveat that this is an incomplete record of the actual numbers who fled from Burma in 1942. There are discrepancies, inaccuracies and omissions. Thousands of people died and have no known grave; others simply vanished into the jungle. The true scale of the exodus can never be accurately calculated, but reports made to the India Office by those who helped to run refugee camps in and after 1942, make the total figure at least half a million people. The majority of these were Indians; some 50,000 were of British origin. It was the only time the British have been true 'refugees': leaving all they possessed, walking into an unknown future and depending on handouts for survival.

Among the thousands of refugees who walked from Burma to India were two members of my mother's family. These cousins are known to have survived the ordeal but their story is a gaping hole in family archives. Perhaps, like other survivors, they had no wish to recall or record an experience in which they lost everything but their lives.

My father was a young lieutenant who almost lost his life in Burma at the crossing of the Irrawaddy River on 14 February 1945. His wristwatch, a 21st birthday present, saved his life. During the longest river crossing of the entire war, he was in charge of one of a fleet of plywood and canvas boats. The engine had been hit so they were attempting to row as Japanese guns fired from the cliffs ahead at Nyaung-U. Two hundred yards from shore, a bullet shattered my father's left wrist, deflected from severing the arteries by his metal wristwatch, which to this day lies at the bottom of the river. Nearly all his companions were killed or wounded. Despite his smashed forearm, 22-year-old Stephen Goodall abandoned the boat to swim. At this point the Irrawaddy is a mile wide, and my father was never a swimmer of any note. Thanks to the skilful hands of a military surgeon who rebuilt the wrist, the only legacy of these events is a 6in. scar up his forearm, and a deep faith in the God whose presence he felt as he swam. For his bravery, Stephen Goodall was awarded the Military Cross.

My father has never returned to Burma, but I travelled there on his behalf to see the country which became the major battlefield of the Pacific War. Burma is a country twice the size of Britain; a Golden Land which captivates and inspires; a visual and sensual feast warmed by the demeanour and generosity of its inhabitants. It is hard to leave and impossible to forget. How much harder must it have been for those Britons who had made their lives there. The scent of jasmine in an English garden evokes smiling children selling jasmine garlands at the roadside, and the rhythmic scratching of a street-cleaner's broom, echoes the early morning soundscape of every Burmese town and village.

Lillian Mellalieu and her family had spent their life in Burma, and she and her husband Gordon represent the warp and weft of this story, as civilians and soldiers shared the hardship of that journey to India. Sadly, Gordon Mellalieu did not receive his wife's letter. In 1943, Angus MacLean, Evacuation Welfare Officer for Refugees, tried to trace him. But such is the speed and unpredictability of war, when millions of men and women are mobilised, that the army failed to track him down. Later, Angus MacLean received a note from the Royal Army Medical Corps with whom Gordon had been serving. It simply stated that on 6 June 1944, Gordon was posted as missing presumed dead after the D-Day landings in North-West Europe. The War Graves Commission does not have a record of a grave and his name is not on a memorial, but there is a curious postscript to the story. In the summer of 1972, the men of The Gloucestershire Regiment commissioned a portrait of Colonel Bagot, their commanding officer during the retreat from Burma. One of those who donated was Gordon Mellalieu.

1

The Golden Land

When the globe was covered with large areas painted red to denote the British Empire, there were fabulous fortunes to be made by choosing a career in one of its outposts. The British had been exploiting the abundant natural resources of Burma (now Myanmar) since the mid-nineteenth century, and the depression which followed the Wall Street Crash of 1929 added to the numbers drawn to this huge country halfway around the world.

Fred Tizzard started life as the son of a Devon vicar and went on to become one of the captains of the Irrawaddy Flotilla Company (IFC), whose launches and paddle steamers carried parcels, pigs and passengers on Burma's two major rivers: the Irrawaddy and the Chindwin – the motorways of Burma. Like all ex-pats, Fred had first seen Rangoon from the water when he arrived on one of the many passenger liners which called there. From Tilbury Docks, it was a long voyage via the Suez Canal, before sailing upriver to Burma's capital city. The first glimpses of Burma were the paddy fields and mangrove swamps of the Delta. As the ship drew close to Rangoon, on either bank were rice mills, tin-roofed warehouses, wooden jetties and timber yards. Sampans bobbed on either side, each rowed by a man standing in the bows, and from the floating bazaar came the voices of women selling fruit and vegetables.

Fred Tizzard had arrived in Burma in 1926, and after 15 years of hard work and frugality, he and his wife Marjorie had created the 'home of our dreams'. A red-brick house beside the Kokin Lake, with cloisters on either side where they drank tea in the shade. Frangipani filled the tropical evenings with scent. Acacia, laburnum, myrtle and the blazing orange and yellow flowers of Flame of the Forest surrounded the garden. In the centre of the lawn stood a tree festooned with orchids, each plant collected from Fred's trips up the Chindwin River. On the drive stood a brand new Austin 7, and at the local yacht club a sailing boat waited for high days and holidays. In July 1941, they had a baby daughter, Rosemary Ann.

Fred was one of many Britons who had sought and made a career in colonial Burma. Unlike him, many hailed from Scotland and the names of the clans are scattered throughout Burma's history. There is even a Scottish church tucked in

Colonial architecture in the heart of Rangoon.

behind what was the Burma Athletic Association Football Ground, now Aung
San Stadium, the home of Yangon FC. Hogmanay was celebrated with nearly
as much fervour in Rangoon as it was in Glasgow. There is no evidence of those
links with Scotland today. Even the street names of the 1940s have been erased
from the city of Rangoon, no longer the capital and now known once again by
its Burmese name, Yangon.

However, in 1941 Rangoon was the centre of colonial life in Burma. The
British had built the grid of city streets around the Sule Pagoda, transforming a
riverside settlement of bamboo and palm leaf huts, into a showcase for empire and
commerce. All streets and avenues terminated at the river which curved benignly
past Strand Road where acres of go-downs, or warehouses, sheltered the produce
of this fertile area of the British Empire. Still gazing majestically over the dockside
is the Strand Hotel, where tourists can drink English 'Afternoon Tea', surrounded
by the ghosts of rubber planters. In their day, the Rangoon skyline was dominated
by the gold-plated Shwedagon Pagoda glinting in the morning sun. Today hotels
for foreign tourists intrude into the cityscape.

Inside the Strand
Hotel.

In the foreground of the city the solid palaces of colonial administration still line wide streets. Amongst them is the terracotta-walled Secretariat, a complex where pith-helmeted administrators in knee-length socks, shorts and ties, shuffled paper to run a country the size of France. The Secretariat's derelict grandness witnessed the assassination of Aung San in 1947, denying him his rightful place in Burmese history. The British first entered that history in 1824 to put the king of Burma in his place. Yet, it was the East India Company, not the British government, which sent a fleet up river to lay siege to Yangon, and discovered a settlement abandoned behind its defensive bamboo wall. Great Britain soon negotiated rights to the lower part of Burma, including the fertile delta where rice crops turned the paddy fields acid green. Sir Arthur Phayre was the first Commissioner of British Burma, arriving in 1862, to spend 5 years establishing British rule. When the present city was laid out in the 1880s, Sir Arthur's contribution was commemorated in the naming of the city's principal commercial street: Phayre Street. Today only the elderly remember which of the broad avenues it was; like other streets in the modern capital it now bears a Burmese name.

The iconic Shwedagon Pagoda. In colonial days most British refused to take their shoes off when entering, despite this being a customary sign of respect.

A surreptitious photograph of the Secretariat: photographs of government buildings, including schools, are forbidden in Burma.

With the British came their administration, honed in neighbouring India; their system of justice and retribution and most enduring of all, education. Encouraged by the British colonial overlords, missionaries arrived throughout the nineteenth century to open schools: American Baptists, Roman Catholics, Methodists and Anglicans. A university was opened to offer higher education to the brightest students and still stands on the campus established by the British. To run this new colonial acquisition an army of administrators, educators and traders was shipped in. However, Burma was not accorded the honour of its own civil service, police or judicial system. Instead it was suborned under the service which operated in India. So, the law was administered by members of the Indian Police, most famously one Eric Blair, who kept law and order in Katha on the Irrawaddy River for 3 years, before abandoning his career to become the writer known as George Orwell.

At the head of colonial society was the governor, an appointee from England, who relied on the professional bureaucrats of the Indian Civil Service for advice on the intricacies of his domain. These elite civil servants were the ruling class and were nicknamed the 'heaven-born', an indication of the exalted position they held in society. Key to this structure was the deputy commissioner or DC, a post created by the East India Company during their conquest by stealth of India in the late eighteenth century. The DC collected and assessed taxes, was judge and magistrate, and acted for the government when it came to law, order and disaster management.

These colonial officials would go out 'on tour' in the dry season between September and April, trekking round the districts on horseback. It was the only practical method to administer a country of Burma's size. With them went a team of servants to cook, set camp, fill the canvas bath with hot water and generally tend to the needs of the Europeans and their horses. Each tour lasted about 6 weeks, and for the entire period they were completely self-sufficient. Every day they shot for the pot and supplemented the game with fresh supplies bought from villages. It was idyllic, without the social restrictions of ex-pat life in the civil station where they were based. During the rainy season between June and September, the men of the Forestry Service and Civil Service returned to their bungalows to complete their paperwork.

With members of the Indian Civil Service came their personal servants: the syces (grooms), bearers and sweepers which the meritocracy had become accustomed to in India. The Burmese in contrast were regarded as work-shy by many of the English sahibs and memsahibs. These British overlords actively recruited labour first from China, then more successfully from India. From the south-east coast of India, thousands of labourers and agricultural workers joined Burma's rice industry particularly in the Delta region, and in the capital city Indians from all parts of the sub-continent were in the majority. A cyclone which hit India's south-east coast in 1897 saw a corresponding surge of migration, and

Rangoon High Court was built by the British. Many of its staff died in the trek out.

a number of famines had the same effect. While every Burmese farmer grew the rice that was one of Burma's greatest assets, it was the Indians who milled it, traded it and provided the crews to transport the crop. The last census of Burma under British rule, taken in 1931, revealed that 53 per cent of Rangoon's population of 1 million people was Indian. Rangoon was an Indian and European city, rather than Burmese.

With the Europeans and Indians came their religions. Rangoon today is still stuffed with places of worship: synagogues, mosques, Hindu and Buddhist temples, and Roman Catholic and Anglican churches. Burmese society is still noted for religious tolerance, and a pragmatic combination of Christianity coupled with animism, exists in many tribal areas. European and American missionaries made little dent in the faith of the Buddhist Burmese, but successfully converted thousands from tribes such as Kachin, Chin, Karen and Kayin. In Kayah State on the Thai border, it was the Italians who brought Christianity at the beginning of the eighteenth century; in Myitkyina and Bhamo, it was the French followed by Irish brothers from St Columban's Mission who proselytised, brought education and nursed the victims of leprosy. In these religious houses were men like Father James Stewart, who would become a hero of the refugee crisis, sheltering orphans as the Japanese marched into town. Later he served with the forerunner of the CIA behind the lines in occupied Burma. Another muscular Christian was cheroot-smoking David Patterson who started his career in Burma as a missionary teacher at St John's College, Shwebo. By 1942 he was a fighting padre for the retreating British Army, comforting the dying, as well as serving soldiers.

Burma boasts extraordinary natural assets: gold, silver, tin and tungsten, rubies, amber and jade to name but a few. This was a country in which to make a fortune, and many did. The trappings of western lifestyles accrued, such as Rangoon's Turf Club and the Pegu or PG Club where the European community gathered. Many Europeans lived in the substantial houses of Windermere Park, today appropriated by Burma's new elite. Then there was the Gymkhana Club which offered football, tennis, squash and rugby to its more athletic members, and billiards to those who were not. This was where the children of colonial families were brought by their nannies in the morning, to bathe and play in the shade. Similarly a club was established in every town housing a small European community. In these darkened buildings reserved solely for Europeans, uniformed servants served gin and tonic cooled by ice, when available, and ruminated over insignificant gossip. Among these colonial administrators so ruthlessly parodied in George Orwell's novel *Burmese Days*, were some who cared deeply about Burma and its people. Men who worked in the great silent teak forests, tending and harvesting the giant hardwood trees which were, and still are, Burma's greatest natural asset. Then there were teachers and lecturers whose legacy can still be traced in modern Burma. Men like Angus MacLean, Head of Mandalay Agricultural College who introduced nine avocado trees from California to an experimental farm at

Baptist worshippers are called to church with this bell made from a Second World War bomb case.

Taunggyi between the wars. Today the town is famous for avocados, and the fruit can be found growing all over Burma.

Burma's surviving infrastructure was planned and built by the British. In the middle of nowhere, a Burma Public Works Department bridge can still be spotted spanning a deep river bed, almost dry in high summer. With the advent of the rains in May it becomes impassable, and rural communities are thankful that British surveyors ordered such iron bridges to be forged in Leeds, and shipped 6,000 miles across the world. The railway, an idea pioneered by the British and transported all over the world, has changed little in Burma since it was built during the nineteenth century. Single track lines, many with old wooden railway sleepers, still puncture the countryside riding on low embankments, connecting communities and offering the poor, a cheap but uncomfortable mode of travel. The wooden stations were also built by the British, though the signs are in Burmese today and few trains and even fewer seats are on offer. In colonial days the stations, rolling stock and freight trains were run by Burma Railways with timetables, refreshment rooms and station staff who were almost invariably from the Anglo-Burmese community.

Like the colonial administrators who fathered them, much evidence of the Anglo-Burmese has been wiped from modern Myanmar, erased by history like a stigma of the empire they represent. As towns and cities have grown, old Christian burial grounds have been moved to new out-of-town locations. In the process headstones and brass plaques are lost and broken. Gravestones from recent burials contain the clues to a small continuing Anglo-Burmese presence, in the mixture of Burmese and European names. Still, just as it was before the Second World War, Burmese society is a marvellous mixture of ancestry. Some families trace their roots back to Portuguese traders in the sixteenth century, with a smattering of Indian blood to boot, all lost in the modern mixture of tribes which form the Union of Myanmar.

In colonial times, which the Burmese refer to as 'the time of the British', children of such mixed parentage could be and often were, an embarrassment and an inconvenience. Christian children's homes, given the soubriquet, orphanage, were founded to accommodate the offspring of colonial administrators and their 'unsuitable' liaisons with Burmese women. One such was the Bishop Strachan's Home in Rangoon. Men who passed the stiff exams to enter the Indian Civil Service and arrived in Burma were given dire warnings about becoming over familiar with 'dusky Burmese maidens'. William Halpin was deputy head of the government High School in Maymyo, the son of a geologist who had 'married' a Burmese woman. As a child he was left in the care of Roman Catholic clergy, who gave him the surname Halpin. His wife, Mary, was the child of a naval officer who 'married' a Burmese girl, but similarly was brought up by clergy. While their mothers sometimes had a role in the children's lives, their fathers were absent: they had returned to Britain, to a 'respectable' marriage with a woman of their own race and a second family. In the days of the decline of the British Empire, the Anglo-Burmese were looked down upon, and regarded as second-class citizens. Similarly the offspring of Anglo-Indian parentage were from an inferior 'caste' in the eyes of many in 'polite' society, or as they termed it 'not quite one of us'. Not all children of these mixed race unions were abandoned by their fathers and many of their descendants survive today. European men did not all simply take Burmese women as their mistresses like George Orwell's fictional forestry officer, Flory. Some married and set up home with Burmese women far from the snobbish drawing rooms of England. The Anglo-Indians and Anglo-Burmese were the backbone of the infrastructure in this corner of the empire. Not only the railways, but the Post and Telegraph Office (another British innovation), and many white collar jobs such as the civil service, customs and excise were the province of these two groups.

Rangoon was the colonial capital, but in summer British administrators decamped to the hill town of Maymyo. The town was founded by a Victorian

The Christian Cemetery, Maymyo.

Bengal infantry officer, Colonel May, on a limestone outcrop rising from the plain some 44 miles northeast of Mandalay. A handful of hilltop villages cooled by a gentle breeze, were transformed into the Burmese town in which the British felt most at home. Adopting the Burmese word for town, 'myo', it became known as May-town or Maymyo. They built teak or brick houses sporting British chimney stacks, and surrounded them with gardens in which they grew flowers familiar from home. Petunias, hollyhocks and pinks are still favoured bedding plants in both private gardens and municipal planting schemes in the town. A grand botanical garden was built by Turkish prisoners during the Great War. An historical conundrum to the Burmese today, as is the eponymy of the Harcourt Butler lake at its focus, named in honour of a long-forgotten colonial administrator. Paths were cut through the surrounding forests to provide shady bridleways where the servants of empire and their families could ride their horses. A tennis club, hospital and wooden bungalows for army families completed this British outpost. Two battalions from British regiments were garrisoned in Burma for tours of 3 years, and they would alternate between the gentile verdant atmosphere of Maymyo and the multicultural clamour of Rangoon. Modern

Maymyo Botanical Gardens laid out by the British.

A timber firm's former 'Chummery' in Maymyo, now a guesthouse.

Maymyo retains its military status, with the Burmese equivalent of Sandhurst prominent in the town. There were also officers from another very British 'army', the Salvation Army, who ran a home for soldiers. Today it is the Chinese and Burmese who seek the cooler air of the hill town, which has been renamed, Pyin U Lin. Second homes are springing up, and the towns' guesthouses and hotels do good business.

Colonial houses in Maymyo are plentiful and sought after in the property market, and there is no evidence of the hurried departure of thousands of British refugees seven decades ago. Yet there are legacies from 'the time of the British'. Leaving Maymyo heading north, the traveller passes suspiciously British-looking cows standing in the shade. Burmese bovines are distinctive with a hump across the withers and hide the colour of bleached wood. However, there are also smaller versions of the familiar black and white Freesians. The Burmese as a rule don't drink milk or eat cheese or butter. However, between the wars, Gurkha farmers from Nepal were attracted by the prospect of better land and an easier life, and since India and Burma were all ruled by the same masters, they emigrated. Their descendants still produce and deliver fresh milk which is sold in Maymyo. Despite living in a culture where milk consumption is historically alien, many Burmese are now adopting milk as a fashionable addition to the diet. The dairy cows themselves are descended from British stock, but are much smaller. Many Gurkha soldiers and their families chose to retire to Burma between the wars, and there are Gurkha communities in other parts of the country whose origins go back to 'the time of the British'.

Scottish companies were quick to forge links with the new colony, among them the Burmah Oil Company (BOC), which had the monopoly on Burmese oilfields until 1901 when Standard Oil joined them. Their main drilling operations were at Yenangyaung, a small town in Central Burma on the Irrawaddy River, where oil had been dug out by hand since the eighteenth century. A forest of wooden derricks grew up and by 1940 there were more than 400 foreign oil workers and their families based there, as well as many local employees. BOC built bungalows for its employees, as well as a hospital and a club, plus a company airstrip a little further south at Magwe. The colonial lifestyle enjoyed by the Europeans based there revolved around tennis, tea parties and 'calling cards' – a practice more familiar to us from the era of Oscar Wilde. Company wives socialised with other Europeans, and although there were Anglo-Burmese and Anglo-Indians, *they* were very much looked down upon by the class-obsessed British. Like the oil industry before and since, black gold brought high salaries and a privileged lifestyle to the British, and the handful of Americans who worked there. Today the oil is running out, and with it the prosperity of the town.

'Brown gold' was the nickname afforded to the teak which thrived on the steep hills all over Burma. Burmese teak is the best quality in the world and the country still has 70 per cent of the world's teak reserves. In the colonial era,

A colonial relic in the oil town of Yenanyaung.

teak extraction was a carefully managed and unmechanised business. Elephants provided the brawn to pull the vast trunks, some 40 metres tall, from forest to river where they were floated downstream. Forestry officers who worked with these enormous animals were a special breed, spending months in the forests which they got to know intimately. Camping in clearings beneath the shade of the enormous teak leaves, they were rugged, practical and far from civilisation, so were used to dealing with any situation thrown at them. So, too, were their wives and families, with husbands away from home for prolonged periods.

The giants of the forestry business were the Bombay Burma Trading Corporation (BBTC) and Steel Brothers; they looked after their employees well. Single young men were accommodated in 'Chummeries', spacious timber buildings with a bar and dining room, bed and bath where they received the comforts of home before returning to the forests. Geoff Bostock, manager of

A little piece of Surrey in the middle of Burma.

Bombay Burma, and his family lived in one of the most palatial private houses in Maymyo – Woodstock, which would be appropriated first for Chiang Kai Shek, leader of the Nationalist Chinese and British ally; subsequently by high-ranking Japanese officers; and today by Burma's own military elite.

These ex-pats lived a lifestyle few, apart from the upper middle classes, were accustomed to in Britain. Armies of servants catered for their needs: cooks and their assistants, nannies and nursemaids, drivers and gardeners. Many women found the only time they were able to look after their own children, was during the long voyage home via the Suez Canal, when the staff remained in Burma. Home leave was given every 3 or more years, and parents sent their offspring to boarding schools in Britain as soon as they were deemed old enough. When the world erupted with war, such families were separated for the duration. Those who worked in the Far East did not always return to Britain for home leave, choosing instead South Africa, New Zealand or Australia, wherever they were closest to at the time. Isolated in their colonial lives, friendships were cemented with the glue of shared experience, enduring down the generations.

What also endured, and perhaps surprisingly survived the ordeal of their escape from Burma, was affection for the land of bullock carts and bridges. The Golden Land left its imprint on Fred Tizzard, Angus MacLean and the other men and women in this story. Gilded memories were rekindled by the smell of jasmine or woodsmoke, evoking the days before their world was turned upside down by war.

2

An 'Unlikely' Attack

Seventy minutes before the Japanese bombed Pearl Harbor, they landed on a beach in Malaya, a few hundred miles from Burma. It was Pearl Harbor which made the news, but it was the landing of Japanese troops in Malaya that would turn half a million people into penniless refugees. The lightning advance of the Japanese Army from Malaya, through Thailand and into Burma, made thousands abandon their homes, jobs and possessions and walk west to India. Thousands died on the way. Entire families were wiped out by disease, starvation and exhaustion. Few spoke of their incredible journey, but they did keep diaries. Many precious items were discarded along the way, but the diaries remained in their packs. The daily routine of that diary entry imposed a sense of order in the midst of chaos. On 7 May 1942 as he trekked out of Burma, paddle steamer captain, Fred Tizzard considered the weight of his pack when he wrote:

> This diary is heavy, but I want to save it if I can. The other diaries that record the joy and sadness of each of us for a quarter of a century are all lost.
>
> FRED TIZZARD PAPERS, IWM

Forestry man Ritchie Gardiner, admitted that during his trek he became addicted to his diary:

> Though I started lukewarm, I found that the interest increased as the days went on and that it required the most discouraging conditions to make me either forget, or not desire, to write up the day's account. I really suspect that it began to be a substitute vice for alcohol (of which of course we had none) for every evening about sundown I would feel the urge to write come over me.
>
> RITCHIE GARDNER, MSS EUR A202 BRITISH LIBRARY

Old Burma hands, who recalled the events of December 1941, claimed that the Japanese community, which included dentists, doctors and photographers, had vanished 2 weeks before war in the Far East began. Certainly one Japanese resident,

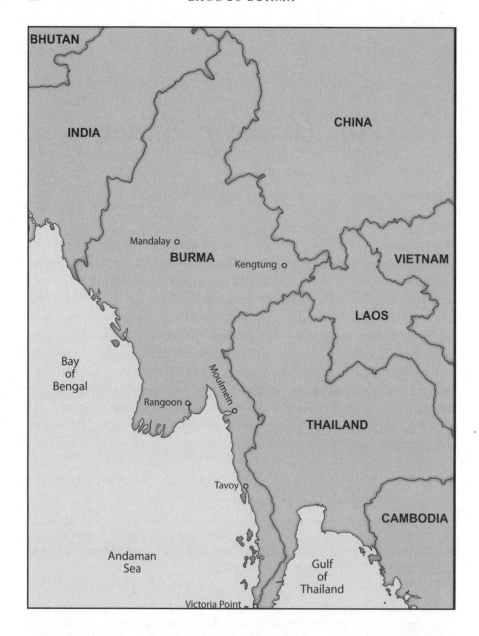

Madame Suzuki, left her home in Mandalay before war was declared and was heard broadcasting on Radio Tokyo soon afterwards. Most Japanese ex-pats had lived in Burma for 20 years and knew the countryside and its people well. It is possible that those who returned to Japan took with them maps of the jungle, trails and footpaths that were used by the invading army to move with devastating speed across the country. Indeed, suspicions of their former Japanese neighbours were uttered by many, but always with the benefit of hindsight. In reality local knowledge often

The Scottish Church in Rangoon is still maintained by Burmese Christians.

Fair weather roads have changed little since the time of the British.

came from the Burmese themselves. There was a growing independence movement, particularly among intellectuals[1] and monks or 'pongyis', as they watched events in India where self-government was talked about quite openly. Japanese propaganda wooed these dissidents with their slogan, 'Asia for the Asiatics'.[2]

Despite war being declared, most of the European community in Burma did not believe that it would come to their doorstep. Blackout curtains had gone

---

1   They ironically called themselves 'thakins', taking the Burmese word for master, often used to refer to Europeans.

2   We now know that Aung San, famous Burmese nationalist and father of Aung San Suu Kyi, was among the Company of Thirty leaders of the independence movement who received military training from Japan and marched alongside the invading Imperial Army, although he later switched sides and allied himself with the British.

up on 1 December 1941, but the restrictions of blackout were heavily resented. Services at the church, which served the large Scottish community working in Rangoon, were brought forward to 4.30pm so that people could get home before dark. Only 2 days earlier, according to diary entries, they had celebrated St Andrews Day with a traditional haggis imported from home and danced eight-some reels and 'stripped the willow' till 3am.[3] All over Burma events were held that night to raise money for the victims of Scottish air raids. Letters from home had brought vivid stories of the horrors of the Blitz. Parents had anguished about the wisdom of leaving their children in English boarding schools where they might be in danger, rather than bringing them home to school in Burma.[4] Few dreamt that they would soon be experiencing similar terrors.

Even the Government of Burma did not anticipate a Japanese invasion. Burma lay secure behind an 'impregnable' fortress – Singapore, which was in reality a partially fortified island standing guard over Malaya. However, the Japanese had four good reasons to invade Burma. By capturing Burma, they would cut off the supply line to China; thousands of lorries carrying Lend-Lease supplies[5] from America were landed at Rangoon, before heading north to Lashio and on to the Burma Road which took them to China. It was a thousand mile trip over terrible roads with hair-raising hairpin bends cut into the mountains on the far side of the Chinese border, but it was helping to keep China supplied in its long war with Japan. A second reason to invade was to protect the territory which Japan was rapidly consolidating to Burma's east: Thailand had kowtowed, Hong Kong was about to fall, Malaya was being overrun, although Singapore was standing firm. Burma was also the rice basket of Asia and stood at the back door to India, the jewel in the crown of the British Empire. Japan's empiric visions included throwing the British out of India. Invading armies had passed over the border between India and Burma in the past, although, admittedly, between the two countries lay some of the most difficult terrain in the world, crossed by a few 'fair weather roads', which in reality were barely more than tracks. The South West Monsoon every May transformed these tracks to swamps and mudslides, surrounded by steep mountains. Streams meandered through the valleys, swelling to impassable torrents with the rains. The forest and jungle between India and Burma was inhabited by tribes who subsisted on what little they grew. Even though the British had ruled parts of Burma for nearly a century, huge swathes of this border country were marked on the map as 'unsurveyed'. A Japanese invasion

---

3   Diary of Jean Melville, IWM.
4   Mrs Anne Farquharson to her parents, 16 May 1940, IWM.
5   Under the Lend-Lease Act, the US supplied war material to the United Kingdom, Soviet Union, China, France and other Allied nations, even before it became a combatant in December 1941.

of India via such terrain was regarded as so unlikely, that only 800[6] British soldiers were even stationed in Burma.

The British government had underestimated the ambition of Japan and more importantly the quality of her army. Those who had seen the Japanese forces in action knew they had witnessed a formidable fighting force. In 1904 General Sir Ian Hamilton was appointed military attaché in Japan. An experienced soldier, whose reputation was tarnished later by command at Gallipoli during the First World War, he wrote enthusiastically:

> Unless I am very much mistaken, this small nation, Eastern to the backbone, is about to testify by the mouth of her cannon that the six Great Powers are not all the world but only a part of it. [I am] staking the last poor shreds of my military reputation... upon a forecast that the Japanese Army, battalion for battalion, surpasses any European army, excepting only the British army at its best.
>
> A Staff Officer's Scrapbook by Sir Ian Hamilton

Three decades later, Japan invaded its mighty neighbour China, waging war over enormous expanses. Those who had heard of the atrocities committed against the Chinese, particularly the Rape of Nanking[7], knew that civilians had good cause to fear them. Nevertheless, the Government of Burma was unprepared for the storm which would be unleashed on its people. Before the Japanese campaigns in Malaya and the Philippines, his superiors informed General Archibald Wavell, Commander-in-Chief India, that 'an attack in force on Burma was unlikely'.[8]

The 'unlikely' attack on Burma commenced with a raid on a small airfield on the west coast of Burma's tail. Tavoy lies at the head of an estuary in the narrow strip between the Andaman Sea and Thailand. It was a town synonymous with tin and tungsten ore, an important raw material in weapons' manufacture. The Tavoy Tin Dredging Corporation and Consolidated Tin Mines of Burma were among the employers with a largely European technical and engineering staff, and hundreds of Indians who formed the bulk of the workforce. There were around 160 Europeans in the town itself, among them William Wood. He and his son were captured in Tavoy, but his wife Muriel and their daughter headed north. Mother and daughter were among those who died by the roadside during the trek to India.

Enemy planes bombed and machine-gunned Tavoy airfield on 11 December. The following day Japanese troops crossed the frontier and British troops guarding

---

6   Papers of General Hutton, IWM.
7   The Rape of Nanking, as it became known, was a six-week period of atrocities (including mass murder and rape) perpetrated by the Japanese against the residents of Nanking, China.
8   Papers of Colonel E.C.V. Foucar, commissioned to write an official history of the campaign.

an airfield at Burma's southernmost tip, Victoria Point, were ordered to pull out in what was billed as a 'strategic withdrawal'. On 13 December, the invasion began in earnest when Japanese troops landed from eight motorboats at Victoria Point. Enemy aircraft now had a base from which to raid more important targets, such as the seat of power in Rangoon.

The capital was unprepared. No deep shelters had been built, and what over-ground shelters there were could only house one-third of the city's 400,000 population. Robert Hutchings, the agent of the Government of India, had warned that evacuation plans should be made, particularly for over a million Indians living in Burma at the time.[9] After Japan signed a three-way pact with Nazi Germany and Italy on 27 September 1940, he foresaw the consequences this alliance might have for Burma. In October Hutchings called on the Government of India, and by extension therefore the British government, to warn Indians of the risks of remaining in Burma. He was particularly worried about thousands of seasonal migrant workers. He felt that they should be warned not to set out as they 'might be exposing themselves to potential risk not only of violent death and injury, but of hardship and unemployment owing to the dislocation of normal routine of the country'. He foresaw that 'they might not be able to return to India, owing to shipping and port difficulties, and to an exodus of persons already in Burma and wanting to return'. He was right, but he was ignored. The official reply to his requests meant death and hardship for thousands. In a confidential report written in 1942 after the exodus, Hutchings wrote:

> The view taken by His Majesty's government at the time was, however, that any action which might be taken either in India or Burma to suggest that an attack on Burma was regarded as certain, or even probable, should be avoided.
>
> REPORT OF THE AGENT OF THE GOVERNMENT OF INDIA IN BURMA

In Burma on 23 December 1941, Europeans were finishing their Christmas shopping and putting up traditional decorations. Scots-born Jean Melville and her sister were in Rowes department store in Rangoon:

> It had a really lovely toy shop. Amongst the offerings for the Christmas of 1941, they had displayed a fine electric train set with a layout of tunnels, bridges, shunting yards; the works.
>
> JEAN MELVILLE PAPERS, IWM

The air raid siren interrupted the peace at 10am. Whereas people on the British home front were well versed in air raid drill, those in Rangoon did not

---

9   1931 Census figures: 1,017,825 Indians (of which 617,521 had been born in Burma).

This bank in Rangoon was bombed by the Japanese in the raids of 1941.

understand that they should take cover, instead many went out into the streets to watch the show. To their delight twenty-four Japanese planes were shot down, but their bombs killed 1,000 of these sightseers and wounded another 2,000. Eyewitnesses reported the accuracy of enemy bombing, claiming this as evidence of fifth columnists. Watsons, a firm importing thousands of American trucks under the Lend-Lease Act, took a direct hit. More trucks destined for China, this time full of ammunition, were parked at the Brooking Street Wharf, another target. However, it was the incendiaries dropped on the wooden homes of the poor that did the most damage. Fortunately many Burmese fled to hide in the paddy fields surrounding the city. The war that few had believed would come to Burma had arrived. By the evening of 23 December, the road heading west from Rangoon was covered with a stream of refugees.

William Newton, a provincial doctor had been watching the build up of Allied troops near his practice in Kengtung, a small town in Burma's east, close to the Chinese border. Since June 1941 they had been arriving to bolster the area's defences, because this remote part of the Shan States was regarded as a likely invasion point. Tracks through the mountainous countryside were improved, supply dumps built and the Home Guard formed. Newton was sceptical that the Japanese would choose this inhospitable terrain as the gateway to Burma, but believed war with Japan was increasingly certain. In need of medical treatment, he left Kengtung in November and arrived a few days later in time for the Walter Locke Football Tournament. The victors were the Customs Club, whose goalie Bruce Stuart would survive the 400-mile trek to India. Newton's operation was scheduled for 8 December; it was cancelled. On 12 December the 55-year-old doctor was redeployed as Assistant Staff Surgeon for army headquarters (HQ) in Rangoon, where he witnessed the first air raid:

> The nerves of the people of Rangoon were severely shaken. Panic prevailed. They were leaving the city by their thousands. I have seen pictures of fleeing refugees and evacuees from Belgium and France during the last war, real ones passing through Shahrabahn in Mesopotamia in 1918, but they were *nothing* compared to these Indians and Chinese who were fleeing with all their possessions in gharries, carts, rickshaws, perambulators etc.
>
> Dr William Newton papers, IWM

As they fled, leaving the smoke and fire of Rangoon behind them, the city lost most of its workforce. Many of these refugees were the labourers, stevedores and dockers on which the prosperous port relied. Without them air raid shelters would not be built, bodies buried and rubble cleared. Jean Melville was horrified as she watched the refugees trailing out of the city.

The natives did not even stop to pick up their own dead, who were lying about all over the place shattered to pieces by Jap bombs. For days after the drains and sewers began to smell so badly, and as there were no conservancy coolies left in Rangoon it remained to some Europeans with the help of a few Indian and Burmese officials, to wash them out to prevent an epidemic of cholera or some such thing from breaking out. Later on conditions did improve a little. People came into Rangoon to work by day and slept outside at night, as at this time night raids had not begun. The market and other shops remained closed, and for several days we could not get any bread until government took a hand and forced certain food shops to open for so many hours a day to enable people to get supplies.

Fred Tizzard had worked with most of his crewmen for 12 years and after the first raid he was concerned for their safety. As he picked his way through the smoking city, he was passed by a horse-drawn hearse, the roof piled high with bedding and trunks. Inside the glass compartment sat a woman, her children and a parrot in a brass cage, all en route for India. The heaviest bombing had been down at the waterfront and the nearby crowded streets were inhabited by the Indian workers. Moored up at one of the pontoons was *Assam*, an express boat which worked up and down the Irrawaddy River. Its captain, chief engineer and the relief commander, Captain Ferris, had been watching the raid from the deck. One of the first bombs fell on the river mud close by. All three men were hit, only one survived. Captain Ferris was buried on Christmas Eve, in a rough unpainted box, lowered into a grave which his friends found ready-dug in the cemetery for someone else. Fred Tizzard was shocked at the number of casualties and wrote in his diary:

> The heaviest carnage was in streets lined with banks, commercial offices, [and] exclusive shops. They closed their doors when the raid began. There was nowhere for the nations to go. Inside heavy concrete walls they would have been immune from fragmentation bombs. True the stock of a high class jeweller might have fared badly with his shop packed with coolies living at mere subsistence level. But that is not why the doors were closed. There were no callous men, no disregard for human life. It was just that no one thought. No one was ready.

Rangoon was a city of many nationalities and languages. Europeans looked down on those they termed Eurasian, the Anglo-Indians or Anglo-Burmese. This was a society where class and social standing were paramount. However, the first raid on Rangoon is said to have changed that, and brought the community together to help the injured. It also changed Fred Tizzard, when war had broken out far away in Europe he had been a pacifist, but the prospect of enemy parachutists landing in Rangoon led him to pick up a gun to defend his family.

On Christmas Day as the chapel bell tolled at 8am, Fred and Marjorie Tizzard carried their daughter to the little Holy Cross Chapel near their home on Inya Road. Rangoon's second air raid blighted the day, but once it was over they held their usual party for the servant's children.

When the Christmas Day raid started, Jean Melville was at home before starting her shift as a hospital volunteer:

> The servants went out into the garden, the mali carrying on with watering the garden and refusing to get in shelter anywhere until suddenly he shouted and made a dash for under the trees. We looked up and saw about 30 or 40 Japanese planes flying to the north of our house making for Mingaladon [airfield] and at the same time we heard the noise of our AA gun fire and of bombs exploding. We dashed across the garden into the trench which was open and from which we could see the planes and see the puffs of smoke.

The 1st Battalion, Glosters were stationed at Mingaladon. Their pre-war role had been to quell riots and keep the peace. As the Christmas turkeys were roasting in the cookhouse ovens, the Glosters were forced to head for slit trenches to shelter from the Japanese planes. They emerged to find the cookhouse flattened. It was the Glosters, helped by volunteers, who toured the streets of Rangoon rescuing the wounded, clearing rubble and removing corpses.

Among the casualties were a mother and her new-born baby, killed when the maternity hospital was bombed. That night much of the indigenous population opted to return to their villages or to shelter in the paddy fields near the city. Women carried children on their backs and household goods piled on their heads in the traditional way. Despite such tragedy, the Government of Burma was determined to prevent the exodus of the Indian labour force which they relied on. Essential workers were forced back to work by soldiers armed with fixed bayonets and night guards were posted to prevent them attempting to escape. The Government of Burma had issued orders that people should 'Stay Put'. Europeans who lived outside Rangoon city centre found themselves besieged by friends wanting to store trunk-loads of valuables until the air raids were over.

Malcolm Taylor was one of the Anglo-Burmese community who joined the Burma Auxiliary Force[10] on Christmas Eve 1941. He was killed fighting for his homeland in February 1945. As Indian labourers abandoned homes and jobs to

10   The Burma Auxiliary Force (BAF), the equivalent of the British Territorial Army, was set up before the Pacific War.

walk to India, he was one of those sweeping the streets and clearing the rubble. When grocery stores shut up shop, as many of their owners became refugees, Malcolm was among those who helped distribute supplies to feed essential workers. By mid-January as the city defences were strengthened, he became part of an anti-aircraft battery, defending Rangoon's military airfield at Mingaladon. When the battery took a direct hit, it was 17-year-old volunteers who quite literally picked up the pieces of their former comrades.

3

Race, Racism and Retreat

It was racism which propelled the column of thousands of Indian refugees to leave their homes in Burma and return to the land of their ancestors. They were far more frightened of the Burmese than of the invading Japanese Army. The cause was the racial tension which had been gnawing at the foundations of Imperial Burma for half a century.

The British Empire was predicated on the superiority of the white ruling class. This does not mean to say that the thousands of Britons who served the empire in Burma were racist, merely that they served in a system which was in essence apartheid. At the top of the heap were the British, while at the bottom were the Burmese. The strata in-between were differentiated by a complicated caste system. There were what the British referred to as the 'better class of Indians', in other words those with education and money. Nadir Tyabji was one example. His father was a businessmen and an elected member of the nascent Burmese parliament, his mother had founded the Zeenat Islam Girls High School in Rangoon and the three of them lived comfortably. Nadir himself, who was twenty-nine when this story begins, spoke impeccable English and had his own car.

The 'better class of Indians' had a club to which Tyabji senior belonged, the Monday Afternoon Club, which aped the British gentlemen's clubs in London. The family mixed with others of the Indian elite such as the Raja of Zeyawaddy (originally known as plain Sahib Sinha from Patna), who had been gifted 20,000 acres of rich agricultural land by the British in the late nineteenth century. Sahib Sinha imported a workforce from Bihar to plough the paddy fields and tend the sugarcane, and their descendants still live there. The wider Indian community had been recruited by the British to help run this corner of their empire. Farm workers, street sweepers and domestic servants were at the bottom of the heap, and moneylenders, merchants and shopkeepers among the more middle class. In less than a century the British had encouraged over 3.5 million Indians[11] to

---

11 *The Burma Delta, Economic and Social Change on an Asian Rice Frontier 1852–1941* by Michael Adas (University of Wisconsin Press, 1974).

emigrate to Burma. Some came for a few years, bettered themselves and returned home. However, Burma was regarded by many from the poorer states as the land of opportunity. Just as the Irish left home during the famine of 1846–47, so the Indians abandoned famine-prone states bordering the Bay of Bengal for a new life. Immigration surges coincided with famine, cyclones and floods. Many of those who looked for a new life in Burma sent a large proportion of their wages home. One of the attractions was the booming port of Rangoon, and the fact that wages were not determined by caste but by the amount and type of work. A lower caste Indian from a poor village was able to better himself, just as immigrants have done for centuries all over the world.

Many migrants were seasonal workers. Indians who arrived to work in the paddy fields for the rice harvest between October and December could then move onto jobs in the rice mills and wharves in subsequent months. It is only a short voyage along the coast from Chittagong to the fertile delta region,

Brooking Street the heart of the Indian quarter in 1941 as the name on this house testifies.

thence on to Rangoon, so many ships such as those belonging to the Irrawaddy Flotilla Company were crewed by Indians. It was down at Rangoon's bustling wharves that racial tension first exploded into violence during an industrial dispute. What had started as tension between the Indian strikers and the Burmese strike-breakers escalated into a race riot; thousands were injured and several hundred killed. In 1938 troops from the Glosters were brought in to control rioters in another explosion of racial tension, which culminated in the gruesome beheading of Indians while praying in a temple in Rangoon. This outbreak of violence revealed the depth of the resentment between the immigrants and the Burmese, and the government attempted to introduce immigration controls. But the 'problem' as the Burmese viewed it, was now a largely resident population, many of whom were second and third generation.

In 1941 Nadir Tyabji saw signs of increased antipathy from the native Burmese population towards his fellow countrymen. He travelled widely with his job as representative for TOMCO, the Indian firm Tata Oil Mills, and knew the country well. In October as he travelled down the narrow coastal district of Tenasserim to Moulmein and Tavoy, tales were told of Japanese intelligence patrols penetrating the area:

> It was on this trip that I acquired a clearer idea of the implications of any turmoil created by a Japanese advance on the small Indian population in the area (mostly small shopkeepers and agricultural labour). I also got the feeling that the Burmese were just waiting for an opportunity to drive the Indians out and take their place in the scheme of things, however ill-equipped to do so. Up till then the Indians were a vital element in Burmese economy – urban and rural – providing a hardworking and cheap labour force for the vital sectors of Burmese economy – agriculture, rice milling, saw milling and transport. On the other hand it was the Indian trader, small or big, who provide the vast distribution and collection network in the rural centres and dominated trade and commerce in the urban centres. These people had begun to get restive and from odd bits of gossip which I picked up at Ye, it became evident that any Japanese advance from the south would result in a massive movement of Indians towards Rangoon as a take off point for the run to India, mainly by the sea route as the quickest and cheapest.
>
> NADIR TYABJI PAPERS, CENTRE OF SOUTH ASIAN STUDIES, UNIVERSITY OF CAMBRIDGE

Today it is estimated that there are 2.5 million people in Burma who are of Indian origin.[12] They are Burmese citizens, the descendants of those who made

---

12   Report of the Indian government's High Level Committee on the Indian Diaspora, Chapter 20.

the difficult choice to remain in the country which had become 'home'. Nadir Tyabji faced the same decision:

> The dilemma for the majority of Indians and other foreigners concerned the grim options offered by the situation, whether to stay back and make their peace with the Japanese or risk the hazards of a trek of some hundreds of miles with wives and children, braving all the horrors inherent in such a journey – lack of shelter and food, as well as disease – compounded by continuous Japanese air attacks and Burmese brigandage along the hill tracks further north. Of course, above everything else, was the clear realisation that a decision to move on, meant the end of a relatively comfortable lifestyle and abandoning not only a well established source of livelihood, but also the various assets created or gathered during their time in Burma. It would also mean starting a new life at the end of the road in India – a nebulous question mark in itself.

★   ★   ★

On Christmas Day 1941, all across the British Empire knots of people gathered round the wireless to hear the news from home. It was bleak. Western Europe lay beneath the Nazi heel; British towns and cities had been decimated by the Blitz; and the Russians were under siege. In the Far East, Japanese troops had moved relentlessly west and that night Hong Kong surrendered after a desperate and bloody battle. But there were high hopes that Fortress Singapore would hold, and Allied reinforcements were on their way.

Two days after Christmas, Major General Thomas Hutton stepped onto Burmese soil. He had been given the job to defend Burma and was horrified by the lack of troops at his disposal. The pre-war garrison consisted of two battalions, roughly 800 men – half from the Glosters, the rest from The King's Own Yorkshire Light Infantry (KOYLI). The Glosters had arrived in Burma in 1938, with their wives and families, to garrison Rangoon. With them came the regimental silver, a glittering record of 250 years' service around the world, which graced the officers' mess at dinners. Peacetime soldiering in Burma was a pleasant prospect of polo and parties, for the officers at least. As war with Japan loomed, many of these officers were 'borrowed' to transform the volunteers of the Burma Rifles into soldiers. By 1942, the Burma Rifles were not yet the hardened frontline troops needed to defend the country against the Japanese. To add to Hutton's problems, there were few aircraft, no intelligence, inadequate artillery and no administration. Add to this the anomaly that although Hutton was on the ground in Burma, the next link up his chain of command was in Java, an island over 2,000 miles away, currently under attack by the Japanese. Important decisions had to be sanctioned via Java, and a reply could easily take a week.

In the perfect weather which typifies Burma at the turn of the year, Hutton toured his new territory. Burma had few metalled roads on which to move an army with heavy guns, tanks and trucks. Reinforcements were anticipated and the only place for them to land was Rangoon. As Hutton took stock, December turned to January and the Japanese crossed a little-used frontier track, taking the mining village of Tavoy on 15 January. Meanwhile, the second prong of the Japanese attack was heading by road over the mountains towards Moulmein. They had to be slowed down if reinforcements were to land at Rangoon.

As Burma became a battlefield, hundreds of Indian tin miners and their families began trudging from Tavoy north to Rangoon. Heading the other way was the army. Bullock carts are wide, and unwieldy when loaded with possessions, but lorry loads of soldiers have to take precedence in time of war. It was a conflict of interest which would be replayed throughout the early months of 1942.

Captain John Graham came to Rangoon from the Punjab in December 1941. He and the rest of 16th Indian Infantry Brigade arrived piecemeal, as reinforcements for the regulars stationed in Burma. They had no jungle warfare training, did not speak the language or understand the religion and customs. Events moved so fast that before they could even begin jungle warfare training, they were sent to defend Moulmein, Burma's third largest city, only 50 miles by air south of Rangoon. As Captain Graham and his men travelled south, they passed through stations where platforms were crowded with hopeful refugees; all heading in the opposite direction, away from the advancing Japanese.

In the early hours of 13 January the train pulled into Martaban, 3 miles from their destination. Captain Graham tried to calm his men:

> As it grew lighter we saw utter devastation, smoking ruins, dead bodies in grotesque positions in the ruins of warehouses. There was no sign of life. It had bad effects on my group of young sepoys[13], some were only 15 years old.
>
> CAPTAIN JOHN GRAHAM PAPERS, IWM

Martaban had been bombed the day before. Nearby was Moulmein, with the outline of its enormous reclining white Buddha visible against the green vegetation. From here Graham and his men were heading up to guard a pass on the Thai border against possible Japanese incursion. As they steamed up river, Moulmein was bombed in their wake. Back on land they marched all night until they reached Kawkareik, a village on the narrow road that led to the 5,500ft high Kawkareik Pass.

These British and Indian troops had the odds stacked against them. There was no accurate intelligence and no up-to-date maps of the area; although the

---

13   A sepoy was an Indian soldier in the British Army.

legendary Gurkhas were also guarding the pass, the Indian Infantry brigade was largely untrained and communications were hopeless. Captain Graham, the Brigade Signals Officer, had to use the civilian telephone line to link up with headquarters because he lacked enough field cable. Wireless sets had a range of 10 miles and were fitted with glass valves, ideal for the dry conditions of the North-West Frontier where Graham and his men had been serving, but 'not suitable for conditions in Burma where atmospherics, dense jungle, and high hills caused wireless signals to fade and become inaudible'.[14]

The village of Myawaddy sits high in the Dawna Mountains almost astride the border with Thailand. On the night of 19 January, the village postmaster Mr Dutt radioed that enemy aircraft were taking off from Maesod airfield in Thailand. The Japanese had already crossed the border by a little used track 50 miles further south near Tavoy, but these planes heralded the main advance of the battle-hardened troops of the Japanese Fifteenth Army. Thanks to Mr Dutt's sharp eyes and ears, troops on the ground had some warning before they were bombed by Japanese Mitsubishi A6M3 Zero fighter planes. Japanese infantrymen moved so swiftly through the jungle that two companies of Gurkhas became separated in the confusion. In a tactic which would be repeated throughout the war, the Japanese launched attacks from thick jungle. The Gurkhas heard bangs and loud flashes like a ferocious thunderstorm, mingled with inhuman cries. Mortar bombs followed and the Japanese emerged lobbing grenades and firing automatics, led by an officer wielding a Samurai sword. This assault was repeated for 5 hours, while the Gurkhas were surrounded. Captain Eric Holdaway won the Military Cross as he and the survivors fought their way out, before melting into thick jungle. Despite the odds against them they managed to rejoin the main British forces a fortnight later. Meanwhile the valiant village postmaster smashed his wireless set and escaped into the jungle alone.

The attack at the Kawkareik Pass was assessed at the time by General Hutton as 'an isolated operation and not the first stage of a general offensive'.[15] Army headquarters still believed the Japanese attack would come via Kengtung in the Shan States and had based the bulk of the defending forces there. While the Gurkhas continued defending their position, Winston Churchill was sent a telegram by General Wavell, Hutton's superior, contending that 'a large scale effort against Burma seems improbable at present'.[16]

The Japanese attack from south and east intensified, as the strategic airfield at Moulmein became the next target. On the morning of 31 January, troops were pulled out of the town, leaving vast quantities of military stores and equipment behind. As the last steamer cast off from Mission Street Jetty, the Japanese reached the quayside. Artillery shells pounded ships as they pulled out into the estuary;

---

14   Captain John Graham, IWM 62/232/1.
15   India Office Records, British Library.
16   India Office Records, British Library.

one sank after a direct hit. A pair of sharp eyes gazing back to Moulmein might have spotted a group of Madras Sappers concealed beneath the jetty. These were the demolition men, always the last to withdraw after blowing up anything which might be of use to the enemy. They had disembarked from the last boat to allow a group of stragglers to take their place. It soon became obvious that no one was coming back for them, so they hunkered down beneath the jetty until dark. Above their heads, the Japanese were setting up guns to attack the departing ships. Under the enemy's noses, these sappers built a raft from petrol barrels, loaded their injured officer on 'deck' and swam the raft 3 miles under cover of darkness, to catch up with the retreating army.[17]

For most of the men in the defending army this was their first experience of battle. Partially trained and poorly equipped they were fighting an arguably far superior force. Reinforcements were desperately needed but Singapore's demand outranked theirs.

In order for troops to land at the docks in Rangoon, the port needed its workforce and they were heading for the hills. A column of thousands of refugees was walking northwest from Rangoon, bound for India. Robert Hutchings represented the interests of the Indian community in his position as agent for the Government of India. On Boxing Day he had offered 29-year-old Nadir Tyabji a new job as his assistant.

Hutchings and a few leaders from the Indian community went in hot pursuit of the refugees, armed with loudspeakers. So desperate was the need for labour that the Governor of Burma himself, Sir Reginald Dorman-Smith, put in an appearance. The head of the column reached Prome, 110 miles from Rangoon. Some of them had been camping outside Rangoon since the first air raid, and were already half starved and in no condition to attempt a long journey. Most were persuaded to turn back, given assurances of work and told they would be evacuated once the job was done. They returned to Rangoon by train at the government's expense.

Meanwhile news of the 'strategic' army retreat was filtering back to Rangoon. On moonlit nights, Mingaladon airfield, north of the city, was bombed. There were no searchlights in Rangoon and air defences were inadequate, in fact the anti-aircraft batteries took it in turns with the air force to defend the city on alternate nights. On 25 January Colonel Brock from the medical service assured his staff that there was 'no fear of Rangoon ever falling in to Japanese hands' and even urged those who were newly arrived in the city to unpack their belongings and make themselves at home.

As the Japanese pushed through from Thailand, Fred Tizzard, his wife and baby had left their home on Inya Road by the Kokin Lake, and gone to live on board

---

17   See p.215 *The Indian Engineers 1939–47* by Lt Col E. W. C. Sandes.

ship. The *Java* was a two-decked paddle steamer, with the upper deck on a light superstructure. As well as trying to come to terms with the realisation that their baby daughter had Down's Syndrome, on 21 January Fred Tizzard had heard on the wireless that the Japanese were near Moulmein.

> Today Marjorie jokes of her 'walk to India' and questions me about the route via Sitthaung and the difficulty of getting a baby out that way. But as I hear her pacing the saloon deck over my head I know there's a load of anxiety in her jokes. And I wish she were safe at Home – I doubt whether it were wise for her not to have gone to India. Possibly our lives are on the verge of tragedy.
>
> FRED TIZZARD PAPERS, IWM

Like many ex-pats, Marjorie Tizzard was reluctant to take ship for India and abandon her husband and a life she loved. Officially the Government of Burma had urged people to 'stay put', nevertheless the docks at Rangoon were crowded with would-be refugees. Rangoon was blessed with frequent and regular ships embarking for South Africa, Australia and India. Soon there were far more people than ships. Touts sold tickets at exorbitant prices. Bribery, extortion and corruption thrived. On 20 January the Government of Burma was forced to take ticket sales into their own hands. From his office in Phayre Street, the commercial heart of the city, Robert Hutchings kept tabs on the growing evacuation. The largest ship calling regularly at Rangoon was chartered to take 2,000 Indians and 800 Anglo-Indians hand-picked from lists prepared by community leaders. Passengers rendezvoused at the Burma Athletic Association football pitch, behind the station and were bussed to the docks. Piles of luggage blocked the gangways and as a result 150 people missed the boat. Of course charters such as this catered for those who could afford to buy a ticket. To prevent another exodus by the city's labour force, the Burma government ordered that no Indian male should be allowed to leave as a *deck* passenger. As wealthy Indians travelled *below* decks, it was an order that ensured the only way out for the poor was on foot.

It was European, and therefore white, women and children who had been given priority on ships leaving Rangoon. The policy of banning Indian males from travelling as deck passengers had been instigated to retain a workforce, but it was a move that was also seen by some as racist. European men were prevented from leaving Burma by a Defence Ordnance, although contemporary diaries and letters pour scorn on those who found excuses to leave 'on business', for urgent 'medical' appointments, or to 'settle children into school'. For some the dilemma was duty or safety. Inspector Shead of the Rangoon police and his family had bought tickets home, but when two ships were sunk by submarines on 23 January off Bassein they decided to stay put; this decision cost them their lives.

Throughout January Rangoon looked like a squatter camp. The city and its suburbs started to fill up with Indian refugees from the south and southeast; those from further north headed for the Rangoon–Mandalay road. Columns of refugees made an easy target for Japanese machine gunners, as their planes dived low to strafe the refugees with machine gun fire. There were inevitable casualties, and even bridges collapsed as panic-stricken refugees surged away from enemy bombers. Without Robert Hutchings and his assistant Nadir Tyabji the casualties would have been far worse. They must have made a striking duo: Hutchings over 6ft tall, whose impressive appearance was crowned with an aquiline nose; and Tyabji, slim and under 5ft. There was a mutual respect between the two men, and Hutchings knew how to delegate and trusted the younger man completely. Tyabji was despatched to Prome to sort out the refugee problem. As he headed north, he passed refugee camps every 20 miles. These had been set up by the Government of Burma and stocked with rice and salt. On 31 January 1942, over the 110 miles between Rangoon and Prome, he estimated there were 50,000 people on the road. The vast majority were travelling in groups according to the areas in India from which they had originated. Tyabji wrote afterwards:

Many had fled leaving behind substantial sums owing to them by employers. Almost none had any idea of the long and arduous trek ahead of them but then neither did I.

As January drew to a close, and the battle for Burma became more desperate, talk on the streets of Rangoon turned to cheap and easy means of escape. Leaflets began to circulate, suggesting a route via Prome, across the Irrawaddy River and along a track through the jungle hills of the Arakan up to the Taungup Pass, then down to the Bay of Bengal. From here small country boats could be hired as far as Akyab where passenger ships called en route to Chittagong in India. Officials at the Indian end of the route found that some refugees even walked to Akyab rather than take a boat. This was an option only for the fittest, as it added 22 days to the journey, whereas from Taungup to Akyab by country boat took 7–9 days and by motorboat 36 hours. The fishing village of Taungup was not equipped to cope with an influx of thousands of people. Only five shallow wells served the village, and the streams were tidal. If and when they arrived, there was no guarantee that refugees would find a boat to complete the last leg of the journey to Chittagong in India.

When he reached Prome, Nadir Tyabji suggested that refugees should be held there until the route could be checked out. The suggestion was not well received by local officials, or indeed the thousands of refugees, in fact there was almost a riot. Part of the explanation for this may have been the antipathy which refugees were experiencing from the Burmese. The Irrawaddy River is a substantial obstacle to cross without a boat, and Burmese police charged Indians to cross the river. After the event, Nadir Tyabji wrote:

> No one had any clear idea of the physical difficulties likely to be encountered by the refugees along the Prome-Taungup route. There was no positive information even in respect of the availability of water and suitable camp sites for such large numbers along the route. The attitude of the tribal population along the Prome-Taungup route, was another worrying factor about which nothing was known. It was obvious to me that the first few batches were likely to face tremendous problems. In the event the first batches of these ill-equipped men and women met with total disaster.

One person who had some inkling of the troubles which lay on the route ahead, was the local Forestry Officer Peter Burnside, who went off to survey the route

The Irrawaddy River at Prome – the enormous barrier that stopped so many Indians as they fled from Rangoon.

from Prome to Taungup. Burnside had seen his wife and family off to India from Akyab, and on 1 February set out to locate water supplies along the path. However, 4 days later, he heard that 880 refugees were almost on his tail. Today a rough B-road runs from Paungde to Taungup through the Arakan Yomas, almost certainly following much the same route as the refugees did in 1942. For most of the journey there is no water source immediately adjacent to the road. Peter Burnside had 6ft square reservoirs dug along the route, and set up rudimentary camps at settlements along the way. He also prepared separate camps for those attempting the journey with a bullock cart. His efforts to divert those on foot down to a narrow path which ran alongside a gushing stream came to nothing. He wrote later: 'Had they done so many lives would have been saved as the path along the stream was cool, easy going and there was unlimited good water.'[18]

Little help was given en route. The government did not supply food, and refugees had to carry provisions for the entire journey. Some families had left their homes in Rangoon at Christmas, and had been living in camps ever since. Their health was run down and they had run out of money. Like a wartime Robin Hood, Peter Burnside cajoled richer refugees to share what they had with their fellow travellers. Many of the rich were not refugees in the strict sense, but they came with cartloads moving house and home.

Cholera is a major killer in modern refugee camps, and in mid-February there was an outbreak at Prome. Officials there saw a way of making a fast buck, and every refugee was required to buy an inoculation certificate before setting out. Peter Burnside received the news by telegram, warning him that there would be a tidal surge of 2,000 refugees a day for 4 days in order to clear the camps at Prome. Instead the route was inundated with 21,000 people, and some of them brought cholera and the problems that came with it. Peter Burnside wrote:

> With the outbreak of cholera along the route at Taungup all labour along the road gradually deserted and so did the police at the camps and some of the first subordinates. Later the majority of the telegraph linesmen also left. One could not expect men to stay at their posts with decaying corpses all round them and no labour to dispose of them.
>
> GOVERNOR'S REPORT ON THE EVACUATION OF BURMA, APPENDIX V, BRITISH LIBRARY

Burnside offered free rations and inflated pay to any refugees willing to help dispose of the dead. The main incentive was priority passage on the first available boat.

The disposal of dead along the road was carried out mainly by sweepers of the Rangoon General Hospital. Here, however, there was a further problem:

---

18 Governor's Report on the Evacuation of Burma, Appendix V, British Library.

Country spirit[19] was needed by them to tackle corpses days old. Not enough spirit was available, but the local licensee was prepared to supply all we wanted at his own price. No go. Tried to conscript the Sandoway opium smokers for this work, but they bolted back the first night at Taungup.

   During all this period of death and disease, doctor after doctor came through Taungup and asked for a priority ticket to Akyab as he had orders (nothing written) to report as soon as possible. That they were rats leaving the country against the law was obvious, but I had enough to do having to threaten people for compulsory service.

Local staff at some of the refugee camps capitalised on the desperation of the Indians to get out of Burma. In the third week of February, Peter Burnside went to intervene, and the officials were so busy extracting money from the hapless refugees that they didn't even notice him.[20] No doubt spurred on by some of these incidents there were refugees who decided to attempt the journey on foot, north along the coast to Akyab, 40 miles or so from the Indian border. There was a route of sorts if they walked along the line of telegraph poles. So many refugees had congregated at Taungup that Burnside offered 10 days' rice supply to those willing to attempt the journey overland to Akyab instead.

   Meanwhile, boats that called at Taungup were almost overwhelmed as refugees attempted to board:

> There was always death by suffocation or drowning lurking around, the crowd were uncontrollable. To put women and children at the head of the jetty in order to get them on early and comfortably was of no avail. As soon as embarkation was started the crowd behind broke through and trampled on all and sundry, barbed wire around the lower deck of the jetty did not stop them; they came over it with torn clothes and flesh and this had to be removed. The crowd could be kept back only by severe beating. I mention this unhesitatingly as there having no doubt been many complaints of beating, but it had to be done to check the mob and wasn't approved of by any sensible person. The local police except for one or two men, were utterly useless, their main idea was to 'squeeze'.

Villagers charged exorbitant prices for rice as demand was so high, and at the height of the rush, the rich paid any price to get a boat, and the poor were unable to get away. Unscrupulous boat men were abandoning their passengers on Ramree Island claiming it was Akyab, in order to get back sooner for other fares. Those helping the refugees did try to prevent the problem by describing Akyab, but the Japanese

---

19   Moonshine – to bolster their resolve.
20   At Kyauktaga Camp on 23 February, Governor's Report on the Evacuation of Burma, Appendix V, British Library.

were already heading down to the coast and this was a problem that could only be solved from the sea. A young naval officer was assigned to deal with the issue.[21]

Hugh Brown had joined Burmah Oil as a management trainee in 1939, but by 1942 had been commissioned into the Burma Navy as a 1st Lieutenant. In early March he was sent on a special mission. At dead of night on the airstrip at Akyab, as Japanese planes rained bombs over their heads, he received his orders to rescue the refugees on Ramree Island. It was up to Hugh Brown to take a boat down and rescue them. It was an extraordinary humanitarian mission, given that the enemy had already taken Rangoon and was spreading west. He managed to scratch together a crew from those Indians loitering nearby, under the premise that they were sailing for Chittagong in India.

> As we passed out of the harbour mouth, the serang[22] put the helm over to starboard on a northerly course. I walked over and put it hard-a-port. This was a bad moment. If there was to be a mutiny, this was when it would happen. It did not which raised my opinion of the Chittagong sailorman. I told the serang where we were going and for what purpose, and that I relied on him and his men to help save the lives of his countrymen. They never let me down at any point though they had plenty of opportunity to do so.
>
> HUGH BROWN PAPERS, CENTRE OF SOUTH ASIAN STUDIES,
> UNIVERSITY OF CAMBRIDGE

At the approach to the village of Kyaukpu on Ramree Island, Hugh Brown could see the refugees, there were so many that the golden beaches appeared black with people:

> Like a tide they converged on the single rickety jetty, some leaping into the water and swimming towards us. I told the serang to go alongside and then to stand off, otherwise we'd be swamped. I jumped ashore, roaring at the crowds to sit down. Frantically they pressed down on me, those in front bulldozed by the throng behind them. I had no alternative but to lash out at the more able bodied among them until, in some trepidation, they retreated.

The refugees had picked the wrong man for a fight: Hugh Brown had won two national heavyweight boxing titles while he was still at Cambridge. Within minutes Brown found an elderly refugee who could speak English and had begun to resolve the situation. Through his interpreter he discovered that many Indian women had been raped and robbed on their journey through the Arakan.

---

21   Peter Burnside arrived in Chittagong on 27 March and after a short holiday was sent to help refugees emerging from the Hukawng Valley.
22   Indian term for boatswain.

Bandits, or as they were then termed, dacoits, are still a feature is some remote areas of Burma. Striking at night on poor roads they lie in wait for farmers on their return from market to rob them of the proceeds. In 1942 many instances of such attacks were reported, particularly during the refugee crisis which provided an opportunity for the unscrupulous.

The 23-year-old naval lieutenant began to distribute rice, dhal (dried lentils) and medical supplies from the government stores with the help of several doctors discovered among the refugees. Dysentery and fever were spreading, and the dead lay unburied. As he realised the enormity of the problem, Hugh Brown's ears detected the distinctive lilt of a Scots voice, and he was astonished to see a sergeant of the Cameron Highlanders and fifteen men, who had become separated from the main forces. With the help of the troops, latrines were dug and bodies buried; other armed stragglers joined them and the lieutenant realised that he had some firepower to deal with the bandits, and that night they lay in wait. Three men were caught in the act of ripping bracelets, nose and ear rings from an Indian woman. To make an example of them they were stripped, tied to trees and publicly beaten with a rope. Once punished, Hugh Brown let them go with the stark warning that they or anyone else caught again would be shot.

Like most Burmese villagers, the locals had fled deep into the jungle as hostilities drew close to them, spurred by the news that the Japanese had reached the fishing port of Taungup only a few miles across the water. However, the next morning there was a procession of people carrying food for the uninvited guests, and a message that the Japanese would remain at Taungup until the refugees had been evacuated. Hugh Brown was sceptical and decided to check for himself. Taking three soldiers, he headed for Taungup, but as they crossed the water they heard screams. Coasting into an isolated island, covered with dense jungle he watched as a Burmese dhow, crewed by Arakanese threw Indian refugees onto the island:

> The rifles of the Cameronians were trained on them and it was no problem to invite the boatmen ashore whilst returning the refugees to the boat, which we took in tow back to Kyaukpu. I neither knew nor cared what happened to the boatmen.

This was one of a few reported incidents, although there may have been others which went unreported. Arakan is the district closest to what is now Bangladesh, and racial tension is usually more strained in border areas. There were other cases of reported kindness to British troops and civilians as they fled from the Japanese. Sir Reginald Dorman-Smith sent a secret telegram to the Secretary of State for India summing up the picture in occupied territory in early February:

Reports from Tavoy do show that the Japanese are treating both Burmans and Indians in a friendly manner. Indeed they are going out of their way to carry their 'let's all be Asiatic together' policy. They are allowing people to leave occupied territory if they want to.

IOR/M/3/785 DORMAN-SMITH TO SECRETARY OF STATE FOR INDIA,

4 FEBRUARY 1942

The Japanese kept their word and under Hugh Brown's supervision an estimated 23,000 Indian refugees took specially chartered ships to India from Kyaukpu. By the time the first ship arrived, the refugees were extremely agitated:

When it arrived, panic set in among the refugees, and some tried to swim out into the Sound. This had to be stopped at all costs and the swimmers rounded up since there were sharks, barracudas and crocodiles in these waters.

An observer who saw the arrival of some of these refugees in India described them for an official government report:

They were in the last state of exhaustion from starvation. I understand that many did die on the beaches and on the ships....I saw some of these refugees when they arrived at Calcutta, and they could only be described as living skeletons.

GOVERNOR'S REPORT ON THE EVACUATION OF BURMA, APPENDIX V, BRITISH LIBRARY

Despite the difficulties, between 100,000 and 200,000 Indians escaped via the Taungup Pass.[23] Some 5,000 are known to have died. A few soldiers are also known to have escaped to India via the delta.

In the chaos of battle after the withdrawal from Pegu, Corporal Sword and about seventy other infantrymen found themselves behind Japanese lines. Realising that such a large group, including a number of wounded, would not be able to slip through undetected, they split into two groups. Both groups were making for Chittagong despite there being 'a mere chance of ever making it, as the west coast is noted for its enormous swamps'. Skirting round below Rangoon, the men managed to avoid enemy patrols, but by the fourth day they had to abandon Rifleman O'Calligan, who was badly wounded and slowing them down. They hired sampans to cross the Rangoon River, which the soldiers had to pay for out of their own pockets.

With a compass and small-scale map, Corporal Sword managed to navigate through the swamps of the Irrawaddy Delta. Some villages were friendly and

---

23   The Viceroy's private secretary G.S. Bozman of the Indian Overseas Department gave this figure in a report dated 14 May 1942. Hutchings estimated 100,000.

Traditional sampans still look the same but today are motorised.

offered rice, beer and cigarettes. In others, they hired bullock carts to save their feet which were blistered and swollen. The men struggled with fever and lack of food as they were forced to skirt towns and villages which had been occupied by the Japanese. Two weeks into the trek, they had a party of Burmese led by Japanese officers on their tail. It was time for a detour.

> We travelled through swamps, long grass for nearly ten miles. There we had to leave two men in a Karen[24] village as their feet were badly swollen and blistered, this reduced our number from twenty four to twenty two to carry on with the rest of our journey. We then made for the jungle so as to maintain good protection from aircraft, and the sweltering sun. We hope to make the coast in the next four days if we are lucky.
>
> 17 Army Ordnance personnel diary (Miscellaneous 90 Item 1324), IWM

In fact they sighted the coast 6 days later. They had spent 3 days climbing through the Arakan Hills, hacking their way through thick bamboo with swords, deprived of sleep thanks to intense cold and insects. When they finally reached Taungup after a 25-day journey they were greeted by hundreds of dead bodies: victims of cholera.

---

24   The Karen are a tribal people, also found in the north.

4

The Fall of Singapore

On 15 February 1942 Britons were devastated by the news that Singapore had fallen. The fortress once deemed impregnable had been taken by the Japanese along with thousands of prisoners. Many of these had been reinforcements arriving to bolster the garrison. Hardly had they set foot on land, than they were captured. A week later the Chiefs of Staff reported to the British cabinet, and made an urgent call for reinforcements to be despatched rapidly to Burma, citing its strategic importance in the region.

> Burma is the eastern outpost of the defence of India, the only supply line to China – whose resistance we must maintain, and a base for future offensive operations.
>
> CABINET OFFICE PAPERS, BRITISH LIBRARY, CAB 66/22/24

Exactly a week before the fall of Singapore, on 8 February, Burma's Governor, Sir Reginald Dorman-Smith, had broadcast on the wireless. Eagerly listeners tuned in, hoping for guidance. His message was that it was the 'intention and resolution' to hold Rangoon, and those not engaged in essential work were advised to 'disperse to areas less likely to be subject to enemy action'. Clear guidance this most certainly was not, but perhaps that was to be expected. Dorman-Smith had been flown in from blitzed Britain on 6 May 1941. Had he filled in a job application today, his experience wouldn't even have got him an interview. Irish-born, Harrow-educated, Dorman-Smith's interest was agriculture not the East, although he had served as an officer in the Indian Army. He won the Hampshire constituency of Petersfield in 1935, and in 1940 Neville Chamberlain made him Minister for Agriculture. It was he who instigated the hugely successful 'Dig for Victory' campaign. When Churchill took over from Chamberlain, Dorman-Smith was not offered a job in the new wartime coalition, instead he was despatched to a prestigious post in a backwater of the empire: Burma. It was to become a poisoned chalice. Dorman-Smith had come from besieged Britain, whose population was united in its aim to repulse the enemy. Burma was a country of tribes, British in name only, swallowed up by the British Empire in 1885, becoming part of neighbouring India. It was only after a series of bloody riots and attacks on the Indian population, that Burma won autonomy in 1937, but its civil servants were still members of the Indian Civil Service. As the Japanese armies swept across Asia, the Empire of the Rising Sun was offering a tasty carrot with the slogan: Asia for the Asiatics. It tempted many Burmese, particularly monks and intellectuals whose political sympathies lay with the movement for independence. One was the hero of the post-war independence struggle, and father of Aung San Suu Kyi: Aung San. The resultant Japanese occupation proved unpalatable, and Aung San's own actions reflected the reaction of many when he switched allegiance later in the war from Japan back to Burma's former Imperial masters.

Singapore made the headlines because of its reputation as an impregnable fortress, but it was the second great city to fall to the Japanese. The great trading centre of Hong Kong had been captured on 25 December 1941. A month later, Winston Churchill received a letter from anxious mother and MP's wife, Lady Georgette Lloyd, whose two daughters were out in Burma.

> I have two precious girls in Burma – they have an uncle (Sir Alan Lloyd) in Delhi, but they have flatly refused, and I'm proud of it, to leave Burma *until* the Governor orders them to.
>
> Sir Reginald Dorman-Smith is very recently appointed. He might imagine that a useless 'gesture' such as that made by the Governor of Hong Kong, would be admirable. I say it would be execrable, and inexcusable, and even the British

The statue of Aung San in the centre of Prome.

government must surely be capable of enough imagination to see where it – delay – may lead. For them, the British women in the East, it is no question of heroism; where are their arms to protect themselves, to take their lives if necessary? To die *fighting*, is given to our men out there. *What of our women?*

INDIA OFFICE RECORDS, BRITISH LIBRARY

In London, the Secretary of State for Burma received other letters from influential members of the establishment, asking about the policy of evacuation of women and children to India. Dorman-Smith, who had two daughters of his own in Burma,[25] refused to order the evacuation because, as he said in a secret telegram to the Secretary of State for Burma:

Morale has definitely deteriorated especially among the Indian community. Servants are now wanting to leave. Both [the capture of] Moulmein and rapid evacuation of European women have contributed. It is now being said that Europeans will look after themselves and leave others to their fate.

GOVERNOR OF BURMA TO SECRETARY OF STATE FOR BURMA, 4 FEBRUARY 1942

Still, the letters kept coming. A week later Dorman-Smith was asked again about evacuation policy; again the question originated with an MP; again he demurred. Steps were being taken to prepare an overland route, and an extra aeroplane was on offer from India, he replied. An unnamed official doubted that the overland route would be ready for many months, and in a scribbled note on the file scoffed, 'The addition of the additional civil aeroplane does not sound very impressive.'

The Governor says that no official encouragement [to evacuate] has been given because it would probably have a bad effect on morale. I think in the circumstances this decision is correct, but I have ascertained from the Commonwealth Office that there is pretty strong evidence that some cases of rape and murder of European women at the hands of the Japanese occurred in Hong Kong. The possibility of the same thing happening in Burma cannot therefore be overlooked, and in the event the question might be raised, why the evacuation of 'useless mouths' was not encouraged?

INDIA OFFICE RECORDS, BRITISH LIBRARY

In fact we now know that among the atrocities carried out at the capture of Hong Kong, was the rape and murder of female nursing staff, and the bayoneting of patients on the operating table. Yet, nothing was to be said to the concerned MP. In fact the governor of Burma did not *order* the evacuation of women and

25   Married to army officers, and in Bhamo at this time.

children from Burma to India at any point. For many European women their sense of duty and the desire to remain at the side of their husbands was paramount. Lady Dorman-Smith herself remained with the governor until the last possible moment, leaving Burma on one of the last flights.

Marjorie Tizzard had joined Fred aboard ship in January, also wishing to be at her husband's side. They had been discussing 'the walk to India' since the middle of January. Marjorie had almost died while giving birth to their daughter Rosemary in July, and was still not strong. With reports of hand to hand fighting in the streets of Singapore, the couple discussed their dilemma far into the night. Fred recorded in his diary:

> Now exit by sea or air is very difficult for her with a baby to carry, no one to help her and no place to go to. It would be a tremendous burden for her, not yet strong in body or nerve after last year's ordeal. We almost decide that she will go, talk of what she might manage to take. Seems a miserable end to our Burma life, which had just become comfortable.
>
> FRED TIZZARD PAPERS, IWM

The mood of those caught in Burma oscillated between optimism and pessimism. Jack Vorley was Director of Evacuation and his wife Helen worked with him as a volunteer, like many they were in denial about the fate of Rangoon, as she wrote later in 1942:

> About the 15th of February I packed up two boxes of our warm clothes, and two small boxes of silver and sent them off on one of the last boats. Actually when I put them on board I had no idea we were about to leave Rangoon, and merely put them on board to save them from bomb destruction, as I thought we'd probably be bombed to hell. Had I known what was going to happen I'd have tried to rescue my curtains, carpets, and all my photos, all of which were left behind.
>
> MRS VORLEY PAPERS, IWM

Events moved so rapidly, as did the Japanese Army, that those caught in their midst could not possibly be expected to predict the outcome. Communications were unreliable and rumours were rife, as thousands of people moved with the ebb and flow of war. Martyn Lees wrote of the last weeks of Rangoon as he and other Europeans knew it:

> Most European officers found work for themselves, our regular employment in most cases being no longer necessary or feasible. The best citizens got little away, fearing that by sending it openly they would cause alarm among servants.
>
> WING CO. J.B.G. BRADLEY PAPERS, IWM

Many treasured possessions were buried in trunks in the garden. Glass, silver and even antique furniture was buried under the garage floor by the Chief of the Rangoon Corporation Mr Walker.[26] Beloved family pets were taken to the vet to be put down, or were shot by their owners. Jean Melville's family gave their dogs, Cockle and Pickle, to soldiers before leaving. On 14 February the Melville family boarded the MV *Maruda* bound for India – there was no lifeboat drill and no life jackets. After 5 days at sea and two submarine alerts, the ship docked in Madras.

Streets in the business quarter of Rangoon became congested as lorries were loaded with records and furniture for the move 'up country' to Mandalay. The city's bankers were inundated with people transferring cash and securities to India, yet the government had made no official order to evacuate. The policy was to stay put: morale must be maintained at all costs. When the banks evacuated on 20 February after the 'E' (Evacuation) notice had gone up, they were criticised and accused of 'precipitating panic'. Yet, the American, Dutch and Chinese banks closed over a week earlier.

Director of Evacuation, Jack Vorley, would have been better informed than most, and decided at midnight on 18 February that his wife and female staff must be despatched north by train. The train took nearly 24 hours to reach Pyinmana, over halfway to Mandalay and safety. His capable wife gathered a hundred miscellaneous refugees under her wing, including the 'orphans' of the Bishop Strachan's Home. There was no food on the train but they managed to get breakfast at Pyinmana. Mrs Vorley was 'taking the dogs for a run' when she heard the distinctive sound of Japanese Zeros arriving to raid the town. The station was so crowded with refugees that few heard them approach. Throwing herself to the ground, she sheltered under a train and emerged unscathed. Two American Lend-Lease lorries and a jeep were commandeered for them, and Mrs Vorley and her rather battered charges continued to Mandalay. Mrs E.M. Bouché had been working for the army defending 'the land of milk and honey' as she affectionately referred to Burma. She was booked on a train from Rangoon to Mandalay, 250 miles away, with her parents and the rest of the family:

The train came at 3 o'clock and there was chaos. Reservation tickets were wrenched off, in fact, what should have been an empty train was filled beyond its capacity on arrival at Rangoon railway station. Civility was forgotten, people just pushed their way about knocking those in their way – no heed was paid to the womenfolk. Parents and children lost one another. There simply was no room for me and my family on this train.

MRS E.M. BOUCHÉ PAPERS, IWM

---

26 Jean Melville papers, IWM

Rangoon Station, an architectural fusion of east and west.

Robert Hutchings had his office in Phayre Street.

Eventually she secured a seat. It was the first in a succession of rail journeys:

> The journey from Rangoon was undertaken with women and children, including expectant mothers all huddled together in two open carriages – not only exposed to the cold and damp at night, but terrible heat by day as we entered the dry zone in middle Burma. There were no seats in the compartment and people took it in turns to sit on the carriage floor. Food was a very big problem as were sanitary arrangements. Some of those mothers sold their babies' artificial milk and used the money as bribes to get on the train.

On Friday 20 February 1942, 'E' notices were posted on trees and walls around Rangoon. This was the order to immobilise all but essential vehicles which henceforth carried an 'E' on the windscreen. This was not an order to evacuate, and it was not until 28 February that the 'W' (Warning) notice was posted, the signal for all except essential workers and last ditchers[27] to leave. The 'E' notice was however an admission that Lower Burma would not be held. On the same day, the Secretary of State for Burma telegrammed the governor urging him to consider offering further facilities for the evacuation of European women (other than those engaged in essential work) and children, from Burma to India:

> Could you consider the possibility of a plan for women and children making the journey by the existing track via Kalewa to Tamu without waiting for the construction of the road. It would of course involve the preparation of accommodation and provisions at each stage.
>
> INDIA OFFICE RECORDS, BRITISH LIBRARY

The Secretary of State had taken advice, and been told that this track would be suitable for women who were physically fit, if it was taken in short stages. Still, he was sensitive to the governor's concerns about morale:

> If such steps involved an appreciable danger of further weakening of morale, they might perhaps still be taken as unostentatiously as possible. Cabinet has not yet decided on question of giving publicity to Hong Kong story, but in any case it is bound to be known in Burma and here sooner or later and seems likely then to give rise to an agitation both there and here for evacuation.

In fact senior civil servant, Reginald Langham-Carter, recorded in his diary one month later on 26 March that the governor was still against any general evacuation.

---

27   Those assigned to ensuring that there was little left of use to the enemy when the city was finally evacuated.

One journalist, who was an eyewitness to the final days of Rangoon, described Dorman-Smith roaming the empty corridors of Government House alone. Less than a year after his arrival, it seemed as though Burma was slipping from his grasp. The entire infrastructure of the capital city had disintegrated.

Many of the police force had deserted and law and order had broken down. Martyn Lees made a sad farewell tour of Rangoon city centre:

> I went down to the station, which was a seething mass of Indians waiting for trains to take them out; from there I went to the sailing club to have a last look. The boats were all bobbing up and down at moorings on a lovely fresh breeze, and dinghies in the shed or drawn up along the shore below it. Not a soul in the place. The Club House just as it had been left, with two inches or so of beer in the glass beer barrel and a few used glasses on the counter. I bitterly resent the idea of a Jap sailing *Kittywake*.

Vivid stories were carried upriver by refugees, of fridges dragged out into the streets and jewellers looted. Fred Tizzard was miles up the Irrawaddy River on *Java*, but marked the day in his diary.

> HOME MAYBE LOOTED TODAY. Crowds of refugees at Prome and Padaung, cholera raging. We remember that our good brandy is left in the house and I miss the pretty things. Today want to fix up an electric fan for Marjorie, but the electric fittings I collected for years are in the house. Drinking water has run out. Item by item we remember the things we've lost and both grin over them. We left the new Bakelite vacuum.

The baby had completed visions of happy family days, but Fred confided his reservations on the page:

> I've assured Marjorie that I'm glad we have our baby. But am I? Marjorie had little hope of having a baby, was ready for disappointment, and by now would have overcome the brunt of it. But Rosemary is with us perhaps for always, just to do our best for her. I know that she's not as she should be. Marjorie hopes at night that she'll wake to find it all untrue – I that somehow the deficiency can be put right. We would miss baby, and are very fond of her, yet I wonder whether losing her might not be better for all three. It is pathetic when I see her wearing the pretty dresses Marjorie made in such love and hope.

Hope, for everyone in Burma, lay with reinforcements sailing across the Bay of Bengal. Some troops had already landed but were waiting for trucks to take them to the frontline. The Desert Rats of 7th Armoured Brigade were aboard a troopship destined to augment the defence of Singapore, when news came over the radio that the city had fallen. They diverted to Burma, docking at Rangoon on 21 February. As the British approached by road, the Japanese raced to get there via jungle tracks. Lightly equipped, unhampered by such luxuries as ambulances, the Japanese kept pace, fast and invisible. Eyewitnesses remember 21 February as extremely dry and hot. Thick clouds of red dust rose from the road as the British column drove along it making for the river. From above, the Flying Tigers of the American Volunteer Group and the Blenheims of the RAF attacked. They had been given intelligence that enemy troops were on the road, but it was a different road. Their view may well have been obscured by the dust. From the ground, soldiers saw their Allied markings and knew they had been the victims of friendly fire. From roadside jungle, the Japanese attacked the column with mortars and small arms fire. By the time the convoy reached the bridge many ambulances carrying wounded had been destroyed, and mules loaded with weapons and radio sets had bolted.

Traffic started to rumble across the bridge that evening, and it looked as if the remaining troops might have time to make it across the river. However, at dawn the Japanese reached the bridgehead, overrunning the main casualty clearing station. Counterattacking, the British pushed them back, and traffic continued across the bridge. It was chaos. Orders were given to destroy the 300 small boats gathered nearby, so the enemy could not make use of them. On the morning of 22 February came the turning point. A lorry swerved and wedged between the bridge girders. No more traffic could cross until it was disentangled. In the village nearby, and on the hills above, the Japanese were gaining ground. British troops were heavily outnumbered and communications almost impossible. Stragglers arrived with tales of ambush, scattered troops and wrecked transport. Believing most men were across, orders were given to blow the bridge when necessary: the Japanese must be halted at all costs. In the pre-dawn darkness, at 5.30am on 23 February 1942, the Sittang Bridge was blown up by the British.

Once the echo of explosives and crash of masonry and metal faded, there was utter silence. Most of the 3,000 British troops were trapped on the wrong side of the river. The silence was broken by jubilant Japanese cries, and the battle restarted. Colonel E.C.V. Foucar summed up the feelings of the men trapped on the wrong side of the bridge:

The alternatives facing them were grim. The 17th Division had now been fighting almost day and night for five weeks continuously in most difficult country, against a superior and far better trained enemy. They were exhausted after their recent efforts... and now they were attacked by two Japanese divisions, and their only line of withdrawal, the Sittang Bridge, had been destroyed.[28]

---

28   Colonel E.C.V. Foucar wrote a history of the first Burma campaign for the Director of Military Training and had access to many accounts and diaries.

At sun up, the damage to the bridge could be seen. The middle span had been blown. Although this was the dry season, the Sittang River still ran fast and deep. It was 500 yards to the west bank, daunting even for an experienced swimmer. Most Indian and Gurkha troops could not swim at all. Captain John Graham and other headquarters staff lashed together planks as makeshift rafts:

> There was chaos and confusion; hundreds of men throwing down their arms, equipment and clothing and taking to the water; some bringing their arms with them on improvised rafts. As we were crossing, the river was a mass of bobbing heads. We were attacked from the air and sniped at continuously from the east bank. Men were seen to cross and re-cross to bring over the wounded. Many drowned. Others who could not face the ordeal went back into the jungle and, working their way north, crossed the river higher up. Some went after dark to the bridge itself and constructed a lifeline across the gap. Although it was under fire, at least 300 men were saved in this way.

Communications were so difficult, that orders to withdraw had failed to reach some troops, who were on the far side of the village. They carried on holding back the Japanese throughout the afternoon. By 7.30pm they were ordered to pull back. Some reached the river and swam across, others were captured. Many were gunned down attempting the crossing. Lieutenant Colonel H.B. Owen, in command of the 2nd Battalion, the Duke of Wellington's Regiment, swam the river with a group of men. His body was found later in a hut, murdered, it was thought by pro-Japanese villagers.

The shattered remnants of the army gathered on the other bank. Many were without boots, sucked away by the waters of the Sittang River. As they trudged along the railway line to reach the rendezvous point, their bare feet were torn by the ballast. Wounded, half-clad and often unarmed, their morale too was shattered.

The disaster at Sittang Bridge signalled the end for Rangoon. Squabbling generals commanded and countermanded the final evacuation. Part of army headquarters set off for the hill town of Maymyo near Mandalay on 23 February. Dr Newton was among those retained with the main army headquarters in Rangoon. His entire working life had been spent in Burma:

> During the last fortnight, life in Rangoon was unbearable. The Japs were now advancing rapidly; our troops were having a hard time retreating and fighting a rearguard action. Orders for complete evacuation of Rangoon were being issued and countermanded. It was all very nerve wracking.

Rangoon was a ghost town, its broad avenues deserted. The only sounds were the occasional clank of machinery, as soldiers unloaded equipment at the docks or assembled vehicles from a patchwork of spare parts gleaned from all over the city. At night a different sound echoed through the streets, as packs of howling, starving dogs prowled the streets looking for food. Fires burnt every night. Birds of prey feasted on any carrion available. Banks, hotels and restaurants were closed, their staff taking refuge with their families in the countryside or in towns further north, away from the fighting. Knowing he was to leave the next morning, William Newton made a final pilgrimage to his old house:

> It was still untouched – the curtains were blowing in the breeze – the pictures, covered with dust, still hung on the walls – the packing cases and trunks containing our silver, glass, crockery, napery, linen etc – stood intact. The old clock was still ticking away and chimed the hour as I locked up the house for the last time. I cannot describe the feelings that came over me as I left all our treasured possessions in that house – things of such great sentimental value to us – things we had collected during 32 years of our married life. Enlargements of Bill and Barbara stood on the tables. Pictures of Bill's family. I had not the heart to destroy these things, nor indeed anything that meant so much to us. I could not possibly have carried away anything with me. A cat which belonged to our next door neighbour miaowed plaintively at me as I left the place; it had gone very thin; there was nothing I could do for it. It was all just too sad and melancholic for words.

Men from the Glosters kept some semblance of law and order, patrolling the empty streets day and night in jeeps. Looters were shot or arrested and brought back to the Mogul Guard Police Station, a gloomy building with small dark rooms which had become the centre of what was left of the administration. Reginald Langham-Carter was one of twelve civil servants left in the city. He was in charge of supplies. When stragglers from the Sittang Bridge disaster turned up, he did his best to feed and clothe them. Uncertainty and depression added to the strain of these last days in Rangoon. Dr Newton described these post-apocalyptic scenes:

> Two thousand convicts of the worst type had been set free to do what they liked with Rangoon. The inmates of the mental hospital were also released. It was pitiful to see these demented people roaming the deserted streets in search of food – people who had been fed and clothed and looked after for so many years, and were completely incapable of fending for themselves. The criminal and the crazy Burmans were setting fire to whatever they came across. Nobody was caught. Law and order had disappeared. British Officers shot the culprits when they came across them but there was nobody to remove the dead bodies. As night fell the sky was lit with fires; a crimson pall shrouded the city; the smell of death and charred wood pervaded the air of Rangoon. The light, power and water services were, however still functioning.

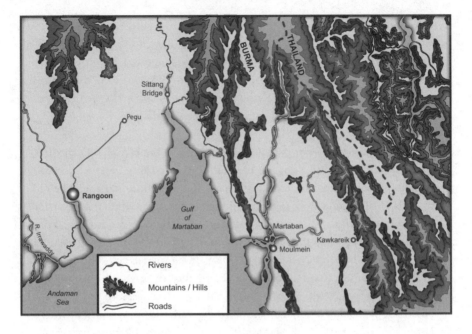

Rangoon mental hospital stood outside the city at Tadagale on the way to the airfield at Mingaladon, in fact not far from the notorious prison at Insein. Of the thousand people who had been cared for there, most had been released into the care of their families, a few others had been sent north to join the flow of refugees. By the time the 'E' notice went up only about fifty of the worst cases were still in residence, and the Indian staff was agitating to leave. A young civil servant was ordered to release the remainder, caused a furore by doing so and reacted by committing suicide, one of the last five officials who did so during the chaos of retreat. He had also taken responsibility for setting free the remaining prisoners. Political prisoners and men convicted of the most serious offences had been sent north to other prisons such as Katha. Several hundred from Rangoon Jail had been put to work in chain gangs cleaning up the city. Whether it really was the remaining ex-cons who were responsible for the lawless state into which Rangoon descended, was debated long after Burma had fallen to the Japanese. Yet, that was the perception of those who witnessed the final days of Rangoon in 1942.

The 'last ditchers' was the nickname given to civilians drafted in to ensure that when Rangoon was abandoned there was little which would be of use to the enemy. Herbert Murdock from Burmah Oil Company was one of ten men flown down to Rangoon to fire the oil refinery at Syriam. They flew in a 14-seater aircraft with a First World War machine gun sticking out of the back window as protection. Last ditchers were chosen for their ability to act under pressure, and were often accountants and office workers rather than labourers. After 2 weeks of preparation the 'D' signal for demolition finally went up and the last ditchers set to work. Armed with 14lb hammers they smashed and distorted pumps and pistons, finally setting fire to the 2 million gallon oil storage tank. With smoke obscuring the skyline, they piled onto a ferry already crowded with Indian troops.

Troops and boat crews waiting to evacuate stragglers indulged in a final drinking spree on looted liquor, while the empty streets echoed with gunfire. Expensive racehorses abandoned by their owners roamed the city, grazing the verges.

At 3.45am on 7 March the last ditchers were given orders to abandon Rangoon. They left wrecked wharves, docks and cranes to slow down the Japanese advance. As the boats from the Irrawaddy Flotilla Company fleet chugged out of the harbour for the last time, thick black smoke billowed high into the sky from the three oil refineries. Power stations, telephone and telegraph offices, petrol dumps and warehouses had all been blown up. The last job was to scuttle those IFC ships which were not moving upriver as part of the evacuation to Mandalay. Among the last ditchers to sail from Rangoon was Captain John Morton. In his report for the IFC board of directors he described their exit, only hours ahead of the Japanese occupying forces:

Many warehouses and wharves on the Yangon River survived the best efforts of the demolition men.

We sailed before dawn after a period of many days of unconscious strain and unreality. We had been ordered to come with nothing except what we stood up in, but were fortunate in most cases to bring a small quantity of hand gear. There were approximately 800 on board and the congestion can be imagined. We lived on tinned rations and a short issue of water, slept anywhere and remained unwashed for five days, nevertheless all thankful for this means of exit under the circumstances.

CAPTAIN MORTON PAPERS, IWM

A small number of Burmese servants had remained with the last ditchers and trusted them to help them escape. However, eyewitnesses saw an army officer refuse to let them board the ship, in case it meant there was no room for a British soldier. They were massacred on the jetty as the ship pulled out.[29]

Once the Japanese entered the deserted capital on 8 March, any chance to get to India by sea was effectively blocked. Small flotillas made the voyage to Akyab, still not occupied by the Japanese although largely deserted, among them was Martyn Lees who sailed from Bassein in the Irrawaddy Delta:

We came out in a fleet of 16 small craft – government river-going launches, IFC Delta launches, a couple of craft captured from the Japanese at Moulmein, the coal barge and other miscellaneous craft led by a sea-going launch in which the port officer Hawley acted as commodore of the fleet. It was roughish for the first day at sea, but the small craft rode the seas unexpectedly well, and it was lucky to have a coal barge with us, which enabled us to anchor a day short of Akyab and coal; some of us went ashore and bathed, quite in the atmosphere of the desert island of boy's fiction. We made Akyab on the fifth day, shepherded by a suspicious fighter plane.

The last ditchers believed that they had left Rangoon 'in a condition to offer little or nothing to our enemies', but they were wrong. The official report on scorched earth policy, compiled from air reconnaissance photographs for the India Office, reveals that the Japanese were quickly able to remedy much of the damage done.[30] The last ditchers made it safely to India, but many among them flew back to Burma to help with the war effort. They landed on the BOC airfield at Magwe which was the new home of the air force.

---

29   Reginald Langham-Carter Diary, British Library.
30   India Office Records, British Library.

5

The Road to Prome

North of Rangoon are the beautifully tended grounds of Taukkyan War Cemetery, where thousands of soldiers from the Forgotten War lie at rest. Many of the black marble gravestones honour unknown soldiers such was the ferocity of the war, and the intemperate nature of the country which became its battlefield. Central to this garden of remembrance is a vast colonnade, its massive stone pillars covered with the names of 27,000 men who died in Burma and have no known grave. So high are these pillars that it is impossible to read the names at the top. Among them somewhere are the names of men who died as they retreated up the road to Prome in March 1942. They were comrades of Alex Morrison, a veteran of North Africa:

Gone but not forgotten, the beautifully tended grounds of Taukkyan War Cemetery.

Life in North Africa was heaven compared to this place; there I had put up with sandstorms, winds that burn like hell till your lips swell up and crack open and your eyes become red and bloodshot. But I can vividly remember Burma, the rubber plantation, a clearing between the trees where dozens of men lay on the ground in rows, badly wounded, with not enough stretchers to go round, on one side being a canvas sheet between a couple of trees where a surgeon worked all night with an oil lamp, as he sawed off arms and legs, men dying like flies, others digging holes to roll them in, several bodies in one unmarked grave.

ALEX MORRISON PAPERS, IWM

These were the remnants of 7th Armoured Brigade who were attempting to fight their way out of Rangoon and head north. Gurkhas and tanks forced a way through the Japanese lines; the wounded were loaded into any available vehicle and, guarded by infantry and tanks, the convoy rolled out:

The final vehicle was being loaded with the last of the wounded who stood any chance of survival over a rough journey. All that were left were the dying, the unmoveable, the hopeless cases, rows of them; a medical officer was going round, giving each an injection of morphia. Over on one side of the clearing lay half a dozen corpses and as I watched about a dozen large vultures, massive birds who stood three or four feet high, were tearing them apart and eating them. Four medical orderlies drew lots to see which of them should stay behind with the wounded and await his fate at the hands of the Japs. By the sound of things they would not have long to wait – a few stray bullets ricocheted through the trees as the last vehicle pulled out and went off up the road. The three officers climbed into my car and as we left, one lone figure, a young medical orderly stood and saluted us.

The tanks lined both sides of the road as a protective shell, allowing the convoy of ambulances and cars to travel down the centre, then accelerate to a rendezvous a few miles further on. Inevitably ambulances received direct hits, but the tanks pushed the burning wreckage off the road to keep the convoy moving. Fighting the entire way the erstwhile Desert Rats made it to Prome 110 miles away.

The road to Prome is little better now than it was 70 years ago. North of Rangoon two main roads fork either side of a range of hills, the Bago Yomas which runs from the north of Rangoon almost to Mandalay. To the west the narrow tar road heads north along the valley of the Irrawaddy, Burma's most important river. The Irrawaddy is also one of the mighty rivers of Asia, formed from the snow waters of the mountains sprawled at the feet of the Himalayas. The road which forks east runs along the valley carved by the Sittang River, the smaller brother of the Irrawaddy. In March 1942 that eastern road petered out to become a jungle track near Pegu, a small town to which the British retreated after the disaster at the Sittang Bridge. Blowing the bridge had been an own goal for the British. Without motorised transport the Japanese didn't need a bridge, although it would have been more convenient. They merely moved upriver, chose a spot where the Sittang narrowed, and troops and mules swam across.

Reinforcements had arrived: the tanks of 7th Armoured Brigade. These lumbering warriors had come from the deserts of North Africa where they had served with distinction. General Wavell had commanded the Desert Rats, and famously at Tobruk they had turned a long siege into a famous victory, and the turning point in the North African campaign. A short, stocky man with a glass eye, he was idolised by his men. On a flying visit to Burma in February 1942 he called on his men to turn Rangoon into another Tobruk. It was not to be. The Japanese outflanked the tanks, moving invisibly through the jungle, to emerge behind the defenders where they formed a roadblock. Retreating troops and tanks were caught at the roadblock and battered by shells emerging from an enemy invisible in the jungle, with nowhere to run to. The tanks, in which so much hope had been invested, were not the weapon for this type of battle. As the British fought their way back to Rangoon, the Japanese cut across country from east to west: they were now blocking the exit up the other route out of Rangoon. The defenders of Rangoon were surrounded. The enemy was approaching by sea and both exits by road were in their hands. Still the order had not been given for the army to evacuate.

It was Brigadier Jackie Smyth who was held responsible for the premature demolition of the Sittang Bridge. He was replaced, as was Major General Hutton – commander of the army in Burma. General Sir Harold Alexander was the new man. He was renowned as cool, calm and collected. The day after his appointment, 6 March, he ordered the military evacuation of Rangoon. Many felt the city was

The road to Prome, narrow and still lined with trees used as roadblocks by the Japanese.

lost without a fight, but as the remnants of the army retreated they had to cut their way out in a bloody withdrawal. General Alexander, a veteran of the Great War, had the distinction of being the youngest major general in the British Army at only forty-five, renowned for remaining on the beaches at Dunkirk with his men, he was the ideal commander of a retreat. Yet, retreat was still not the official policy in Burma.

Cliff Jones, a motorbike despatch rider with the 1st Battalion, the Glosters, had not been at Dunkirk, but all soldiers could imagine the hell those men had gone through, trapped between the German Army and the English Channel:

> It seemed like another Dunkirk. Many who had hardly prayed before were not ashamed to pray that night, as we waited expecting the worst, hoping against hope for deliverance from some quarter. Many individual deeds of bravery were performed of which no mention will ever be made.
>
> Throughout the next day we were dive-bombed, machine-gunned, and shot at by an invisible enemy amid a din enough to wreck the strongest of nerves. As suddenly as obstacles presented themselves so suddenly did deliverance come this time. The road was opened and like the children of Israel crossing the Red Sea we crossed into temporary safety. Our battalion was the last to go through, as it was detailed to fight the rearguard action.
>
> CLIFF JONES PAPERS, GLOUCESTERSHIRE REGIMENTAL ARCHIVES

To add to the hell of the retreat, the letters from home which sustain soldiers on a foreign field were absent. Former missionary David Patterson had been at the battle for Sittang Bridge, and when Rangoon was abandoned, had just been appointed chaplain of the 17th Division when he wrote home to his mother:

> All forms of communication have at present broken down. I have received no letters for months, they must be heaped in a huge pile somewhere. All the men are in the same state, there must be really enormous piles of mail somewhere, but whether they are in India or Burma, I don't know.
>
> DAVID PATTERSON PAPERS, CENTRE OF SOUTH ASIAN STUDIES,
> UNIVERSITY OF CAMBRIDGE

Padre Patterson had spent his working life in Burma as a teacher and missionary:

> It is a terrible thing to see fighting going on in the country you have been living in. I have seen all the places where we are in peace time, and seen the villagers happy and gay in their silk clothes, and now to see the same places filled with Indian soldiers and deserted by the inhabitants is terrible.

Cliff Jones recalled similar scenes of chaos:

Having reached a point 21 miles from Rangoon on the Prome Road, we were
informed that the enemy had broken through and captured Pegu and also had
crossed over and cut the Prome Road – our last lines of retreat, none by sea or
river. At Hmawbi we found the road choked with troops, transport, tanks, cars,
one hopeless chaos and a beautiful target for Jap bombs. The order from the
CO was 'every available man to the front'. This manoeuvre savouring of 1914
tactics failed to achieve the required result in the splendid and gallant attempt to
remove the Japs from their impregnable positions. We suffered severe casualties

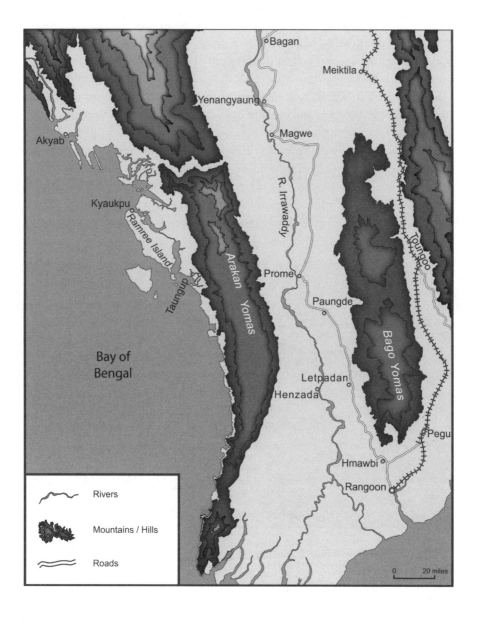

(72/700) and to many the position seemed hopeless for Japs were on our front
and flanks and the burning city of Rangoon in the rear.

Just south of Prome, road and river meet. Fred Tizzard had been moored at
Prome waiting to pick up the last ditchers from Rangoon since the third
week in February. With him were Marjorie and Rosemary Ann, so he was
understandably impatient, concerned that the Japanese would cut off their
escape. Since the Irrawaddy Flotilla Company had come under army control
in December, company boats had transported everything, from refugees to
petrol and stores. Coal was running short and looters were helping themselves
to anything portable. His future looked bleak. Quite apart from the dangers of
invasion, the entire infrastructure of his adopted home was systematically being
wrecked by Japanese bombing or Allied demolitions. While he waited for the
last ditchers, Fred Tizzard helped refugees onto boats heading north. Some were
packed onto the motor launch carrying the garrison from Bassein in the delta;
others onto larger IFC ships going upriver to be scuttled. The beautiful paddle
steamers built in Scotland and brought halfway across the world, were all sunk to
prevent the Japanese using them.

The tracks alongside the Irrawaddy River were bloated with dust raised by the
bare feet of thousands of refugees plodding north. Many queued to be ferried
across the Irrawaddy heading for the mountains of the Arakan Yomas. If they
survived the climb over the Taungup Pass, and the descent to the coast, there was
the chance of a boat to India. Thousands more hoped to find a boat going north

These river launches are the same as those used by the Irrawaddy Flotilla Company before
the war.

to Mandalay. The British were adamant that they could hold Upper Burma, and drive the Japanese out from there. Meanwhile, Japanese troops were pouring into the country. These were men who had fought at the capture of Singapore and Hong Kong, or were hardened after years of war with China. The remnants of the British Army were depleted, exhausted and included half-trained soldiers who had learnt their craft on the run. Morale was seriously low.

On 12 March 1942, General William 'Bill' Slim landed at the dusty airfield at Magwe. His rapport with his soldiers would transform the morale of this beleaguered army. It was not an auspicious landing. The airfield was deserted, telephone unmanned, lined up on the airfield were thirty-eight aeroplanes, the sum total of the Allied air force in Burma. Hailing a truck of Burma Rifles passing by, Slim hitched a lift to the RAF mess a couple of miles away. When he expressed surprise that the planes had been left unguarded, the flyers cheerfully told him that was the army's job. Nine days later the Japanese zeroed in on the airfield at Magwe, with devastating results: a handful of planes survived but the defending army's air cover had to withdraw to India. Throughout the rest of the defence of Burma, the Japanese held the skies, although Allied pilots were able to drop supplies to those making their escape. Lack of air support was just one of Bill Slim's problems.

The new general had arrived not knowing what the overall object of the campaign was to be, but he decided that to break the Japanese run of success, a counterattack must be launched. A lack of intelligence was a huge handicap. On the staff was one Japanese speaker, and as no prisoners had been captured and interrogated, all intelligence was gleaned from the bodies of the dead. This yielded little and what it did was often out of date. The question of reinforcements was academic now that Rangoon was in Japanese hands. Slim and his boss General Alexander would have to make do with the forces to hand.

American General Joe Stilwell was in charge of the Chinese armies and was famously acid-tongued, earning him the nickname 'Vinegar Joe'. Stilwell was critical of the distribution of British Forces, remarking on 14 March after a meeting with General Alexander:

70,000 [men] on the [British] rations [list] in Burma and [only] 12,000 at the front. The difference is scattered round the country in Frontier Guard detachments and the Burma Auxiliary Force. Every 'home-guard' puts on shorts and a Sam Browne[31] belt and climbs on the ration wagon. But nobody goes up front. There it's just a couple of brigades of Indian troops, one brigade of tanks and about five battalions of British troops. But G-2 [intelligence] had

31 A Sam Browne is a leather belt with a strap across the chest worn by officers in the British Army.

no idea how many Jap divisions are in Burma. Neither did assistant G-2. They finally found a guy who did.

THE STILWELL PAPERS, 1948

Fighting and retreating, the British moved slowly north, losing men and equipment with every day. Halfway along the road to Prome lies Letpadan, a village which sprawls either side of the main road. The Glosters were still acting as the rearguard, but at Letpadan they scored a small victory. Knowing that Burmese fifth columnists were passing intelligence to the Japanese, the Glosters feigned a withdrawal, pulling out of the village into the surrounding jungle. Once the bait was taken, the famously iron-willed commander Lieutenant Colonel Bagot surrounded the village. As the Japanese leapt from the windows of houses where they were bivouacked, they were skewered on the bayonets of the British. In the midst of the dark days of retreat this was a fillip to morale which was still celebrated three decades later, gracing the comic *Victor and Wizard* as their cover story in August 1978. Almost at the same moment a daring commando raid was made on Henzada, a town on the Irrawaddy a few miles west of Letpadan. It was led by a young Major Mike Calvert, who would later make a bigger mark in the annals of history as one of the leaders of Orde Wingate's Chindits. At the wheel of the boat which took the soldiers downriver was Irrawaddy Flotilla Company's Captain Rea, who won a Military Cross for his bravery.

For the Japanese these were merely setbacks. The British were heavily outnumbered and outgunned. At Prome, Allied generals made a stand on a line

Letpadan – scene of the Gloucestershire Regiment's victory.

drawn due east to Toungoo, in the eastern valley bordering the Sittang River, where the Chinese under US command were advancing to meet the Japanese.

Without adequate intelligence, often the first Allied troops knew of the enemy presence was the shriek of red tracer bullets and cries of 'banzai' emerging from the jungle gloom. The signature Japanese tactic was to race through the jungle to either side of the main road, fell a tree across the road, post snipers in the trees on either side of the road and wait to ambush the opposition. Prime locations for these traps were sections where there were tall trees lining the roadside, confining transport to the highway. Alex Morrison was driving a staff car with 7th Armoured Brigade as they approached just such a spot:

> We came to a dirt road on our right which led off the tar road, a large clearing on one side, jungle on the other, with rows of large teak trees four or five feet in diameter, perhaps forty feet in height, the typical formidable barrier which confined our tanks mainly to the road. There were rows of similar trees on each side of the main road, an ideal spot for an ambush, for the vehicles would be forced to use this part of the road for at least two miles.
>
> ALEX MORRISON PAPERS, IWM

The colonel leapt out of the car to take a close look at this bottleneck. A bullock cart slowly rumbled towards them loaded with hay, the epitome of Burmese rural life:

> It seemed a very peaceful scene – until one single shot rang out and a bullet passed through the rear window of the car and out through the windscreen. I hit the road as a second shot tore through the roof. At the same time I sighted the sniper, a figure high up in a tree overhanging the road. I fired instantly and a Jap came crashing down, to land in a heap on the road. Another Jap ran out into the road behind us. But I was expecting this to happen and dropped him too. As I got in we exclaimed, 'The bullock cart!' It was Japanese, for I saw flashes of machine gun from under the hay as we tore away, and I had a quick shot at it, an S bend in the road ahead gave us safe cover, as we sped along at about 80mph.

The rest of the brigade were several miles away, but Morrison and his colonel sped back to warn them. They were too late to be effective. By the time the convoy reached the bottleneck, the road was blocked. Every available man had to grab a rifle and fight, knowing that they were trapped.

> The battle went on well into the early hours of the morning, before two tanks managed to get chains round one of the trees which blocked the road and drag it to one side, leaving enough room for a vehicle to squeeze through. It was becoming light as we started the old routine, dashing through the bottleneck at

Bullock carts are still made
to the same design and still
crowd the roads.

intervals. We lost several lorries, one loaded with small arms ammunition, and
only one man, the driver. I was scared stiff when my turn came to move. I could
see the shells exploding on the road in front of me and the wreckage of vehicles
scattered about, bodies spread on either side, dead Japs hanging by their feet in
trees. I put my foot down on the accelerator and tore up the road. A very calm
voice beside me, the Colonel's, said 'Do your best young fellow, do your best.'
Just before we reached the road block we found a tank burning like an inferno
and taking up half the road, a body spread across the other half of the road in my
path. I must have hesitated for a second, but the Colonel said in my ear: 'Keep
going. Keep going.' I felt the bumps as we almost jumped over the body, the
Old Man banging his head on the roof of the car. A couple of shells exploded
nearby and we felt the impact of a lump of shrapnel hitting the radiator and
tearing a gash across it, almost cutting the bottom tank of the radiator in two.
But I kept going and we ran the car till it seized up. We stopped, I poured petrol
over the car and set light to it.

At the end of March, the Glosters hit a roadblock a few miles south of Prome,
when they reached the village of Paungde. Cliff Jones lost two close friends in this
ferocious battle in which the Glosters were heavily outnumbered by the Japanese.

After retreating through the night we took up positions roughly 200 yards to the north of the village of Paungde. I prepared to dig in but alas we did not reckon with the rapidity of the Japanese advance using the same old, but always successful tactics, the enemy pushed up a small force, and occupied the village itself, unknown to us, and but for the fact that we had sent out a patrol in the early morning, we would not have been aware of the enemies nearness. This patrol was ambushed losing a scout car, the driver being killed. Word was sent back to the CO and we were awakened from our troubled and restless sleep by the now familiar cry 'Stand by for action'.

Cliff Jones papers, Gloucestershire Regimental Archives

One of the many problems the army had to cope with, throughout this fighting retreat, was the lack of equipment, in particular communications equipment which barely functioned in the testing conditions of the Far East. At Paungde, it was the battalion bugler rather than the radio which signalled to the Glosters:

At 0700 hours the attack began and our troops advanced slowly towards the village. Needless to say the din was terrific – mortar bombs exploding, the noise of automatic weapons and the heavy sound of small guns which the Japs had brought up to oppose us. About the actual fighting in the village I am unable to say much, but what I gathered from several of our men who were in action on different sectors, it was a bloody and ghastly ordeal. Many men of our battalion who went into the attack never came back, and included in these were two of my best friends. One, I learned afterwards, died in attempting to bring out a wounded comrade. He died as he lived, doing kindness to others. The other friend was badly wounded at the head of his section and fell in full view of the enemy. Several gallant attempts were made to get him out, but murderous enemy fire pinned down our men, so he had to remain where he lay. The battle raged all day and at 1600 hours, the CO ordered a general retirement to positions three miles back. We had suffered heavy casualties – every third man coming back was wounded and many died before they could receive proper medical care. To the people at home this little affair was another routine announcement – 'Our troops retired to prepared positions'. What an entirely wrong impression this oddly worded report gives to those who can't see and don't realise the agony and suffering that the men involved have to bear.

When the remnants of 7th Armoured reached Prome, they found it had been heavily bombed. Trees smouldered at the roadside creating a tunnel of heat, and the sky glowed red overhead. One after another, the towns by the roadside leading north beamed a telltale red glow into the sky. The Japanese had crossed the Bago Yomas between the Sittang and Irrawaddy valleys, and the defensive line between

Prome and Toungoo was no longer defensible. The oilfields at Yenangyaung and Chauk would be the next targets.

The further north you travel along the road from Prome, the more the landscape deteriorates into a desert. Vast quantities of dust rise from the roads and paths as travellers make their way across the plain. Not that it is entirely flat, hills and hummocks covered in dry scrub are plentiful. Poking their lollipop heads above the plain are the toddy palms from which skilful toddy-tappers extract the juice to make jaggery. Found all over south-east Asia, it tastes somewhat like fudge, and is sold at the roadside in misshapen lumps to be used in cooking and traditional medicine. The landscape becomes hotter and dryer closer to Yenangyaung, and the toddy palms are replaced by acacia trees and oil derricks.

Oil had been hand dug from the plain alongside the Irrawaddy River for at least 200 years before the British arrived in the nineteenth century. Once the ancient kingdom around Mandalay had fallen in 1885, the oilfields were ripe for exploitation. David Cargill, a Scots merchant founded Burmah Oil in the same year and the company brought in new technology which drove oil production up. In 1909 a pipeline was dug to take the crude oil produced at their main oilfield at Yenangyaung, to be refined into petrol 275 miles away near Rangoon. It made Burma self-sufficient in oil and soon the company was exporting it to India. When the Japanese invaded, the oilfields and their associated refineries immediately became strategic targets, and in the fighting retreat during early 1942, the battle of the oilfields was one of the most desperate.

In the middle of a violent thunderstorm, the Japanese attacked in a battle which concentrated on two river beds, Yin Chaung and Pin Chaung. Captain John Perkins, of the 11th Sikh Regiment, was in the thick of the desperate fighting that ensued:

> The Japs infiltrated across the river [Pin Chaung] to establish a road block cutting our main force off from the Chinese who were to relieve the situation. So when we came across, we saw what appeared to be Chinese but what actually was the enemy. Scorching sun, dead tired troops, terror stricken mules unattended, no water to quench an unending thirst.
>
> CAPTAIN JOHN GRAHAM PAPERS, IWM

In the heat of the plains in mid-April, men drank from the radiators of army lorries and jeeps, and from any ditch or puddle within reach. On 15 April the last ditchers began the systematic destruction of the wooden derricks, plugging of wells and wrecking of all and any equipment which might be of use to the enemy. A sheet of flame fuelled by millions of gallons of crude oil rose into the sky and sent smoke as far as Bagan, a plain by the Irrawaddy covered with 4,000 ancient temples. Captain John Perkins and his men were beneath that toxic cloud:

Tranquil Pin Chaung – scene of desperate fighting in 1942.

Yenangyaung was a mass of bombing debris and every oil derrick seemed to
be a sheet of flame. In the sky as far as you could see was a thick pall of black
smoke which shut out the sun, a terrifying spectacle, unnerving. As we passed,
a derrick crashed across the road behind us, blocking our retreat. Although we
were completely safe from air attack, because of the thick low lying smoke.

Throughout the battle, one non-combatant emerged unscathed. Gemma, a dog
owned by a company of Madras Sappers, became separated from her company.
Two days later she was found curled up in a wrecked car. Two weeks later she
unwittingly acted as a diversion during the defence of Monywa on the banks
of the Chindwin River, west of Mandalay. The Japanese crossed at dawn and
attacked from some deserted houses. As British troops retreated, the Japanese
raked the ground with machine gun bullets in the paddy fields nearby sending
up spurts of dust. Instead of taking cover, Gemma ran about in the open
investigating the bullet marks with her tail up. She served as a useful distraction
drawing Japanese fire which would otherwise have been aimed at the troops.
The last sight of her was surrounded by a hail of machine gun bullets, aimed
from only 50 yards away! Once the firefight was over, the British went to try
and retrieve what equipment they could, and again found Gemma curled up
inside an abandoned car.[32]

32   See *History of the Madras Sappers* by A.E.W. Sandes (1956)

The railway line runs alongside the road heading north to Prome.

The repercussions of the destruction of the bounteous Burmah Oilfields would reverberate for nearly a quarter of a century. With the advent of the Socialist government in 1962, BOC was thrown out of Burma and the oil industry was nationalised. BOC took the British government to court to claim damages for the wartime sabotage of the oilfields. Although they won their case in the House of Lords, the War Damages Act was passed in 1965 which retrospectively exempted the government for such destruction in time of war.

6

Flights and Superstition

Bamboo blossom is a rare occurrence and lies at the root of a Burmese superstition. Blossom appears the season before the bamboo dies, on a cycle of 40 or 80 years. In 1941 wise men and astrologers noticed the phenomenon in the bamboo forests of north-west Burma, and forecast a great calamity. The last time this had been recorded was in 1884 during the reign of King Thibaw. A year later Thibaw was deposed and the British annexed Upper Burma. Burma is still a land where astrology can sway decision-makers and belief in black magic is common. In 1941, the village elders near the jade mines at Hpakant were convinced that the flowering of the bamboo foretold disaster. A few months later, unexpected clouds of brilliant green parakeets flew over Indawgyi Lake nearby, poisoning the waters with their droppings; this was seen as another omen of disaster. The Kachin fishermen whose villages border the lake reported that huge shoals of fish were killed. The Japanese would come, foretold the astrologers, cause havoc, death

Indawgyi Lake, the largest in south-east Asia; supplies were landed here for the Chindits.

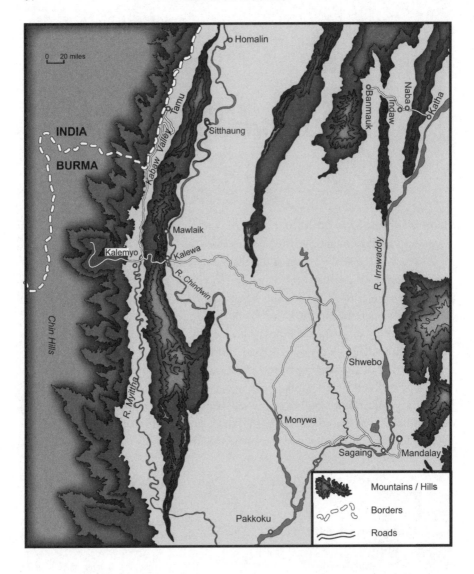

and destruction in Burma, then leave as quickly as they had arrived. In essence the wise men's prediction was fulfilled.

The Burmese do not share the common British mistrust of the date Friday the 13th, but in 1942 there were 2 consecutive months when the date fell on a Friday: February and March. Fred Tizzard's wife Marjorie pointed out to him that the river boat captain had signed his will on Friday 13th. Sailors are often superstitious by nature, and Fred considered the comment significant enough to record in his diary. On Friday 13 February the couple had steamed from the pretty village of Nyaung-U on the east bank of the Irrawaddy to Pakkoku on the west bank, 6 hours upstream. By Friday 13 March Baby Rosemary had developed

A road built by the British Army in the Chin Hills.

bronchitis, and her mother was exhausted as she tried to look after her daughter in temperatures which were soaring as the country entered the hot season.

Marjorie had led a charmed and blessed existence in Burma until now. She and Fred were devoted to each other. He refers to her in his diary as 'a wife in a million'. Both had been brought up in the shadow of the Great War, when the lives of so many couples were shattered by death and disability. Hardly surprising that they were unwilling to separate in the face of invasion, but Fred had been ruminating on the prospects for his wife and child, and was convinced that there was now no choice. His diary gives clues to the options they considered: setting up home in Maymyo, providing Upper Burma was held; setting up home in Bhamo, in the far northeast close to the Chinese border, and at this point still considered a safe option; and finally, to remain onboard *Java*. Fred believed the latter to be the safest option because the ship could help provide a means of escape. With extraordinary prescience he dismissed the Bhamo option, saying that if the British were driven north of the oilfields at Yenangyaung:

> Our army may retreat to India and leave folk in Bhamo stranded... and if Burma falls, the exit may be too fast for baby. If she goes it will be very hard for her and lonely for me on *Java*, for these difficult days have been happy days.

While the *Java* was moored at Pakkoku, Fred heard reports of the road west from the town which had been reconnoitred by men from Burmah Oil. Unlike many commercial firms in Burma, the Irrawaddy Flotilla Company did not organise the evacuation of its families, and many of the men who served on its boats died in the struggle to escape to India. Whereas Burmah Oil executives made early contingency plans for their 400-strong workforce and their families based in central Burma. In January 1942 two oilmen were despatched to recce a route overland to India from the oilfields at Yenangyaung. They travelled in a camper van, taking a rough road towards the Chin Hills. When this petered out, the duo followed a fair-weather road into the Kabaw Valley, a finger of land sandwiched between the Chin Hills to the west and another range of hills on the east. The path ended at Tamu, where there was a steep climb over the hills to the Indian town of Imphal. It was a route which became familiar to many soldiers from the Fourteenth Army, when they fought their way back into Burma later in the war.

When the oilmen returned they described the road as 'very bad'. They revealed that the van had been forced to travel at an average speed of 10mph; there was nowhere to buy supplies of food or petrol en route; and pronounced the route unsuitable for women and children.[33] Three staff were sent to Rangoon to stock a lorry with stores to set up camps and food dumps necessary for the journey. BOC took its responsibility for the welfare of its employees and their families seriously. Unlike the Government of Burma, BOC realised that the evacuation of women and children was a prudent response to the Japanese invasion. Despite the

---

33   Michael Porter papers, Burmah Oil Co., IWM.

Teak logs on the Irrawaddy River, still part of Burma's transport network.

shortcomings of the roads, the BOC families set off in a convoy bound for India at the beginning of March.

Similarly, the Bombay Burma Trading Corporation (BBTC) was the first of the British companies to organise the evacuation of families before it was too late. BBTC, known in London as Wallace Brothers, was a trading house, with its roots in the timber industry, and foresters spread over vast wild tracts of land throughout Burma and across into Thailand. The corporation was blessed with staff whose job made them familiar with the hills, and the dense areas of forest which covered them. However, there was an even greater blessing, in the guise of hundreds of elephants, still routinely used in the teak forests of Burma to this day. When the British first began to exploit Burma's teak, the corporation had imported beasts from India and Thailand, as well as capturing wild Burmese elephants and training them for logging. They built up a herd of over 6,000, soon replacing them with calves born to captive elephants, which were easier to train. Teak is native to India, China, Thailand, Laos and Burma where it grows best on steep hillsides which are inaccessible to machinery, hence the importance of trained elephants. Trees can grow to 40 metres tall and have pretty but insignificant white flowers, which have been used for centuries as a medicine.

Over the last 200 years, the Burmese have developed a method of seasoning the wood prior to felling, by ringing or girdling the scaly bark by cutting a 6in. strip round the trunk. This kills the tree but leaves it standing to season evenly over the next 3 years until it is felled. The great quality of teak is its density, which also prevents it from floating while still green. Girdling allows the wood to season, and become light enough to float down the network of rivers, when it is felled. This can only be done once the monsoon has swelled rivers to sufficient size to carry the teak trunks. When the nineteenth-century founders of the Bombay Burma Trading Corporation saw the potential of Burma's teak industry, they built a network of saw mills to exploit it. The great shipping lines, which carried freight and passengers around the world, had decks built from teak. As the Royal Navy expanded in the closing years of Queen Victoria, and during the run up to the First World War, its sailors strode decks made from Burma teak. With the outbreak of the Second World War, more Burma teak was required for the fleet. After war in the East was declared in December 1941, teak production went into overdrive.

The Van Milligen family lived in Chiang Mai where Evelyn Van Milligen was manager of the northern teak forests of Thailand, or Siam as it was known at the time. As soon as they and other Bombay Burma families heard the news of Pearl Harbor on the wireless, they set off with what they could carry to walk through the mountains and jungle to British Burma. Twenty women and twenty children set off with Frank Burden as guide and protector – the Japanese were sweeping across Thailand which had capitulated without a fight. Of those children, only one survived the journey, the youngest, Pamela Van Milligen, who was 5-years-old. Despite suffering from malaria for much of the trek, Pamela was carried to

The route from Sitthaung to Tamu taken by organised convoys of army and timber families.

safety by Frank Burden, whom she had been drilled to call Father Number 2, in case of capture. Nineteen children were buried along the track through the Shan States in eastern Burma. Pamela's father meanwhile, who had gone to warn the Bombay Burma timber crews who were out of touch deep in the teak forests, was captured by the Japanese, but managed to escape by dressing as a woman! After a terrible journey, which Pamela's mother never spoke or wrote about, the bedraggled women arrived in Maymyo where they were taken in by other British families, and later flown to India. Perhaps it was this experience of the women who had walked from Thailand, which prompted Geoff Bostock, manager of Bombay Burma, to prepare a secret evacuation plan. In January 1942 he researched and put together detailed routes, lists of stores and equipment right down to the number of buckets and tinned baths, plus the names of evacuees. Copies went to four other managers, who were advised to use the situation in Singapore as 'a guide to future movements'. When evacuation was considered necessary a coded telegram would be sent:

AGREE DEPRECIATION STATISTICS NECESSARY

Forestry launches which chugged up and down the Chindwin on a regular schedule were told to call in at every telegram office on the river in future. All was to be done in the utmost secrecy. Indeed, the Bombay Burma Corporation's early evacuation

Logging elephants moving camp as they have done for 200 years.

of families was heavily criticised in some quarters. Official policy was still to 'stay put': the British could not be seen to abandon Burma. But whatever the official policy, many civil servants had already sent their wives and children out of danger.[34]

Foresters often took their families up country with them, and their only contact with the outside world was a wireless set. In theory this kept them up to date with war news, but in practice the corrugated topography of Burma meant that reception was intermittent. Jimmie Williams, who acquired the soubriquet 'Elephant Bill', had been with the Bombay Burma for 20 years, and his expertise with elephants was rivalled only by that of the Burmese elephant handlers or 'oozies' with whom he worked. Jimmie and other forestry men lived in jungle camps in the teak forests, where they knew every track, rock and hillock. Jimmie was unaware that the BBTC had begun to prepare an evacuation scheme for families, until a letter arrived at his camp brought by a runner. He packed up, and headed west to the Chindwin River where the families were gathering in case evacuation was deemed necessary. As he emerged from the wilderness, it became obvious that the Indian population was on the move. Trains, boats and roads were crowded with refugees. It was February 1942 and Singapore had fallen.

---

34   E.g. Reginald Langham-Carter, who had evacuated his wife and daughter by plane on 1 January 1942.

Geoff Bostock called a halt to all forestry work in the Chindwin area, elephants and their handlers were returned to base and loaded with food, bedding and the few possessions allowed. A week after the fall of Singapore, on 23 February, a procession of fifty-six elephants, twenty-two women and fifteen children, plus camp cooks, servants, coolies and a doctor, left Mawlaik on the Chindwin led by Geoff Bostock. It was the first of two caravans of Bombay Burma families. Coolies carried 400 ducks and 200 chickens, and the elephants were loaded with fresh vegetables, tin and canvas baths, tents and bedding. It was superbly organised, after all Geoff Bostock had worked for the company for 25 years and routinely set off into the teak forests equipped for a long stay in camp. Among this first group was Geoff's wife Evelyn. The first stretch of the journey from the Chindwin River was along a 6ft wide track, a narrow fit for the laden elephants. The women walked, as Evelyn recounted shortly afterwards:

> We were all very fit though and I thoroughly enjoyed it. The walking was some of the steepest and most difficult I have ever seen, but the scenery was

Maymyo Railway Station little changed.

magnificent. You can imagine how hard it was to get all those children up, and we had also four expectant mothers, two of them pretty near their time. They had to be carried over and I was sorry for their coolies.

BOSTOCK FAMILY PAPERS

This prudent and timely evacuation was relatively comfortable. Camp equipment like tents, canvas baths and bedding were carried by the elephants, and Jimmie Williams and other timber men, used their intimate knowledge of the area to organise campsites near water. Nonetheless it was a tough climb on a rough bridle track over hills 5,000ft high. Tiny children were carried in 'dhoolies', a sort of canvas chair slung between bamboo poles. To the children it was an adventure at first, but soon the routine of early morning starts and long days travelling became tedious. As Evelyn described in a letter home afterwards: 'Called at 5.30am, off at 6.30 after a hasty cup of tea and a saucer of porridge gobbled in the midst of rolling up the beds, screaming children, trumpeting elephants, cursing men and yelling coolies.'

Compared with the experiences of those who were to follow on the trek to India, this was a fairly gentle expedition. It was not yet really hot, and the track had only a smattering of other refugees on it. Every hour's walking was followed by an hour's rest, and after reaching camp at midday the party slept for the afternoon, had their evening meal and slept till dawn. To feed their enormous frames, elephants have to forage at night, but the oozies tied the animals up and cut bamboo, branches and grass to feed them, rather than allow them to graze the forests to feed themselves. An elephant has to drink 50 gallons of water and eat 495 pounds of foliage per day to obtain sufficient calories to work. In the forests the beasts work for 3 days followed by 2 days' rest, working 18 days a month with 12 days' rest. In the interests of the BBTC families, this routine had to be ignored, as did the annual cycle of 3 months' rest in the hot season from March to June. However, when water ran short, it was the elephants which had priority and the families who went without. The worst stage of the journey was after the elephants were left behind, and families travelled by lorry down the hairpin bends in the mountains of Assam to the railway station. Tightly packed in, with temperatures beginning to soar, it was a filthy, sweaty and uncomfortable experience. Others followed on this route, among them the Edwards family who ran the Salvation Army soldiers' home in Maymyo. Jim Edwards was in charge, and although as a European male he wasn't allowed to leave, his family were given their marching orders 10 days after the fall of Singapore. On 26 February Jim Edwards saw his family off at Maymyo Railway Station to take the line to Amarapura, across the Irrawaddy and on to Monywa on the Chindwin. Although it was a hot and crowded journey, the women and children were provided with free food, and had been inoculated against cholera before they left. They walked between prepared camps. Florence Edwards had two children, aged 9 and 19, and kept a diary for most of the journey:

[At] the evacuation camp made & planned by government & how we enjoyed
a real bath & plenty of water. Everything is just planned for everybody to be
made as comfortable as possible. All made of Bamboo & Grass walls. Plenty of
Hot & Cold water for all. Am hoping that it will be like this all along the way.

EDWARDS FAMILY PAPERS

They stuck to the Chindwin River as far as Sitthaung, taking a similar route to
the timber families. The camp system was rudimentary for those who took to the
road in good time, as Florence wrote in her diary on 9 March:

What a time we had on Monday. Left a very decent camp early on Monday
morning then 2½ miles to the river, ferried across in a small boat & then waited
for the bus for 4 hrs. After going hungry for 6 hrs we expected to have food
when we arrived at Tamu Camp, but when we arrived we found all the others
who had walked, still waiting for food. Nothing prepared, Mr Atkinson kept us
waiting for about 4 days before we went to 57th Mile.

The wives and children of the Glosters had been sent up to Maymyo for safety
after the first bombing of Rangoon, where they doubled up with families of the
KOYLI. But the regiment had been told *not* to evacuate them. Such was the speed
of the Japanese advance that only 6 weeks later military families were offered places
on evacuation convoys, but the military families were accompanied by elephants
to carry their baggage and food. The campaign was not yet lost and some military
families wished to remain with their men. Official historian, Colonel E.C.V. Foucar
wrote after the exodus:

The moat outside the ancient town of Shwebo, a former capital of Burma.

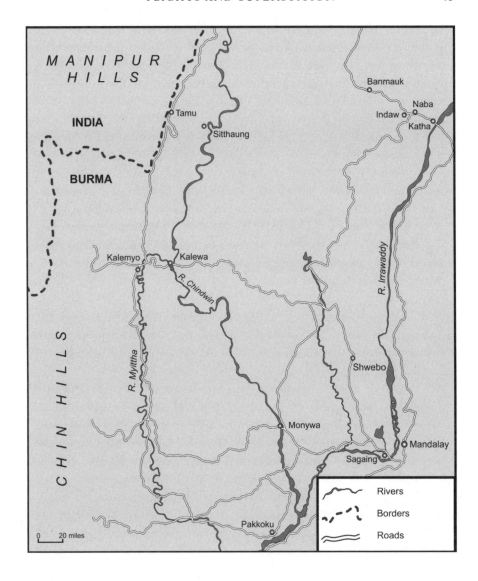

This campaign must have been the only one in modern times in which a British Army has had attached to it a large following of women and children. It was an unhappy state of affairs and apart from other drawbacks it affected efficiency. Many military families or members of them, particularly those of men in the Burma Frontier Force and Burma Military Police were lost on the overland route to India. Leaving Burma late these families were exposed to the terrible conditions encountered on these routes. This fact gave rise to an understandable feeling of bitterness at the absence of effective arrangements for the safe evacuation of dependents of fighting troops.

COLONEL E.C.V. FOUCAR PAPERS, IWM

On 6 March 1942, with the fall of Rangoon imminent, it was announced that air evacuation would be offered. In fact it was a half-hearted scheme which consisted of one aeroplane and a jungle clearing. Reginald Langham-Carter, ex-secretary to the financial commissioner in Rangoon had flown his wife and daughter out with a Dutch airline on 1 January. He volunteered to help with the air evacuation. Shwebo is a moated town, north of Mandalay and a few miles west of the Irrawaddy, and was not an ideal location as he recorded in his diary after arriving there on 10 March:

> It is a small place and could not cope at once with the influx of refugees. The first batch were mostly army wives from Maymyo, who were accustomed to a good deal of comfort and found in Shwebo only bug infested beds in an old wooden barrack, trees still being cut down on the space that was being made into a landing ground, and no planes yet able to arrive. Some went back to Maymyo at once. Rumours abound.

When Langham-Carter arrived at Shwebo, he met Geoff Bostock fresh from chaperoning the women and children of the Bombay Burma Trading Corporation. The bush had been cleared, leaving space enough for a small plane to land:

> We have made frenzied appeals for more aircraft but still only have the one Chinese National Airways [Aviation] Co plane with an American pilot. Each adult evacuee can take only 33 lbs of kit, each child under 12, 16 ½ lbs and babies nil. Some of the Indian passengers cheat. One woman, after being weighed, secretes a sewing machine under her sari but is found out and the machine confiscated. Most people's kit is found to be overweight and it is pathetic to see them having to take out one cherished possession after another to bring the weight down. They can weigh as much personally as they like. Most find wearing extra clothes impossible in the heat but a few fly nearly double their own weight with fur coats, extra underwear and so on.

Nadir Tyabji, the representative of the Government of India, had been handed what he termed 'the most thankless job on the evacuation platter', the selection of passengers for each flight. There were only forty seats available each day, and thousands who laid claim to them. The business-minded 29-year-old came up with a scheme whereby the well-off were allowed to pay for twenty seats, but could only use a few of them. He then had the power to decide which deserving cases took up the 'spare' seats. One such was an old school friend, Akram Khan, who had made a fortune by winning a government contract to operate lorries on the Burma Road. These volunteer administrators were overwhelmed by the number of people arriving every day on foot or by train at Shwebo. With the organisational abilities honed as an experienced civil

The cliffs at Nyaung-U, where Fred and Marjorie walked before they parted.

servant, Langham-Carter introduced a telephone system to coordinate the number of arrivals by train and car; how many evacuees were in camp; and how many had been flown out. The police organised buses to meet refugees at Shwebo station and take them to the refugee camp which was run by a missionary who had fled from Lower Burma, Padre Dyer. As refugees checked in, receipts were examined to see who had paid and who had travelled in hope. For 3 weeks the system ran with relative efficiency, then on 28 March CNAC (China National Aviation Corporation - the first commerical airline in China) signalled that it was no longer safe for them to operate from Shwebo. The war had come too close.

Evacuation flights had also been operating from the former Burmah Oil Company airfield at Magwe, and as the second week of March drew to a close, Fred Tizzard became increasingly anxious to ensure his wife was among the passengers. However, Marjorie fretted about travelling alone with the baby. This was before the era of disposable nappies, pre-packaged baby food and other modern conveniences. Already worn down by the constant care of her daughter, his wife was not resilient enough to make the journey alone. Rosemary's birth at the Dufferin Hospital in Rangoon had been prolonged and difficult, and she had to cope with the fractious baby without a nanny, despite her lack of strength. On Friday 13 March Fred confided to his diary:

This morning she was worn out by worry over going alone and strain of seeing after baby without Nanny, so she demanded a peg[35] of whisky before baby's bath. As *Java* may not return downstream again Marjorie really should fly to India from Magwe today, but she is herself too poorly. I wish both had been away long ago. Marjorie doesn't want to go because she came out to be with me, and says her going throws all anxiety on her alone, yet it may become hard to carry on the job with them here. Just now the Japs seem content to stay in Lower Burma.

Two days later on 15 March Fred nursed his daughter for the last time as he carried her ashore. He had persuaded his wife to leave. As he hitched a flat, or cargo lighter, to the *Java*, he waved at his wife standing on shore in her favourite old rose pink frock and pith helmet. Had they left it another day, the story might have ended very differently. Marjorie flew from Magwe on 20 March. The following day the airfield was bombed. For Fred the decision for her departure was a relief, but alone in his cabin, despite his punishing workload, regrets overwhelmed him:

'I'll never get back again,' said Marjorie and I know it was true, almost certainly. How cruel is the tragedy, that I should have a wife like her, one in a million, who wanted only to stay, and I wanted nothing as much as her willing comradeship through all that may pass till peace returns – but it's 7 months too late, and with Rosemary to save, whatever trial she may bring to life ahead of us. My life here is so easy, food found for me, John[36] to look after my needs. M bears all the burden. In spirit she's here on *Java* to help, I know, for she wished only to stay and to here her thoughts fly back, but she has no help and is very alone. Should I have let her take the chance and stay? How I wish that I had done, I admit that I wish it – yet would it have been only selfish if I had. Was it taking less sacrifice from her to let her stay, or to drive her to go? Is it a great mistake?

Fred Tizzard articulates the feelings of so many faced with the dilemma of abandoning homes and loved ones. Thousands were unable to record the pain of separation, or if they were, the diaries and letters were lost. Fred left whole days of his diary blank, except to note the untidy state of his cabin, which he saw as analogous to the state of his mind. On 26 March he received the news that his wife and child had reached Calcutta: they at least were safe.

---

35 A peg was a colonial expression for shot.
36 His personal servant from Rangoon.

7

The Road to Mandalay
Where the Flying Fishes Play

The road to Mandalay is not the romantic prospect which Kipling would have us believe from his poem, and it is the rare river dolphin whose back curves playfully above the water: there are no flying fishes on the Irrawaddy River. But then Britain's favourite chronicler of the East visited Burma for only half a day.[37]

---

37 *The River of Lost Footsteps* by Thant Myint-U (2007).

The Golden Palace where the penultimate king of Burma died.

Side street on the outskirts of Mandalay, little changed since colonial days.

Before the days of air travel he would not have had access to Mandalay, the city of fabled palaces which has become such a byword for romance and mystery. Perched on a crook in the Irrawaddy, it is a sprawling city in the hot central plains. Modern visitors rarely attempt the journey by the inadequate roads which serve the country, opting to land at the international airport several miles beyond the city limits. Refugees heading for the security of the former capital in 1942 were forced to make the journey either by road, rail or boat. In those days, Mandalay was famous for three things, rubies, opium and brothels.[38] It was a pretty town of wooden houses with cinemas and a racecourse, and substantial British and Indian communities. From the veranda of the European Club, one could watch polo on the fields half a mile away on cool evenings. There were tennis courts for the athletic and inside the teak clubhouse military bands played for tea dances. Green baize tables were the focus on tropical evenings, when the clicking of ivory mah-jong sets or the mannered banter of bridge occupied the British elite.

At its centre stood the giant square-moated Fort Dufferin with its crenellated red stone walls. Within these walls King Thibaw had ruled as the last king of Burma

---

38   Captain Graham papers, IWM.

Fort Dufferin is still a military base so no photos are permitted, this is the moat and Mandalay Hill behind.

before his kingdom fell to 'the trousered ones',[39] and the capital moved south to Rangoon. In 1942 the town was once again destined to become the capital of the new divided Burma. From this base the army would attempt to hold Upper Burma, just as King Thibaw had held out against the British in the late nineteenth century. However, the troops who were withdrawing to Mandalay were an exhausted army, unused to jungle warfare, with second-rate and often inappropriate equipment. With the fall of Rangoon and Lower Burma they had lost their line of supply from the sea, and while the air force was able to drop supplies from bases in North East India, the monsoon was due in May, and the enormous rolling rain clouds would make visibility increasingly difficult. The Japanese on the other hand held the ports and did not bother with such complexities as supply lines, preferring to stay mobile and live off the land by looting from the inhabitants.

Helen Vorley was a woman with nerves of steel who had survived a direct hit on the train coming north from Rangoon, then gathered up survivors and organised transport for them. When she arrived in Mandalay, she found it under siege: on the outskirts of the town were refugee camps housing between 50–70,000 people. These

39   A nineteenth-century Burmese nickname for the British.

had been set up by Angus MacLean, one of the many Scots who had made a career in Burma, in his case as Professor of Agriculture and latterly as head of the Agricultural College in Mandalay. Initially when MacLean was asked to set up the camps, he apologised that he would not be able to give the job his entire attention, as the college's exams were held in the first half of February and had to take priority. Within a week he was overtaken by events. A hundred Anglo-Indians, who were on their way to India, needed a pit-stop at Mandalay while the rest of their journey west was arranged. They were a foretaste of the sea of refugees heading for Burma's second city.

On 2 February the first wave of the refugee column arrived. Separate Muslim and Hindu camps had been built a few stops down the railway line west of the city. The Muslim camp was largely male, and housed in two mosques augmented by temporary huts. Latrine trenches were dug, but used by only half the refugees. The camps were run by volunteers although in a report written later, MacLean was critical of the resident Indian population who did little to help with a few notable exceptions. Although he visited every day, he found the filth of both camps difficult to stomach, and called in an overworked Indian doctor to vaccinate against cholera. Still, the flood of refugees was growing, and the medical staff was unable to keep up.

Robert Hutchings, agent for the Government of India, set up a small mobile office in Mandalay during the third week of February. His young assistant Nadir Tyabji was in charge:

Water is short in the dry zone round Mandalay, so the local well is still the parish pump.

News from Rangoon became increasingly alarming and the most disturbing aspect was the dichotomy between the government version on the radio and the first-hand accounts from evacuees from Rangoon and Toungoo indicating that the Japs were almost knocking on the gates of the capital, and that general evacuation had been ordered. And then came the famous broadcast by the Governor of Burma one evening assuring the population that the British-Indian forces had consolidated their position around Rangoon and that the Burmese capital would prove to be a second Stalingrad. I remember telling my staff that evening that Rangoon was finished and that we were to prepare for the final exodus from Burma! So much for credibility.

NADIR TYABJI PAPERS, CENTRE OF SOUTH ASIAN STUDIES, UNIVERSITY OF CAMBRIDGE

Inexorably the Japanese invaders moved closer to Mandalay. On 14 March, a week after Rangoon fell, Jack Vorley attended a meeting with General Hutton and Governor Sir Reginald Dorman-Smith, at which he was assured that Upper Burma would be held. He was appointed Commissioner of Evacuation and told that a new road from the border town of Tamu through the Naga Hills to Imphal would be ready by May. With this in mind, he was told, it was imperative that all refugees be kept in and around Mandalay. As a career colonial servant, Jack Vorley[40] would not have refused his new post, but he had been handed responsibility for the evacuation of over a million people: the non-indigenous population of the country.

---

40   Jack Vorley was with the forestry service.

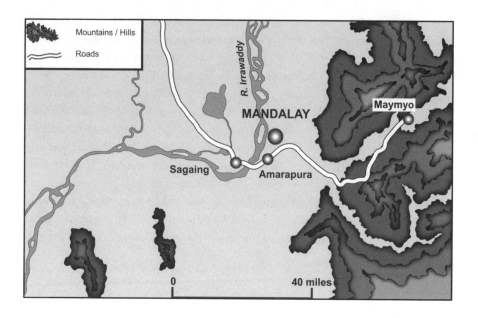

As the Japanese extended their bombing raids to towns further and further north, the flood of refugees became a tsunami. On 19 March Dr William Newton took a train from Mandalay station, on his way east to Taunggyi to treat the wounded in hospital:

> The railway station was in a state of confusion and chaos. The refreshment room was not functioning. The entire platform was littered with refugees from down country. I managed to get a seat in a third class compartment on a train which did not leave until the next morning. We passed two or three trains laden with refugees, hanging on everywhere; some were on the tops of carriages; people were warned not to ride on the tops because in some places there was very little clearance between the tops of the carriages and overhead bridges. In spite of these warnings, people would climb up and were consequently swept away when trains passed under these bridges, many to their deaths and others to very serious injuries.
>
> WILLIAM NEWTON PAPERS, IWM

En route to Taunggyi, the train puffed into Thazi, where it remained for two nights:

> The filth on the platform was indescribable. Refugees were everywhere. There was nobody to attend to the sanitation. The station staff were demoralised; they went into the jungle in the early morning, fearing the Japs would bomb the station and would not return until after dark. Thazi had been bombed by the Japs; the civilian population had all run away to the adjacent jungles. The next morning the driver had to be persuaded to take the train up to Shwenyaung. En route several of the stations were without any staff at all; they had run way.

Communications in Burma were in such a parlous state, that William Newton arrived in Taunggyi only to find that the hospital was packing up to move further north.

Whereas Jack Vorley and others in charge had anticipated that people would take refuge for a few days before moving on, the scale of the flood had not been anticipated. Anxious and exhausted refugees reaching Mandalay often wanted to walk no further. Soon land round the railway station became an unofficial camp, and 2,000 people were forcibly moved to Amarapura, another former ancient capital a few miles to the south. There were few latrines dug and it was here that the first case of smallpox was reported. Jack Vorley brought the casualty into Mandalay Hospital himself. On 21 March the first cases of cholera were identified, overcrowding and inadequate sanitation helped to spread the disease and soon hundreds of people were dying every night.[41] Bodies were found on the streets and by the famous moat surrounding Fort Dufferin. Many of the Indian sweepers, who dealt with rubbish

---

41   Papers of Helen Vorley

Horse and cart still act as taxis in modern Burma.

in colonial Burma, had already left Mandalay, heading for India. Burial was difficult as the clay soil developed deep cracks when temperatures rose as they rapidly did at the end of March. The hospital called on Angus MacLean for advice and help.

> The hospital needed a place to bury corpses. The mortuary was a bamboo shed on the edge of a field clear of the living quarters. The cemetery was near the south west corner of the (college) farm. Mandalay cemeteries were places to avoid in the hot season when the ground was rent by a network of deep fissures reaching even to the graves with their flimsy coffins. The filling of the rents with burnt paddy husk was a palliative but not an effective measure to prevent the nauseating conditions which prevailed. Now ancient bones, and some not so ancient, littered the surface where their rest had been disturbed to make room for the latest victims of violence and disease. A great square pit, a truck arriving with old bamboos and drums of kerosene, indicated the less conventional means of disposing of the dead.
>
> ANGUS MACLEAN PAPERS, CENTRE OF SOUTH ASIAN STUDIES,
> UNIVERSITY OF CAMBRIDGE

Every train and boat disgorged more refugees, who were now intercepted south of the city to ease congestion, and to prevent consequent pollution of the Irrawaddy River. But this was far from ideal, as Angus MacLean was too well aware:

> Men and women, family groups and orphans, infants and aged, poured in a tragic stream on foot and from railway trains in to these camps south of the town. In the mass the habits of these people were disgusting and repulsive; the conditions they created in the crowded lines were foul for latrines were available. Conditions in the south of Mandalay for assembling large numbers of such people could scarcely have been less suitable. The first essential is water – ample supplies of drinking and bathing water – but there is little water of any kind between the muddy Mandalay Canal many miles distant to the east and the Irrawaddy, and the refugees were not permitted to come near this river. Wells are few and the water is of indifferent quality. There is little natural shade in the area where the trees are chiefly of the small leaved acacia species and the Palmyria palm. Finally the clay-like soil baked iron hard in the hot weather and riven by cracks is difficult to dig, and useless as an absorbent. Sanitation in such conditions is well nigh impossible.

All over Burma there are traditional Buddhist 'zayats', shady platforms where the traveller can rest. New refugee huts were based on these simple bamboo and palm leaf structures, and MacLean ordered the digging of more trench latrines. A firm of Indian merchants in Mandalay agreed to supply the camps with food and the deputy commissioner footed the bill. A Hindu school teacher was installed as camp commandant. Despite his revulsion at the filthy refugee camps, Angus MacLean was deeply compassionate:

> Only those who made intimate contact with this movement could realise the extent of the tragedy in which the refugees were involved – the uprooting from homes however humble, the onward urge that no argument or reason could quell, the inevitable toll of exertion, of exposure, of disease and when these things conquered, the amazing calmness with which individuals faced the end.

Nadir Tyabji tried to corale his fellow countrymen into organised camps, but the camps were 6 miles out of town, too far for these exhausted people.

> This had led to families just dumping themselves on any open ground along the city roads creating critical public hygiene and health problems, not only among the refugees but also the local population. This also resulted in a running feud between the Burmese and refugee Indians, resulting in senseless loss of life and property on both sides.

Mandalay river bank, playground, bath and launderette to the locals.

As war news percolated through from the south, tensions increased, and Indian refugees became the scapegoats for years of resentment against their fellow countrymen. It escalated into street fighting, with resident Chinese siding with their Burmese neighbours against the Indian interlopers. During the riots, shops and homes were torched and when order had been restored 600 lay dead and some 3,000 injured.[42] Refugees were an easy target too for Japanese lone raiders which machine gunned their roadside bivouacs. Tyabji called for desperately needed cholera vaccine to be sent over from India. Once inoculated, with the requisite yellow card in hand, refugees could cross the Ava Bridge, the gateway to their onward journey to India.

The Ava Bridge was the only bridge to span the Irrawaddy River, and represented the route to the west and freedom. On the far side is Sagaing, a vast district lying between the Irrawaddy and Chindwin rivers and stretching up to the Indian border in the north and west. No preparations had been made in Sagaing to deal with the thousands of people heading for India, so the order was given to close the Ava Bridge to refugees. Inevitably these orders were ignored by soldiers wanting to make a quick buck. On one occasion a non-commissioned officer charged 1,500

---

42   Nadir Tyabji papers, Centre of South Asian Studies, University of Cambridge.

The strategic Ava Bridge, in 1942 this was the only bridge crossing the Irrawaddy River.

refugees a price of 8 annas apiece to cross.[43] With available soldiers and officials either at war or involved in the refugee crisis, few extra hands were available to police every boat crossing from east to west bank to check for passengers.

Despite the refugees and cholera epidemic, Mandalay was still relatively untouched by the war itself until Good Friday, 3 April 1942, when Japanese Zeros appeared in the sky and transformed the city with their bombs. Scientists from the Pasteur Institute in Rangoon had relocated to the Agricultural College, which was now serving as an overflow area for the military hospital. It was 11am and Angus MacLean was about to leave the college for a meeting, when a Burmese messenger ran in, covering his ears with his hands. The Zeros bombed with impunity, Mandalay had no anti-aircraft guns:

> Good Friday came like most days at this season hot and cloudless but the sky was dust laden with a strong breeze from the south. Listening rarely to the Tokyo radio I knew nothing of promised bombs as some afterwards claimed to have known. In the basement where the Pasteur Institute had been evacuated and was producing serum, the red lights on the cold storage chambers flickered and died. The power station had been hit, or the lines were down. The college water supply came from two wells 180 feet deep, and had to be pumped to the surface by an electric compressor.

---

43   Governor's Report on the Evacuation of Burma, Appendix V, British Library.

The death toll was 2,000. The railway station took a direct hit as did the hospital. With immense practicality MacLean adapted a steam engine to run the college water pump, knowing that the improvised hospital at the college would have to cope with more casualties. A hot dry wind fanned the flames to a frenzy, and great columns of dense black and grey smoke billowed up into the sky:

> Motor vehicles and bullock carts were soon streaming to the college with their mutilated loads. I drove through the bombed area over a mesh of wires with wrecked pony carts and carcasses strewn along the roads.

The heat was so intense that some bodies were incinerated on the spot, leaving nothing but a mound of ash at the roadside. In the random nature of war, a horse was killed, keeling over with its burden, but the owner on top of the cart was untouched. Eyewitnesses reported streets littered with corpses, and there was an apocryphal story that the vultures became so bloated that when they perched on the electricity wires, their weight brought wires and poles crashing down. It was 120 degrees in the shade and once again Mandalay faced another health hazard as bodies decomposed where they had fallen. The human population was decimated, but the number of flies escalated: a fly population doubles in a few hours in extreme heat.

Men from the Burma Fire Service, fought the blaze but the old teak buildings which were clustered closely together, allowed flames to leap from house to house. Bombardier Malcolm Taylor, who had been at the wheel of the first lorry leaving Rangoon, helped to remove bombs from an ammunition dump ringed by fire. He and other army drivers ferried patients from the Home for the Poor to safety in a convent, which was away from the heart of the fire. Mandalay was still smoking when writer and explorer, Frank Kingdon Ward drove into the town 4 days after the raid:

> On the outskirts of Mandalay were the railway yards and destruction. Fleets of engines stood cold and motionless on the tracks; further along were shattered coaches, wrecked wagons and twisted rails. We passed the deserted roofless station. The business quarter of Mandalay had ceased to exist. It was a city of the dead – an unburied Pompeii. Nothing remained but smoking ruins, charred tree stumps, cracked walls, twisted telegraph poles and tangles of wire. Taxis half melted by the heat, formed funeral pyres for the charred skulls of their drivers, who had perished with them. The main road had become an inferno, people had been roasted alive.
>
> FRANK KINGDON WARD PAPERS, CENTRE OF SOUTH ASIAN STUDIES,
> UNIVERSITY OF CAMBRIDGE

Japanese bombers scored a direct hit on the Upper Burma Club within the confines of Fort Dufferin, smashing the highly polished teak dance floor and teak pillars supporting the roof. However, the military installations within the fort were largely unscathed. Wounded Chinese soldiers who tried to shelter were machine gunned from the air.

> Across the blackened wilderness I caught sight of something which seemed infinitely beautiful in the midst of this awful desolation: it was the shining moat which mirrored the red crenellated wall and tapering pyramidal spires of Mandalay Fort. We crossed by the South Bridge where lotus leaves floated on the wide water and passing under the high wall, gained the park-like interior which had been untouched by the Blitz. Even Thibaw's palace, tawdry with its garish glitter of glass pillars and heavy wooden carving seemed a thing of taste after the utter destruction of the Western town. Outside the East gate under the shadow of Mandalay Hill, we spent the night in the mess of the Burma Rifles. As night fell, swift and menacing, the lurid glare in the sky told us that Mandalay was still burning down towards the river, four miles away.

Down on the river, Fred Tizzard had also seen the glow of the burning city as he steamed upstream on the *Java* which had become a hospital ship on 31 March. Often the *Java* had to run up river at night using a searchlight, despite the risks of air attack. There was such a shortage of fuel that soldiers had to break up the wooden charpoys on which they slept, to keep the steamer running. Fred had got word that his wife and baby daughter were safe in Calcutta, and was able to concentrate on navigating the Irrawaddy whose waters were dropping daily as the heat increased. The Irrawaddy has a shifting mass of shoals and sandbanks. Modern river traffic has the benefit of small river boats which patrol each stretch marking shallow areas with the quivering top sections of bamboo. There are also white markers on the banks by which boatmen steer from mark to mark. Captains designate crewmen to plumb the depths using lengths of bamboo, to check clearance. Despite all these precautions, even ferries which regularly run up and down river still run aground, and have to wait to be towed off. Sometimes male passengers are asked to get off the grounded boat in midstream to lighten the load and then heave. Fred Tizzard had known ships to run aground, and remain there for days waiting to be rescued. Fortuitously, Fred had run aground as he headed towards Mandalay, so the *Java* arrived there 5 days after the Good Friday bombing. The city was largely abandoned.

> There are no dust clouds on the shore now. Little wheeled traffic there, the dust beaten smooth by refugee feet. A coolie half dead of cholera on the gangway. My men are determined to go. John despite his having made his final decision 'to stay with my lord till the end' is falling over himself in eagerness to go too. Opened the linen chest for the last time to get a few things and unframed the pictures. The ache seems over now, when I think of old days it provokes a happy smile of memory rather than pain.

One of Fred and Marjorie Tizzard's proudest possessions, their car, remained onboard the *Java*. On 10 April Fred drove the car into Mandalay to sell it. He drove on roads empty but for decomposing bodies and the tangle of wires and rubble left from the bombing. The Methodist and Anglican churches had been burnt, and a press report later in Britain described how Clement Chapman the Methodist chaplain had sung hymns in the shell of his ruined church before taking his black cocker spaniel and leading 250 people to safety in India. Fred's last sighting of Mandalay was on 28 April as the IFC boats were sunk to prevent them falling into Japanese hands, he watched with regret as the ships he had known for much of his working life settled heavily into the deeper channels of the Irrawaddy.

> Lorries blazing on deserted Mandalay shore when we passed at 8am, a fire in our dockyard, some launches sunk and others settling down. Looked my last at Maymyo hills where Marjorie and I hoped now to be enjoying our holiday, and in the afternoon saw Mandalay Hill disappear. Our leaving Mandalay means the end of all M and I have planned out of this career. But it is no good worrying as I did over lesser things months ago – now we must live just for the day and await what the rest brings. A little refugee boy in one green stocking and one khaki has saved one roller skate!

Now skippering a launch, Fred Tizzard continued to ferry refugees up river away from the Japanese, although privately he felt many of them were not in good enough shape to make the cross-country trek to India. One of his last acts was to donate the tinned baby milk, which he and Marjorie had bought for Rosemary, to a refugee family. On 3 May he abandoned his career as a captain in the Irrawaddy Flotilla Company, and stepped ashore at Katha to begin the trek west.

Many of those in Mandalay were refugees from Rangoon, like Mrs Bouché who had arrived from the capital by train barely 6 weeks earlier. She had found a temporary home with friends. After the raid, thousands were homeless and desperate to escape before the country was overrun, which many felt was inevitable. Trams and buses transported them out to fields in the countryside near a lake,[44] the site of a new refugee camp. There were a thousand people but no tents, so they settled down under the shade of almond trees.

> The authoritative powers strutted about the camp with little cards inserted in their topees[45] indicating their jobs – administrative, food, rations, complaints etc. Burmese labourers were in great demand and made good money. With their tools and thatti[46] they built us homes – homes we will never forget, even

---

44   Possibly near Amarapura.
45   Topee – another word for pith helmet.
46   Thatti – woven grass mats used in traditional Burmese houses for walls.

though they did not have ceiling or a carpet on the floor! Mother Earth was never more appreciated. Our home was just about 12 feet square and the height of the partitions was just about 2 feet off the ground, but it was privacy and we were glad of it. The order for the oil lights to be extinguished was trumpeted at 10pm. Several people were the proud possessor of the good old Hurricane Lanterns. Here and there in the soft light afforded by the stars one could distinguish young boys and girls, some singing and dancing, others eating – and it was not uncommon to hear loud bursts of laughter. Parts of the camp started community singing to the accompaniment of a guitar and ukulele.

MRS BOUCHÉ PAPERS, IWM

After 6 days the Bouché family packed their suitcases and bedding to take the bus and train to the only airfield still in operation, Myitkyina:

My little daughters took a last look at the beautiful dolls they had treasured and they rose to the occasion obediently because they had to be left behind for other little girls to play with – perhaps we should have let the girls have their dolls, but what are toys when people and pets were to be considered – some pets had to be put down.

Angus MacLean remained in the city during the chaotic last days. His concerns were for the college staff and hundreds of estate workers on the college farms. Like many of those in charge of a Burmese workforce, he made sure they were paid, but was horrified to hear that a band of Indian soldiers then robbed them at gunpoint. That any of his estate workers remained was a tribute to him. Mandalay was days from occupation by the Japanese, and while the British could leave, the local population had families. He wrote afterwards:

Hotly as I resented these desertions at the time, I must admit in retrospect that to remain called for courage and a strong sense of duty and of loyalty. Some had these qualities. The large bazaars and markets were deserted and food was most difficult to obtain. Most of the shops had been destroyed, lighting was unobtainable and over most of the town, water. The few British officials and businessmen in the civil lines spoke grimly of corpse water from the moat. There were said to be piles of undelivered letters in the post office where one might sort one's own mail, if one had time.

The infrastructure so carefully built by the British Empire had crumbled. There were others who would not or could not leave, among them the inhabitants of the Roman Catholic Leper Home on the road to Maymyo. MacLean donated the college supply of seed rice to tide them over for the months to come.

The priests opted to stay put at the Roman Catholic Leper Home outside Mandalay.

Military news when it was communicated to civilians was bleak. The Japanese were breaking through in the Shan States to the east, and the Chinese armies were in retreat. Casualties were still arriving at Mandalay, both Chinese and British, and the railway was still operating, after a fashion, although many staff had left for India. In the last hours before Mandalay was abandoned, Angus MacLean received word that a hospital train was stuck in the hills near Tonbo on the road to Maymyo:

> There were still fowls at the farm, the white leghorns we had cherished as a poultry demonstration. The farm superintendent had as many as my cook could deal with killed, and these were cooked during the forenoon. The mornings milking from the cows, before these were handed over to the Burmese farm tenants, was collected and with as much drinking water as we could load once again, made the run to Tonbo in the early afternoon. The hospital train was in the station where we received a very cordial welcome from all on board.

Tonbo station is a rural halt on the railway line built by the British between Mandalay and their beloved hill station Maymyo. The wounded were fresh from the fighting near Lashio in the Shan States, further up the line. Maymyo and Mandalay would soon be overrun. The sappers were laying charges to detonate the one and only bridge over the Irrawaddy, and the explosion would signal defeat and the retreat to India. After serving in the trenches of the First World War, Angus MacLean had spent his professional life in Burma. His love of the country is evident in this description of his last night in Mandalay:

> There was one of the sharp storms of wind and rain normally so welcome at this season, affording as they did a brief respite in the long hot weather, but that evening there was no blessing. The scent of moist earth like incense of gratitude and the harsh but amusing chorus of the frogs passed unheeded in the mood of depression which settled upon me, dark as the over-clouded sky. All who had made some claim upon me had gone. College and farm were deserted and empty. I the last to go – the morrow held no task to challenge but also to inspire – no task but that of escape for which there could be no enthusiasm for it seemed desertion. Marauding deserters were abroad. The convicts from Mandalay jail had been released. Roving Chinese troops added to the disquiet.

As he meditated alone, by some extraordinary chance the electricity supply came on in the pre-dawn darkness. The imposing pillared building, which today is part of Mandalay University, echoed his mood: 'The high light in the bowl in the college hall was lit as in the nights before war came – one small dim light in a great darkness of the land and of the spirit. This was the end, a strange and sombre passing.'

His wife, Marie, was on her way to Myitkyina with the staff of the Maymyo military hospital, to fly out with the casualties. On Monday 27 April Angus MacLean celebrated his fifty-first birthday alone, and left Mandalay to walk to India:

> Out on the trunk road we joined a thin stream of cars coming from Mandalay and perhaps Maymyo. There was no military traffic. At the fork for Sagaing there were British sentries but we were not held up and drove into Amarapura where none were afoot and where no lights showed. As we rose to the great bridge there were again British sentries but we were not challenged. The toll gates were open. We drove slowly through. Somewhere on the bridge roadway, planks and ropes lay ready in preparation for the destruction of a span. Dawn came not like thunder but imperceptibly.

As British infrastructure crumbled the principal casualty had been communications. The telegraph office in Mandalay was the pivot of communications in Upper Burma, and had taken a direct hit in the Good Friday raid. Soldiers were often completely unaware of the current state of play, events were changing too quickly.

On 29 April, 24 hours before the Ava Bridge was to be demolished, a solitary Burmese soldier arrived in Maymyo with orders for anyone remaining to get out via Mandalay. The Japanese were heading for Maymyo through dense jungle to the east, planning to approach the hill station and surprise the garrison without using the main road. Speed was called for. Still, to escape they had to negotiate the twenty-three hairpin bends running from Maymyo to the plains, plus the 44 miles to the river. Some Burmese soldiers reacted to the news by deserting, others knew their villages had already been overrun and decided to stick with the British forces and trek to India. George Vellacott left Maymyo at 1pm on 30 April. Fifteen miles short of Mandalay a runner met them with the news that the last paddle steamer was leaving the dock at 4am the following morning. As the soldiers marched grimly on in the dense dark of the tropics, they heard the crump of explosives as the sappers blew the last span of the bridge adjoining the western shore. It was one minute to midnight. Two hours later the weary soldiers arrived at the shore. They had made it, but had passed many stragglers on the road. Commandeering an abandoned Buick, George Vellacott raced back and forth along the Maymyo Road picking up stragglers and piling them onto the car. On one trip he had twenty-two soldiers of different nationalities on board.

When the last paddle steamer left Mandalay at 5am, towing two flat bottomed barges it had a mixed cargo of women, children, bullocks and soldiers. All were bound for Bhamo, upstream through the second defile. As they headed north they travelled away from the Japanese, but also towards a wall of mountains that separate Burma from neighbouring China and India. Not one of those on board was equipped for a journey across those mountains. The only map in their possession was a road map of India, with Burma inset at a scale of 50 miles to the inch.

The day after the Ava Bridge was blown, Alex Morrison was hunkered down in a ditch with twenty-four other men, trapped on the wrong side of the Irrawaddy River. They had abandoned the possibility of taking vehicles across on rafts, and silently waited for the enemy to close in. They were surrounded:

> Jap mortars opened up, shelling us from both sides. Our fighting padre gave a service in the open, despite the shelling, bombing and machine gun fire. We sang Abide with me. He was a great man our padre – imagine him in battle, Bible in one hand, revolver in the other shooting Japs left and right as he repeated: 'God forgive me, God forgive me.' After the service was over. All hell broke loose.
>
> ALEX MORRISON PAPERS, IWM

Darkness fell so quickly as he and his pal Shorty were pinned down by fire at the river bank, that suddenly the two men realised they were alone. They fell into an exhausted sleep, and woke to find themselves surrounded by Japanese soldiers. The captured men were marched to a jungle clearing where they found sixteen others. Here they were lined up in single file and loaded up like pack mules:

I realised that they had kept us to carry their supplies. A rope was slung over my head to hold a metal ammunition box to my back, and this was about fifty-odd pounds in weight. In Indian file we set off north. I noticed that several of the boys had wounds, two or three looked pretty bad. Within a couple of hundred yards, one lad dropped to the ground. He was stuck with a bayonet four times and we carried on, through the night.

Over the ensuing 5 days the new coolies plodded on with blistered feet and raw chafed backs. Two more soldiers were bayoneted when they faltered, and left by the path. However, fortune smiled, and they were ambushed again, this time by 5,000 Chinese soldiers. After 30 hours rest and with salt rubbed on their wounds to help prevent infection, the remaining British soldiers joined the Chinese, to discover with astonishment when they stopped at a lake to bathe, that a large proportion were women. The Chinese were aiming for home, so the six Britons parted company with their allies. They were given weapons and food to help them on their way. Of the six, one was a wounded soldier from the Royal Signals Corps nicknamed Sparkie. The other five took it in turns to carry the stretcher dodging Japanese patrols as they went, but the enemy was on their tail:

After a very brief encounter we withdrew north as fast as we could; but for three or four days they followed close behind us. During this time Sparkie was in great pain, his legs black and odiferous. Then he decided that he would go no further and rolled off the stretcher. He had plenty of guts this lad; knowing we had a chance without him and knowing also that he was dying, he had decided to make a stand against the enemy on his own. The Japs were close behind us as we left him propped against a tree, a Jap Tommy gun loaded by his side. Anyway it would be a quicker death than the gangrene could give him. After a handshake, our last Chinese cigar alight in his mouth, we moved off quickly, still north. Ten minutes later we heard a Tommy gun firing in short bursts. We stopped and listened in silence. We heard rifle fire. Then all was quiet again.

8

The Last Battle

Monywa and Shwebo: two towns 40 miles apart. Shwebo an ancient capital surrounded by a picturesque moat, and Monywa, hot and dusty, strategically placed on the Chindwin River. Two armies, British and Japanese: the British in retreat at Shwebo making a dash to cross the Chindwin; the Japanese already in

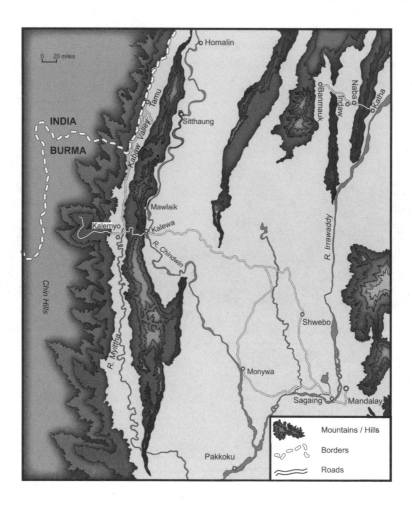

place on the river at Monywa racing to intercept their opponents. Two modes of transport: the British by road; the Japanese by river. Neither road nor river led either army by the most direct route. The Chindwin deviates from a direct course as it flows down to the Irrawaddy below Pakkoku, even indulging in a few hairpin bends. As the Japanese attempted to ferry their troops up river in the first days of May, water levels were at their lowest, and even experienced boatmen ran aground. As for the British on the capricious pot-holed tracks leading northwest to their destination, these crossed and re-crossed dry river beds deep in sand. The few higgledy-piggledy bridges thrown across rivers might be suitable for bullock carts travelling at snail's pace, but were not built for army trucks. The two armies were destined to clash where road and river meet: near Kalewa.

After desperate fighting in pockets all over central and eastern Burma, on 28 April General Alexander issued Slim with orders to retreat to India. Japanese speed and superior numbers had beaten the Allies. Stilwell and his Chinese had won some fierce battles, notably retaking Taunggyi in the Shan States. Communications were so poor that Vinegar Joe had led from the front in some operations. Once the retreat was decided, Stilwell opted to take the Chinese out from Katha, higher up the Irrawaddy. Chinese stragglers were scattered across the countryside, and fond of stopping passing trucks at bayonet point to hitch a lift. As ever, rudimentary rural bridges were too weak for the vast numbers of tanks and lorries on the move, so Eric Yarrow and his engineers were sent to shore them up.

Kalewa on the banks of the Chindwin, where the British turned and headed for the hills.

Before the sappers had even finished the job, vehicles were streaming through in a seemingly endless line. There was but one intention now to get out of Burma and to get out as an intact force. That it was a retreat nobody can deny, but it was only fair to say that the main withdrawal was always organised and never out of control.

SIR ERIC YARROW PAPERS, IWM, DESCRIBING A BRIDGE OVER THE MU RIVER

The roads were jammed and the retreating army was under attack. Colonel Bagot of the Glosters created a small mobile fighting unit, nicknamed Bagot Force to delay the enemy. Fifteen miles north of Monywa, they held them back for 4 days allowing the rest of the army, crawling along pot-holed roads at speeds of no more than 10mph, to arrive at the Chindwin. As vehicles constantly broke down, and were abandoned, others drove lorries back to pick up stragglers. Inevitably refugees tagged along behind the retreating army and soldiers cooked up improvised meals along the roadside to feed themselves and the refugees struggling in their wake. Eric Yarrow and his sappers had blown up bridges and saw mills, any building with machinery of potential use to the advancing Japanese. Now they turned their demolition skills to the road, laying charges to crater the surface and slow down enemy vehicles in their wake. Yarrow recorded in his diary:

A typical wooden bridge on the road to Banmauk.

The work took about an hour and a half. Before fixing any of the charges we pushed a three-ton lorry down a slope on to the road which proved to be a most effective block. Fired the charges just as it was getting light, although I felt sorry for the refugees which were waiting to get through.

The army was to rendezvous at Shwegyin, a small sandy bay where a stream meets the Chindwin, overlooked by steep jungle-clad hills. It lies a few miles south of Kalewa. Their route was via a cup-like depression in the hills to the northeast. This depression, known as the 'Basin', was about half a mile long and some 400 yards wide at its broadest point, and also overlooked by commanding hills. Tanks, jeeps and lorries assembled in the basin as troops queued to board the paddle steamers hefting them across the river and to safety. It was an achingly slow process. Six paddle steamers acted as the ferries: each could hold 600–700 men, but only two lorries and two jeeps. Queuing men were employed cutting firewood to feed the steamers' boilers. However, the Japanese found them. Zeros bombed from the air and their troops moved up to attack, so the British were forced to load the boats at night because the embarkation jetty was too exposed to air attack. A couple of hundred yards upstream, the Irrawaddy Flotilla Company captains knew a sheer cliff which they could snuggle close to, protected from the enemy. The wounded were lowered down the cliff on ropes to the boats waiting below.

For 6 long days and nights the crossing continued, while rearguard troops, including the Gurkhas, grimly held the Japanese at bay. Tanks which had landed at Rangoon only 3 months earlier were torched in a vast bonfire, as were lorries, stores and other heavy equipment. Finally at 5pm on 10 May[47] the army let loose every bullet, mortar and shell they couldn't carry over the mountains to India. This sudden onslaught of artillery quietened the Japanese as the British Army turned to leave. The glow of burning lorries and jeeps punctured the gloom as they climbed the steep path to the west. Turning the noses of their steamers upstream the IFC crews headed north to transport other troops. Several hours upstream at Sitthaung they joined other boats, and moored side by side across the river to act as a temporary bridge allowing remaining troops to cross, before they were scuttled. In the last 20 years, high scrap metal prices have encouraged entrepreneurs to winch up the carcasses of twenty of these Chindwin workhorses. Some have been cannibalised to provide water tanks and even walls, in a country where nothing goes to waste.

As the British headed west, army mules found it almost impossible to follow the steep and narrow paths in the darkness, many fell over ledges, others were pushed out of the way. Progress was slow, an estimated 1mph. The path was hopelessly blocked with troops and animals, and those at the rear should have been an easy

---

47   Captain W. Hutcheon papers, Irrawaddy Flotilla Co., IWM.

Winched out of the Chindwin River, the boiler from an IFC boat sunk at Sitthaung on 14 May 1942.

target for the Japanese, but they were not pursued. It was not an easy escape through the hills. In places the track was barely wide enough for a man to walk, and there were waterfalls to cross on ledges 6–8in. wide.[48] Many men ran out of food but plodded on. Once at Kalemyo there was a haphazard convoy system which ferried the wounded and sick ahead to Tamu, returning for others afterwards. Some walked barely 40 miles, others walked the entire way to the Indian border.

Mixed with the troops were hundreds of refugees, who provided useful camouflage for some of the rearguard. Among them Mike Calvert, who with two of his men was stranded on the wrong side of the river, watching his comrades vanish into the darkness. Having swum across he found himself in a village full of refugees and Japanese soldiers. Undeterred he borrowed a sari from an Indian family, and despite his hirsute appearance and height, passed undetected before the noses of troops from the Imperial Japanese Army.

Today Tamu is a pleasant town on the border with India, but at the beginning of the rainy season in 1942 it was a village crowded with refugees. This was the

48   Owen Gribble papers, IWM.

last town before an unknown wilderness which stretched up into the Naga Hills, full of headhunters and unknown danger. Queues of people ranged outside the Telegraph Office, hoping to send a telegram or make a telephone call to loved ones in India to reassure them that they were still alive. A year later they were still there as a journalist reported in May 1943:

> Patrols entering Tamu last autumn found it a 'city of the dead'. Skeletons still reclined in derelict cars, sat at decaying tables, lay in collapsed beds. A ghost town, the pagodas' doors bolted and barred, its idols smashed by rude sacrilegious hands.[49]

Gruesome accounts were printed in many British newspapers, describing the skeleton still grasping the telephone receiver inside the Telegraph Office; others slumped by the counter waiting to use the phone. The Telegraph Office no longer stands on Tamu's main street, the two storey wooden building was pulled down by the present owners, and replaced with a smart new shop built in the Chinese style which is so fashionable. Behind the store though, the teak timbers, shutters and doors from the old building have been recycled into a single storey storehouse. The well and tall tree which once stood nearby are gone, but remembered by those who played under them as children. However it is possible to see exactly what the Telegraph Office looked like, because on the other side of the road still stands the building which was the manager's home in colonial days, but is now a private house. A memory lingers in the town, of the road to India covered with a black column of refugees as far as the eye could see. There are gruesome stories of nine Indian refugees, forced to kneel in a ditch, then beheaded by a Japanese officer. There is a memory too of one of the last acts of the departing British before they crossed the border. A huge piece of roadside waste ground, now used as a football pitch, was the dumping ground for hundreds of cars, jeeps and lorries which transported many of the escaping troops and civilians. An enthusiastic local described how they were set on fire, and the mangled carcasses lay rusting there for many years. A thriving scrap metal market has long since taken advantage of such bounty left behind by the British. Although there is plenty of evidence of it still on Burmese roads today, as some of this scrap has been cannibalised to make new hybrid trucks.

Today the road from Kalemyo to Tamu has more bridges in its 80 miles than any other in Burma. There are fifty-four substantial wood and iron constructions, crossing a landscape veined with streams and rivers running from the range of hills both to the west and east. Many of these bridges bear the hallmarks of British construction, but date from efforts to recapture the country from the Japanese.

---

49   Undated and unsourced cutting from the Sir Eric Yarrow papers, IWM.

Tamu Post Office looked
like this until it was
demolished.

Burmese Farmers on the
road to Tamu carrying
produce to the Indian
border.

It is the Indian government which built the current road, and shored up the vital bridges to encourage cross-border trade. This is the Kabaw Valley, a fertile, pleasant, green valley with rich agricultural land, but it was one of two Burmese valleys which earned the title, the Valley of Death, during the year 1942. Seven decades ago farmers had not tamed the jungle which bred malaria in the rainy season, and gave the Kabaw Valley such an evil reputation.

The border point at Tamu was where many of those who had made their lives in Burma took their last look at the country that had been home. They converged from many routes. Lieutenant Colonel I.G. Scott of the Burma Frontier Force had collected stragglers from Kalewa on the sandy bank of the Chindwin River. From Kalewa a metalled road now winds along the banks of the Myittha River, the only river in Burma which runs backwards, as the locals say, i.e. from south to north. The road meanders from village to village with a fine view of the rocky riverbank below. Timber company elephants spent much of March and April 1942, hauling logs to bridge the rivers along this route, and to shore up the road. The road from the Chindwin ended at Kalemyo, where the road to Tamu begins:

> The road as far as Tamu is unsurfaced and as there had been no rain it was thick with dust. It was burning hot and the whole countryside had a parched

The British retreated through the hills bordering the Myittha River.

look. There was little enough water for the army and the position was made much worse by the thousands of refugees, mainly poor Indians, heading for their country. Everywhere they camped became foul ground, and they camped everywhere! All one could see for miles and miles was a steady stream of refugees and with water in very short supply there were queues at each and every water point. Many dropped dead from exhaustion and their bodies were left to rot in the sun. We buried many a body and rendered what aid we could but there were so many that it was beyond our capacity and we had first to look after ourselves.

LIEUTENANT COLONEL I.G. SCOTT PAPERS, IWM

Throughout the campaign in Burma, the army struggled to maintain the health of their troops, who succumbed to a bevy of tropical diseases. More men were casualties of disease than of battle.[50] Once the army had crossed the Chindwin River, the main aim of officers like Lieutenant Colonel Scott, was to extricate the men to India, where they were needed to defend the border against the advancing Japanese forces. Humanity urged them to bury the dead, but it was imperative that they remained fit. Cholera had first appeared on this route when three people were diagnosed in the third week in February.

Watching his fellow countrymen die by the roadside was Nadir Tyabji, assistant to Robert Hutchings, the agent for the Government of India. After running the Indian government's refugee office in Mandalay, he too was on the road to Tamu and viewed with horror the physical condition of his fellow countrymen:

To assess their physical condition one has to remember that most of these evacuees had been on the road for over a month living on subsistence rations with little or no physical resistance left to cope with conditions to which they were totally alien. Many were afflicted with cholera, and all I could do was to see them break away from the column, stagger or crawl to the water holes at varying distances from the track, take a few sips of the water already fouled and collapse, never to get up again. It was a traumatic sight to see dozens of bodies round each waterhole. Some we were able to bury in shallow graves but there were others who had wandered away into the thick forest to find a peaceful and solitary ending, with their visions and dreams disappearing in misty silences.

NADIR TYABJI PAPERS, CENTRE OF SOUTH ASIAN STUDIES,
UNIVERSITY OF CAMBRIDGE

There are many such reports of distraught refugees vanishing into the jungle to die quietly alone.

---

50   See Slim, *Defeat into Victory*, p.177, 'In 1943 for every man evacuated with wounds we had one hundred and twenty evacuated sick.'

Whirlpools and sandbanks are among the dangers to be navigated on the Chindwin River.

Rudimentary camps had been established at the roadside every 20 miles, but for weakened refugees these were too far apart. Even soldiers in their late teens and early twenties found 20 miles a day a punishing distance in extreme temperatures on a poor diet. Nadir had been working hard since he took the job as Hutchings' assistant on Boxing Day, but he was a fit young man. The vast majority of his compatriots managed 7 miles a day, forced to survive the extra 2 days without food, on the meagre rations saved from previous camps. Their daily rice ration was a handful a day.

> Apart from the water holes, which were mostly some distance from the track, one had to watch the heart-breaking sight of young and old, men, women and children collapsing on either side of the track and having to be left behind as the remorseless tide moved on. Many of those who lay along that track happened to be individuals I had come to know. I lent a hand in burying them and carried on.

Ration cards showing the basic food which had been issued to each refugee had been organised. Although there were villages along the route their Burmese residents had little to spare to augment these starvation rations. When soldiers from an Indian Mounted Battery arrived at Htinzin, 30 miles from Tamu the villagers thought they planned to loot their food stores. In fact the soldiers wanted to buy some bamboo matting to make shelters, but they didn't speak Burmese and the Burmese didn't speak Hindustani. A villager ran to get help from some Chin Rifles nearby, who arrived to sort out the Indian soldiers, whom they assumed were Sikh or Punjabi deserters. In the ensuing gunfight, two men were killed outright and the British major commanding the Mountain Battery was shot through the neck and took a bullet close to the lower half of his spine. Six others were wounded. The villagers of Htinzin had good reason to be wary of Indian soldiers. Diaries and memoirs of the trek are full of incidents when these men went on the rampage in Burmese villages. One of the most brutal racial incidents was recorded by Captain John Perkins. As he helped ailing Irish Sergeant Major Kirkland, through the Naga Hills, they were passed by some men from the Burma Frontier Force, who were usually Burmese or Anglo-Burmese. Then they were overtaken by some Indian soldiers, as Perkins wrote:

> Immediately there were shots echoing round the valley. Kirkland and I went to investigate and found that they had murdered two unfortunates for little more that a pocketful of rice. Two sepoys were looting the bodies, whilst their companions had done a bunk on my arrival.

Despite his bedraggled appearance after 3 weeks up to his knees in mud, with his uniform in tatters, Perkins announced himself in Urdu as a British officer.

> Discipline there was none, so after suggesting they stood up and explained themselves, which didn't appear to exactly agree with their wishes, for they took no notice, I then threatened to shoot. By this time my sergeant major not understanding the conversation became a bit anxious for my safety – me too!

What follows in his account has been crossed out in the version deposited in the Imperial War Museum archives. But it is still possible to decipher the words: 'After a pass being made at me with a bayonet I shot my friend and Kirkland did likewise with the other, so after a fashion the other unfortunates were avenged.'

The gnawing undercurrent of hunger must have turned many previously rational human beings to such inhuman behaviour, and a few incidents are recorded. When Lillian Mellalieu and her family set out on the trek there were four siblings, among them her younger brother Eric. In her farewell note to her husband she mentions that Eric has left them, but she does not refer to the circumstances, which almost certainly contributed to the death of her parents and sister. The only survivor of Lillian's family was her youngest sister Irene. It is thanks to her that we know that 16-year-old Eric absconded with the family's rations, perhaps driven mad by the mud, corpses and rain.

The first monsoon rains drenched Tamu, an unimportant village of about a hundred houses, on 25/26 April 1942. There was a vestige of colonial administration, a court house and the ubiquitous 'dak' bungalows used by visiting officials. The telegraph line to India ran through the village, hence the telegraph office. Refugee camps had been built but when Nadir arrived he noticed a neatly marked off plot of about 5 acres with somewhat better-built huts large enough for ten people:

> On enquiry I was told that the enclave was meant for non-natives – Anglo-Indians or native sahibs as the case may be – and I knew instinctively that this was going to cause trouble. It was blatant discrimination.

The camp had been set up by the Government of Burma, but Nadir had been given a free rein so he interpreted the ruling liberally. The inherent racism of colonialism was criticised by many throughout the crisis, and there is evidence aplenty in the accounts left by those who were there. Nevertheless, these were British attitudes typical of the colonial era. One European travelled part of the journey in a large car which carried five people and five dogs. Colonel Henry Shortt was born in British India in 1887, he had served all his life with the Indian Medical Service, latterly in Burma. When he heard of the numbers of refugees heading for the Indian border state of Manipur he expressed his horror in his diary:

> They would be an undisciplined mob, would foul all the jungle tracks, and bring with them malaria, dysentery, possibly typhoid, typhus and very likely cholera to mention only the most likely diseases; such a mob would endanger not only the civilian population of Manipur but, out of hand as they would be, would inevitably spread infection to the troops assembling to stem Japanese invasion.
>
> COLONEL SHORTT PAPERS, IWM

Yet Colonel Shortt was one of those who organised cholera vaccines and medical help in the string of refugee camps, along the route from Tamu into Assam. However, this was once again an apartheid system rationalised by the need for law and order:

> For reasons of discipline these camps had to be kept for Europeans and Anglo-Indians as they could be kept in reasonably disciplined control, whereas if opened to Indians they would be overwhelmed by undisciplined crowds.

A separate line of camps was constructed for Indians. The two routes became known as the White and Black routes,[51] although in the governor's official report

---

51   Governor's Report on Civil Evacuation, British Library, p.53.

Tamu is now a much larger town than it was in 1942.

on the crisis it is claimed that there was no resentment shown by refugees at the time. If the refugees were divided by race, they were certainly divided by wealth. Porters had been recruited from over the Indian border, as well as some Chin tribesmen. Early evacuees had the advantage of better weather and a less crowded route, but were ripped off by the porters who took advantage of them, inflating prices to six times the normal rate. Officials had to step in and set a fixed rate for the route through the hills from Tamu, but for the poor who had been on the road for several weeks or even months, this was still beyond their reach. If porters carried their food it helped refugees' chances of survival.

Refugees streamed into the bottleneck at Tamu from all parts of central Burma. Most travelled by a combination of boat and train. There were even some who hired buses at exorbitant rates from Pakkoku on the Irrawaddy River, a trip which took 2 or 3 days. But they arrived at the border in a better physical state, more able to undertake the trek into the hills. If Robert Hutchings and Nadir Tyabji could have plotted the transport options on a vast map the situation would have looked more intricate than that in Churchill's war room. Sadly, they had no such tools. Solutions were tried until they were found not to work. For example, government convoys were organised on the route pioneered by the Bombay Burma families, from Sitthaung on the Chindwin, 36 miles over the hills to Tamu. However, there were too many problems. When the families of men of the Burma Frontier Force and the Burma Military Police were sent by convoy from Mawlaik, also on the Chindwin, there were more accusations of racism. The British government back in London was sensitive to the press coverage which resulted in April 1942, and tried to suppress a photograph of European women waiting to be evacuated by air. The Ministry of Information, Near East Division sent a worried memo about the photos taken by Rogers of *Life* magazine:

> These go to Cairo from where they are distributed. It is of course extremely difficult to prevent photos of this kind from getting to America and other countries direct, but it might be useful if we could warn Cairo to be extremely careful in what they pass for publication, and to stop if they can or to discourage the circulation of anything which seems to support the stories of preference being given to Europeans.
>
> INDIA OFFICE RECORDS, BRITISH LIBRARY

The photograph appeared in *The Times* on 15 April in a round-up of war news. Dressed in pith helmets, a small group of white women and children are sheltering from the sun under the wing of a plane. There was some rationale behind this preferential treatment, as already outlined by Governor Reginald Dorman-Smith. In a secret telegram to the Secretary of State for India, summing up intelligence reports from occupied territory in Tenessarim down the tail of Burma, he reported that the Japanese treated all fellow 'Asiatics' kindly, whereas the fear was that such treatment would not be shown to the Europeans.

Perhaps he also had in mind his refusal to order the evacuation of women and children earlier in the year. Dorman-Smith had been privy to the unreleased information of the rape and murder of European women at the fall of Hong Kong on 25 December 1941. Coupled with the intelligence reports received from occupied Burma, maybe it is not surprising that he acquiesced in the discrimination in favour of the white minority. On 14 May 1942, he sent a telegram to the Secretary of State for India, excusing and admitting that preference had been given to Europeans in the final days of the airlift, because they knew that Indian women and children were 'generally left unmolested'.[52]

---

52   India Office Records, British Library.

Broad leafy streets run down to the Sule Pagoda in the heart of Rangoon.

Missionaries and their wives sit beneath a painted awning made of bamboo and newspaper at St John's College sports day in 1934.

The European boat club in Rangoon, it was used as a brothel by the Japanese during the occupation.

The man with the dragon tattoo, just visible on his right forearm: Fred Tizzard at his desk in more peaceful times.

Marjorie Tizzard in pith helmet, stands next to a pile of coconuts in Taunggyi Market.

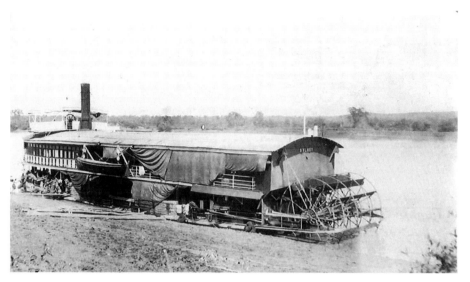

One of the paddle steamers captained by Fred Tizzard during his career with the Irrawaddy Flotilla Company.

A creek near Tavoy, the town where the Japanese attack began.

CONVOY "MAYMYO NO.1".

CIVIL EVACUATION OFFICE
MAYMYO
E.O. No. 1240 dated 25 F b 42.

To ......*Mrs. Edwards*.......
.......*Salvation army*. *One child*

PASS: KEEP THIS WITH YOU.

    This is Evacuation Pass No...*2.7*... from Maymyo under the Government Voluntary Evacuation (Civil) Scheme, Maymyo. Your must have your meal and then be at the Railway Station, Maymyo, ready with your luggage and family to embark by 8 o'clock p.m. on .....*2.5.3.*.. Feb 1942.
/0 —
    Accommodation on the train will be allotted to you.

    Attached are Pass No.....................
....
for those travelling in your charge.

Camp No..............
Compartment No...............

G.R.A.

Subdivisional Officer,
MAYMYO.

Evacuation Pass given to Mrs Edwards for her place on one of the few government convoys.

Army wives set out to walk to India with their unwieldy suitcases.

Sappers setting explosives on a railway bridge: Eric Yarrow's photos survived despite dropping the camera into the Irrawaddy River during the retreat.

British missionary David Patterson's car crosses a Burmese river by raft, then is hauled up the bank by elephant power.

Baggage elephants from a refugee convoy take the winding path through the hills to India.

Burmese villagers waiting to sell food and drink to
refugees arriving on the west bank of the Chindwin River.

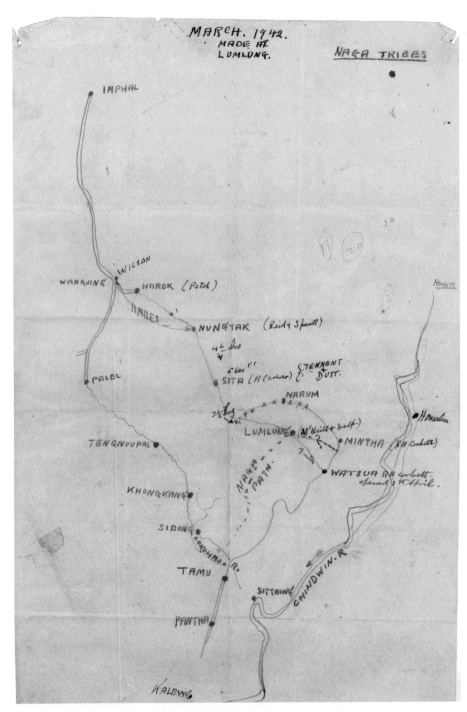

Hand-drawn maps were all most walkers possessed to guide them through the mountains to India.

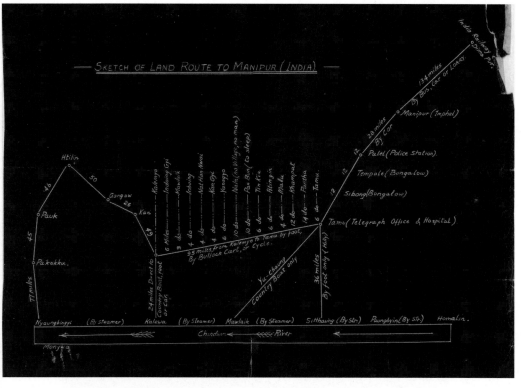

The map used by a Burmah Oil Company employee to escape to India.

Eric Yarrow's men rest in a Naga village during the long walk to India.

Soldiers on the Chindwin River during the retreat in May 1942. Eric Yarrow is in the foreground on the left.

As the terrain deteriorated vehicles were immobilised to prevent the Japanese making use of them.

Crossing the Irrawaddy by sampan, soldiers head towards enemy lines to blow up a bridge.

A Shan ferry constructed from bamboo to carry passengers and vehicles across river.

Men from the Bombay Burma Trading Corporation lash teak logs together as makeshift rafts to float down river.

Left: Timber company families trekked along jungle tracks on the Burma–Thai border to escape from the Japanese.

Below: Carrying what they can, barefoot Indian refugees at the start of their journey through the hills to India.

Spattered with mud, exhausted refugees descend to the Imphal plain. Behind them men shore up a landslide caused by the torrential rain.

A little boy and his sister at the end of their journey. Many children succumbed to disease and malnutrition en route and their bodies were claimed by the jungle.

9

The Old Man of Banmauk

In the cool gloom of a traditional teak house, an old man remembers how the soldiers came in 1942. He is tattooed from knee to hip with trees, flowers and animals pricked out in blue. The tattoo artist worked for 2 weeks, a week on each thigh, with no anaesthetic or antiseptic. Two weeks of fever followed, thus a whole month of life was lost for this piece of body art. A rare sight today, these tattoos are a symbol of manliness, although he happily admits that it was painful. In May 1942, with a wife and four young children U Khin Shwe abandoned his

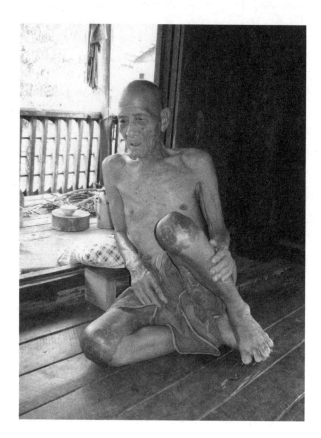

Ninety-year-old U Khin Shwe shows off his tattoos at his home in Banmauk.

home in Banmauk and fled through the jungle to the next village. It was a scene repeated all over Burma as the country became a battlefield in the Pacific War. What makes this story different is that this man is an eyewitness to the retreat of the British Army: a nonagenarian is a rarity in modern Burma.[53] Soldiers meant trouble, he explained before an assembled posse of great grandchildren. Be they Japanese, Chinese, American or British, soldiers were foreign and armed.

His village, Banmauk, lies on a rough track between two great rivers, the Irrawaddy and the Chindwin. Almost due west through hills and jungle stands Imphal, the capital of Nagaland and the destination for thousands of refugees fleeing from the Japanese. Columns of refugees, military and civilian, descended on this village after coming ashore at Katha. Some had come down by boat from Bhamo, close to the Chinese border. Bhamo had been considered a place of safety for some time, and civilians and the wounded had been brought upriver from Mandalay. By the end of April the town was congested. An Irrawaddy Flotilla Company captain, T.F. Musgrave, described the last few weeks in the town as 'unadulterated hell':

> During the last fortnight it was the hardest job imaginable to keep the steamers running. I had to pay double wages and during the last week had to give the crews 100 rupees per day to keep at their posts, between all hands. Money was no object.
>
> FROM PAPERS IN CENTRE OF SOUTH ASIAN STUDIES, UNIVERSITY OF CAMBRIDGE

Bhamo was the headquarters of the Roman Catholic St Columban's Mission. These Irish fathers kept urging Captain Musgrave to leave, as many others were. But on the morning of Sunday 3 May, their message stressed that there was not a moment to lose. Japanese troops marched into town 3 hours later.

From Bhamo the river flows swiftly through the second defile, where vertical cliffs dive into waters estimated to be 100 metres deep. Forest clings to the rocky shore, and pagodas perch at the water's edge. A rock with a faint resemblance to a parrot has been painted in garish red and green. In the rainy season, boatmen know they are in trouble if the parrot's beak 'drinks' from the river, as the water has risen too high for safe passage.

Little has changed since 1942. Today, passenger boats call at the few villages along the riverbank, on a 'schedule' which is at the whim of the shifting sandbanks and demands endless patience. Cargo and passengers share a crowded space, with bench seats for the lucky, and floor space for those who are not. Each village is heralded by an invasion of women and children selling drinks and snacks from dugout canoes. The hawkers jam the aisle, as passengers attempt to gather string-

---

53   Average male life expectancy is 57.

The dramatic second defile of the Irrawaddy below Bhamo.

tied parcels, cardboard boxes and carrier bags to disembark. Once through the crush, dry land is reached by walking a plank laid crookedly from deck to shore; outstretched hands are always there to prevent accidents.

In May 1942 boats were even more crowded, filled with panic-stricken refugees. Hungry refugees needed feeding and welcomed the tasty snacks and drinks offered. Katha was the terminus.

The town of Katha is little bigger now than it was in 1942 when the High Court judges, staff and families were evacuated here from Rangoon; a strange location for Burma's seat of justice, until you consider the solid walls of the prison which was built here by the British. This was George Orwell's beat as a policeman, and the miscreants he arrested would have served their sentences behind the high terracotta walls, just as they do today. The Katha Tennis Club still proudly bears the date of its foundation, 1924, and if the future novelist ever picked up a racket this is where he would have played. In 1942, Katha was the jumping off point for one of the easiest routes used in the retreat from Burma. In fact a track, unmarked on modern maps, is still known to those who work for the Burmese Ordnance Survey Department as, 'the evacuation route'.

George Orwell lived in a house just like this in colonial Katha. The cottage with the chimney was the kitchen.

There is no evidence or memory today of the refugee camps which sprawled on the outskirts of Katha in 1942. When Fred Tizzard arrived among the teeming crowds there, he met Jack Vorley, the commissioner for refugees:

> He had work for each of us in helping the evacuation of civilian refugees. Briefly he sketched the situation. Train services had ceased, no more refugees could reach Myitkina to fly out. The only other line of escape was 250 miles of almost unknown river and jungle through which only an occasional forest officer had ever passed. The thousands of Eurasian and Indian refugees still congested round Katha must be divided into two classes, the Stay Puts, which would include the sick or elderly and most of the women and children, and the Walkers, including all fit enough to face the arduous journey. The Stay Puts were to be distributed in surrounding jungle villages, where village Headman would be very heavily bribed to show them hospitality until British rule returned.
>
> FRED TIZZARD PAPERS, IWM

Tizzard had brought a launch piled with refugees from the burning city of Mandalay, upriver to Katha:

So here among the Stay Puts must end the journey of my little lad with the one roller skate, and all the other 450, whose husbands and fathers are now tramping home to India and expect to find them waiting there. The tragedy is no one's fault. A single line railway and one aerodrome were never intended to cope with an exodus of this dimension. The Japs have moved too fast for us. Nothing was ready, for no man's flight along this wild route had been expected, but everything possible was being done to make it easier.

Angus MacLean was also another volunteer here. He questioned why no preparations had been made along this route:

> The Katha route to the Chindwin, one of the few possible lines of escape which must have been considered and discussed by many when the news from Malaya and Lower Burma stunned us, was long but it was not extremely difficult as were the routes from Myitkyina. The first section was well known to men of two timber firms and to some forest officers. With some small effort, bridges could have been strengthened to stand up to light motor traffic.

These Europeans had the luxury of travelling by car until road conditions deteriorated. Then they hired a bullock cart, one of many which had been working up and down the track carrying supplies and refugees. All but the weakest carried backpacks:

> I had been warned that my shoulders would chafe under the unaccustomed rub of the pack straps, so thought it well to break them in under a light weight before they had to bear my full load. Even 14 pounds weighs heavy towards the end of the first day.

From Katha those on foot had a gentle walk uphill before dropping down to the railway town of Naba, a small but important junction on the main line between Mandalay and Myitkyina. Food supplies were still coming up the road from the south. From Naba the route went to Indaw and finally Banmauk. Vast teak forests along this route are still worked by elephants, which move from logging camp to logging camp accompanied by their oozies and a pack of dogs. Fred Tizzard's description reveals what it was like seven decades ago:

> The track ran level, through teak forest that cannot have been worked for many years; they were the tallest teak trees I have ever seen, some 70 or 80 feet high. The bullocks went slowly, the driver grumbling that they had worked too long yesterday. So some of us impatiently walked ahead, which later proved unwise. Soon the party was strung out over half a mile, in twos and threes, exchanging news of friends and reminiscences of the last few weeks.

Naba Junction is little more than a pinprick on the map, but was swarming with refugees in 1942.

From Fred Tizzard's diary we get a picture of the group he walked with, many of whom had helped with the organisation and feeding of refugees. Helen Vorley was awarded a medal for her role in helping refugees at Mandalay, where her husband was based as evacuation commissioner:

Ahead walked Mrs Vorley wife of the Evacuation Commissioner. Sturdy and efficient in her khaki shorts and sports shirt, a water bottle slung on one hip, her revolver on the other, she smokes like a chimney constantly reaching for the cigarette case in her hip pocket. I'm a he woman, she tells me and do not doubt it. She will last through with no complaint, in spite of her being six years in the tropics without a break. With her walks Forrest, who has evacuated and evacuated since first the Japs drove him from Tavoy. He must be over 50 which is not young for a man who has spent half his life in this climate. Emaciated with sickness, and now suffering from dysentery, he may become a problem. But he is game.

Close behind them walk Marjorie and Flossie, two Eurasian teachers from Rangoon, who have worked on evacuation. Marjorie marches in a black silk shirt more suited to a city. Marjorie is tall, Flossie short and sturdy. They chatter and joke all day. Both are bursting with energy, sometimes they run to catch another member of the party. Unless their light town shoes give out they will complete the journey without turning a hair. Women seem to have an endless reserve of stamina to call on when faced with prolonged physical strain. Otherwise some of us would never have been born.

Also in this group were Dr and Mrs Jury who despite being in their sixties insisted on carrying their backpacks rather than put them in the bullock cart. Dr Jury was an American who had been head of Judson College, part of the university in Rangoon. The college was part of the legacy of the first American missionary, Adoniram Judson who arrived from New York in 1812. In 5 years he had achieved his first convert, but the success rate increased when Adoniram proselytised to the Karen tribe. The tribe were animists, but among their legends were stories of a great flood, a woman born from a man's rib and a lost book which would be brought to them from across the sea. American Baptist churches are still found all over Burma, and Judson Baptist Church still stands in Rangoon on the main university campus north of the city.

With Dr and Mrs Jury walked an unnamed women referred to by Fred Tizzard only as the Matron:

> The Matron was in charge of Bassein Hospital before war came to Burma. Since then she has worked in many hospitals. She is not yet middle aged, but worn out by overwork and disappointment. She is uprooted, employment and pension gone, anxiety over how she will live at the journey's end seems to drain her confidence that she will reach it. Then there is Miss Chapman in short blue skirt and blouse, shoes that seem suitable, but may not have 200 miles wear left in them. She is a Missionary, one in charge of a Rangoon orphan's home. Her orphans went up to Myitkyina to fly out. She is short, fit and hardy. No nonsense about her, full of confidence.

Whatever the physical state of the refugees, speed was vital. In the chaos of the army withdrawal, no one was quite sure how far north the Japanese had managed to penetrate. Each new group of refugees, and in particular soldiers, brought rumours from the road. Jack Vorley organised his volunteers to set up camps, and food dumps along the route:

> I got to know Vorley and to like him. He was a Forest Officer before becoming Evacuation Commissioner. There is nothing remarkable about Vorley. Of medium height, medium build and middle age, he speaks slowly in a quiet voice, and rarely. He seems the right man for his job, one who moves steadily and methodically along a set course, unmoved alike by sudden enthusiasm or disappointment. He took little share in today's argument, and let argument work

itself to a standstill. He lay resting under a tree after several weeks of almost ceaseless work, but was ready to listen attentively to any constructive idea.

We have another eyewitness account of the members of this group from Angus MacLean, the Professor of Agriculture from Mandalay. From his diary we know that Fred Tizzard had acquired fluent Hindustani and a fair knowledge of Burmese during his years navigating the Chindwin and Irrawaddy Rivers:

> It was his crisp 'Chelao, chelao!' as if from the bridge of his ship that marshalled the lagging coolies and got us under way each morning. He supplied the only map apart from my rough tracing of the first part of the route and a list of names. This map we poured over daily but several tracts were unsurveyed and in Manipur few of the villages were marked. Tizzard usually kept an eye on the rearguard.

Janet Lindop also walked at the back ensuring no one was left behind. The energetic Jack Vorley led the way, while his wife walked more slowly and 'disliked heartily paths skirting cliffs and log bridges thrown across streams'. Flossie and Marjorie were the youngest members of the group, and like modern teenagers weren't dressed for a trek through the jungle.

> In their case there could have been no training for the long jungle marches but they never faltered nor did they lose their modesty. Marjorie was worried at times by the sores which her feet and legs collected until they became a patchwork of sticking plaster. Neither had adequate protection when the rain came but not once did they seem despondent. With courage and simple dignity they earned in full measure the credit which has been accorded freely to their community. They marched light and usually in the lead.

Both Tizzard and MacLean are unanimous in their faint praise for the medical member of the party.

> The Sikh doctor whose name I did not learn, short and somewhat overweight for his height. Caught in the operating theatre at Mandalay Civil Hospital when the early April raid was made on the town, he was rather overwhelmed by events. He had brought few medicines with him. He was full of questions about the route ahead but hardly rose to the occasion and the traditions of his profession when as we advanced more deeply into strange country, men lay sick in the villages along the way.

In fact when one of their porters was bitten by a snake he did save the man's life, but as the dead and dying became more frequent along the route he showed little compassion. Many of these were soldiers, Chinese, Indian and British, in ones and twos. Fred records men from the Glosters and KOYLIs, most of them patients from the hospital ships abandoned at Katha. He found one man abandoned outside a small hut, naked to the waist lying on a bamboo mat. His friends had left him there 6 days earlier, too weak from dysentery to go any further: 'He was pathetically happy just to have someone to talk to, showed me snapshots of his home near Gloucester, and seemed unconscious of his poor chance of ever seeing it again'.

Other walkers were always in sight, discarded items of clothing or valuables marked the route, the ash of camp fires lay by every stream and river. Janet Lindop had brought her dogs, as had many other Britons. Only a few survived the journey. Fred Tizzard recorded one encountered en route:

> A mangy, starving pup crept from under the roots of a banyan tree and tried to follow us. At the first deep water we crossed it turned back shivering to wait for another party. A few minutes later I started at the sound of a shot close behind me. A soldier had disposed of the pup.

The 90-year-old in Banmauk has no memory of the hordes of civilians who passed through his village, only the troops. Among them was the man in charge of the Chinese Fifth Army, General Joe Stilwell. His diary and the letters he wrote home to his wife, show exactly why he acquired the nickname 'Vinegar Joe'. He routinely ranted about the 'bloody limeys' to his wife but worse was reserved for the Japanese: 'When I think how those bowlegged cockroaches have ruined our calm lives it makes me want to wrap Japanese guts round every lamp post in Asia'.[54]

By the standards of the day, the 58-year-old general was considered old. Yet he famously set a pace that was not just punishing but sadistic in the demands it made of those who accompanied him. He marched at 105 paces to the minute, a speed which is more like a fast jog.[55] Among his companions was Frank Merrill, who would become a legendary figure and lead Merrill's Marauders, the American equivalent of the Chindits, fighting behind enemy lines in the latter part of the war. Yet during the hasty exit from Burma, Merrill fainted from heat exhaustion and was forced to rest, while the general himself, some 20 years older, was still leading the way. Another of Stilwell's companions on the march was Dr Gordon Seagrave, an American missionary doctor, who recorded the journey in his diary:

> We followed a path that passed through jungle, crossing a stream they call the Chaunggyi several times until we came to a sort of gorge; and then there was

---

54   *The Stilwell Papers*, 1948
55   As timed by the author in running shoes over flat tarmac!

no road at all. The General and his Hkamti Shan[56] guide led us splashing down the stream bed. The General sets the pace and is followed by the American officers; then comes a small group of heterogeneous officers; then the English; then our group; and finally the General's Chinese bodyguard. The General has been carrying one of the Tommy guns. From ten minutes to, until the hour we have a rest, and then fifty minutes of marching. When we started down the river, the Americans at first stopped and snatched off their shoes and rolled up their trouser legs. Later they gave up in disgust, and all plodded right through. One or two have cut off their trouser legs and made shorts of them. It was dark before we stopped for the night. The general would have kept on if there were not so much chance of his men getting badly hurt stumbling around in the dark.

A Burma Surgeon by Dr Gordon Seagrave (1944)

---

56   Hkamti is a town on the upper reaches of the Chindwin, close to the Patkoi Mountains. Shan tribesmen are to be found predominantly in the Shan States in eastern Burma next to the border with China.

A river cuts through hills near the Indian border, another obstacle to be crossed by fleeing refugees.

Among Seagrave's companions were several unnamed British Quakers, conscientious objectors who were members of the Friends Ambulance Unit. They had served with the American and Chinese forces. As Stilwell urged his entourage forward, men began to flag. The sharp-tongued general had no sympathy and wrote in his diary: 'Christ but we are a poor lot. Hard going in the river all the way. Cooler, all packs reduced to ten pounds. Limey's feet all shot. Our people tired. Damn poor show of physique.'

Rivers had to be waded down or crossed with monotonous regularity, but once the walkers were over the Mangin Taung, the rivers were big enough for rafting. Stilwell's Hkamti Shan guide organised bamboo rafts of the type which are still a common sight on Burmese rivers today. Enormous lengths of bamboo form the superstructure, and once floated to their destination, the poles are sold as scaffolding to the construction industry. A solid hut with pitched roof provides the crew with accommodation, plus an earth hearth for cooking, exactly the model which the Stilwell party used. The Burmese nurses and British Quakers wove a rattan roof to protect them from the sun, much appreciated by Dr Seagrave:

We men live in our underpants and the girls in nothing but a simple longyi[57] strapped up under their armpits. Every time we get hot we drop over the side for a swim. It is nice to be able to sleep again. If we aren't swimming we are sleeping. Tun Shein[58] has built us a little native fireplace of mud amidships, and we have weak tea and a bit of black sticky rice, which he begged off a native. Every so often our tummies rumble. We are better off than the others who don't know the customs of the country.

Monsoon waters had not yet swelled the Uyu River, the route down to the Chindwin River:

The first hours were easy. We had a Hkamti captain at the bow and a helmsman at the stern. We men only had to jump to action when we got to shallow water. The Hkamti have taught us to be patient and not try to pole faster than the current, for when we pole too rapidly, the several sections of the raft tend to pull apart. We had to pull them together once during the morning and attach them with reinforcements of full-thickness rattan.

General Stilwell was adamant throughout his trek, that they take the path less trodden to avoid refugee-borne diseases, and he had a local guide. Fred Tizzard's group were without a guide on a route used by thousands, and when they arrived

57   A longyi is a 5 yard tube of material, tied at the waist, worn by men and women.
58   Tun Shein was one of the Burmese who accompanied the group.

General Stilwell and Dr Seagrave travelled on a bamboo raft just like this.

at the Uyu River were without the skills or tribesmen to build a raft. Local Shan
tribesmen were recruited, but it meant a 2-day wait. After some heated debate
round the camp fire, the party led by Jack Vorley divided into walkers and rafters.
As Fred Tizzard recorded:

> Finally we decide that our unwieldy party must split. Twenty is too many. It
> complicates cooking, and delays the morning start. Besides it will take the
> raftmen two days to build rafts for twenty. Most of us feel that we should not
> delay and Chinese troops are almost overtaking, Indians are getting ahead to
> foul camping sites near water, and each day wasted increases the risk of the
> Japs being in Homalin before us. Several of us were determined to abandon
> the rafting and to walk on alone, although it may double the distance we
> have to march. Some cannot possibly tramp all the way. The less fit must go
> as far as possible by raft. Rafting would be easier for all, but all those fit and
> young enough to walk should do so, and not hold back the whole party while
> a needless number of rafts is constructed. I am glad that Vorley shares this
> view, for I would not like to leave him. Most of us know what we should do,
> but one or two whose feet already give trouble wanted to join the walkers,

rather than wait a day longer here. They could not be dissuaded. So I made the brutal sounding suggestion that all who joined the walking party did so on the understanding that if they could not carry on they must just drop out. On a raft one can rest now and again, but a walker unable to carry on might jeopardise the whole party's escape. One or two men prepared to protest, but Vorley, as leader of the walkers, smiled and said nothing, so my ungentlemanly motion was apparently carried.

However, their plans were all for nothing when the Shan raft-makers disappeared after their women were threatened by roving Chinese soldiers. Using an old raft as a template the amateurs attempted to replicate it. Fred had his doubts that it would survive a voyage, but went along with the rest of the group's efforts. As 2 more days passed, Indian refugees tramped past, and the walkers decided not to wait any longer for raft construction and set off down the river bed. As the river broadened out there was a blue sky overhead, the rains had yet to break and along the banks Fred Tizzard saw the golden flowers of the Padauk tree high above his head. To the Burmese the tree symbolises love and romance, as well as strength and durability. They feature in the legend of a seventeenth-century soldier king who when he was far from home would think of his beloved when the Padauk tree was in flower. In these forests on the way to the Chindwin, Fred's thoughts turned to Marjorie and to happier times when he had walked with her in such beautiful surroundings:

Today I went round a corner of the gorge to wash my flannel shirt scouring it round and slapping it on a log native fashion. Then lay for an hour in the now hot water, naked but for sun helmet. Just lay and thought. A brilliant blue jay settled close to me like the jays Marjorie never tired of admiring. The last weeks have been so busy, it is a luxury to have an entirely idle hour, with nothing to do but lie braced against the current so that the stream does not wash me slowly downstream and think. For 3½ years I have been waiting for a holiday, and now I have it. There could be nothing a more complete change from my work. I have always wanted to set out on a walk on which there was no turning back. While serving on the Chindwin I tramped in the evening along jungle paths. It is a long time since I have felt so completely peaceful. The last 18 months have been all anxiety, always a worry to thrust itself into my mind a few minutes after I woke. My mind is on holiday. There is no longer any need to plan. No more is required of me than of the humblest coolie walking out with me, I have only to put one foot in front of the other, the same as he.

Bird sounds were punctuated by shrieking monkeys and shrill cicadas, the latter filling the forests with a sound like the drills of demented dentists. Fred's daily routine was to wash his shirt after lunch while the walkers rested in the heat of the day, then write his journal:

IFC paddle steamers could navigate as far upriver as Homalin, the colonial post office survives.

We had to be content with a place where fire had swept through a bamboo thicket, leaving the ground thick with ashes and the bamboos blackened. From the stream bed I lever up large stones to Miss Chapman. Wood spared by the jungle fire was difficult to find. I lay aside a stack of it for the morning tea, with dire threats to any who might burn it and make me find more in the dark, with maybe a snake also. First we made tea in our one big aluminium cooking pot, boiling the water well as the stream may be infected with enteric and I issued it with my little saucepan. The cooking pot refilled we boiled the rice ration and in my capacity as victualler I stirred in one dessert spoonful of Marmite. There were several complaints tonight. Flossy protests against too little milk and sugar in the tea and there is a chorus of endorsement. Miss Chapman complains that although one spoonful of Marmite colours two gallons of boiled rice, it imparts no flavour. Both quite correct, I thought the rice a repulsive mess, but it cannot be helped. Later on maybe hunger will provide a piquant sauce to it.

British refugee diarists all recorded their consumption of Marmite, Horlicks, Glaxo Klim and other staples of colonial life. But in fact the vitamin B in Marmite was essential to prevent Beri-Beri, a debilitating and potentially fatal disease of the nervous system. The destination of all those on this route was Homalin, a hard paddle 2 miles upstream from the confluence with the Uyu River. A few British colonial buildings survive, including the Post Office, but in early May 1942 war news had barely reached the handful of ex-pats living here. Within days war came to their door, when a Japanese patrol boat moored up beneath Strand Road. Villages north of Homalin had been warned not to help the British by the Thakins[59], who threatened to burn villages sympathetic to their colonial overlords. The Burmese nurses walking with Stilwell and Dr Seagrave had no shoes by this stage, and were bleeding profusely. Although the shops had pulled down their shutters, one of the Burmese with them persuaded the village headman to co-operate, and the women bought canvas tennis shoes.

Both Stilwell's group and Fred Tizzard's party were just ahead of the monsoon, which began to fall as they climbed over the Naga Hills. For much of their journey they had relied on the stores they carried and food purchased from villages along the way, which were largely friendly and shared what little they had. They had no idea of the reception they might receive in the Naga Hills where the tribesmen were renowned for one thing: headhunting.

The Burmese left behind had no inkling of their future, but it wasn't long before they discovered the brutality of their new overlords. Stories abound in villages today of the torture of those who worked for the British during the colonial era, particularly those who had been interpreters. In Regency England, a whole generation of children grew up with the spectre of Napoleon Bonaparte as the ultimate deterrent if they misbehaved. Following the invasion, Burmese parents used the threat of the Japanese to instil obedience in their offspring in the same way. Fear of Japanese soldiers was so strong during the occupation, that teenage girls were encouraged to dress like men and cut their hair short. The latter was a particular sacrifice, as waist-length hair is considered a sign of beauty still sported by heroines of Burmese soap operas today.

---

59 The name adopted by the pro-independence movement.

10

Food, Fripperies and Footwear

What would you rescue if the house was burning down? When asked the question, most people would opt for treasured possessions: photographs of family, the necklace left to them by their grandmother, a favourite painting. People forced to abandon their homes, and escape as refugees, usually have a little more time to consider what to carry with them. But their thoughts veer towards sentiment, what they are leaving behind, their life, friends, job and family.

The diary kept by Fred Tizzard throughout his escape from Burma, is peppered with references to the possessions he and Marjorie are leaving behind. Throughout his trek through the jungle wilderness of the Burma–India border, Fred carried a little silver teapot, which he knew was precious to his wife. During the 5 week journey, he periodically reviewed the items in his pack, discarding things he felt he could do without, such as a razor.

Lillian Mellalieu was another who decided to carry a collection of silver *objets d'art*; many children carried a precious doll or teddy bear, some were lost on the route, others were given to Naga children in villages which gave them food and shelter.

As the cherry blossom flowered along the banks of the Irrawaddy, Fred Tizzard, packed his daughter's teddy bear, which he would carry all the way to India: 'April 15th, Packed my get away pack, getting in all I planned, with no space for food. Her silver tea set goes in her pigskin zipper, with Rosemary's blue bear.'

Those who had chosen to live and work in Burma, were not like the expatriate oil workers of today, able to fly home every few months on leave. Fred Tizzard had not been home for 7 years. Men who worked for the civil service routinely returned to Britain on leave, but their physical, if not their spiritual, homes were in Burma. They enjoyed a lavish lifestyle with the trappings appropriate to their position in colonial society. On the outward ship from England packing cases of china, linen, glass and silver accompanied the mem-sahibs when they came to join husbands for a life in the east. The temptation was to choose from these valuables, rather than items which might be of practical use on a trek of several hundred miles. Thanks to sentiment, a handful of items from the Glosters' regimental silver survived the retreat, secreted in officers' packs. The remainder was buried in the jungle en route, but stolen during the war. The tattered regimental colours were flown out and now hang in Gloucester Cathedral.

Men such as Jimmie Williams of the Bombay Burma were used to life in the jungles and forests and carried more practical items. Nevertheless, they were not equipped with the sort of lightweight kit that a modern expedition would routinely take for a march of 300–500 miles, through a hostile environment. Organisations such as Raleigh International advise those trekking in the jungles of Borneo for example to wear 'Goretex' boots, and take a spare pair of laces, plus knee-length leech socks made from fine cotton, which prevent leeches from sinking their jaws into the flesh. As added leech prevention they recommend gaiters to cover any gaps, such as where boot meets sock above the ankle. A 1940s-style prophylactic was to don a pair of ladies' silk stockings under marching socks.[60] Today kit is carried in a lightweight modern rucksack with a waterproof liner, and trekkers sleep in synthetic sleeping bags lined with silk or cotton. These are easily dried if bedding gets wet. Many refugees recorded using a pillow case as an improvised rucksack, as their standard luggage of the day was a suitcase, which was awkward and unwieldy to carry. Raleigh International's adventurers are issued with trowels to dig improvised latrines; toilet rolls; provisions for at least 5 days; and a compact stove which runs on methylated spirit. They all carry scissors, a penknife, can opener and 3 litre water bottles and supplies of purifying tablets, although expedition leaders have researched the routes and know where to find clean water. On each expedition there is a medic, trained in expedition medicine, and a comprehensive medical kit including a stretcher and saline solution. Expedition organisers also suggest a roll of gaffer tape, for unforeseen emergencies. Above all the expedition leaders act as guides, are equipped with maps and know the route they will be taking.

From eyewitnesses we know that many trekkers in 1942 carried heavy items inappropriate on such a journey. Harmoniums, sewing machines and even gramophones and records were not unusual items seen on the road to India. In the case of many Indian families a sewing machine was probably their most valuable possession and the tool of their trade. One family left with their possessions carried on eleven bullock carts. These included canteens of silver cutlery, and a grand piano! Some refugees began the journey as if they were moving house, rather than running for their lives. Soon the paths between Burma and India were littered with such fripperies, as exhausted refugees struggled up hills and across rivers. Packs were lightened regularly on the journey. Those who could afford to, or were persuasive enough, hired coolies to carry their possessions. Usually coolies came from the local tribes in each area, but some groups persuaded Indian

---

60   Alastair Tainsh – 'Keeping Fit in the Jungle'. Talk given to the Bengal Club, January 1943.

refugees to act as their coolies, hoping to keep their services for the entire trip. Using porters may seem a luxury, a typical example of the arrogance of empire, but it could make the difference between survival and death. There was little food available along some paths, and on the Burmese side of the border, there were few camps where refugees could get a meal. Porters enabled the walkers to be better provisioned, particularly if they were elderly, became footsore, or developed one of the many diseases which were rampant among these malnourished, frightened people. It was hard to recruit the animist tribes of the Naga Hills in May, because they were busy preparing fields, and appeasing the spirits of the land or 'nats'. This often required them to go into retreat for 10 days at a time. The carrot used to lure such tribes was opium, while the stick was the threat to burn their villages if they did not comply. Herbert Mitchell, superintendent of the Naga Hills district, was unable to raise porters because news had spread of Japanese bombing raids on villages nearby. One village of nine houses ignored his warnings, so he took a party of eight Royal Marines and burnt the village to the ground. This was not an isolated incident; other Britons resorted to the same method.

Many refugees, of whatever ethnic background, were not used to hiking long distances through difficult countryside. They were office workers, bank clerks, waiters and railway officials. The thousands of soldiers who walked to India were often no better off. Men from the Glosters, KOYLIs, Burma Rifles and those who had arrived to reinforce them, had all been fighting in the fierce heat of the plains of Lower Burma for 5 months. In such battle conditions, units became separated and stores went astray. As they fought their way north, men became so thirsty that they drank from car and lorry radiators when no other water supply was available. Survivors of the Sittang Bridge disaster lost all their kit, and many servicemen were walking wounded. Captain John Perkins, an Indian Army officer was attached to army headquarters and hastily assembled his pack before leaving Myitkyina by train on the first leg of the journey. Thanks to the quartermaster he had access to medical supplies including quinine to protect against malaria, and potassium permanganate which was used to sterilise water, although the taste was obnoxious and the water turned pink. In fact on the trek the bottle broke, and the crystals burned through several pairs of socks in his pack. Supply lines had been so stretched and disrupted that he could only muster a small heap of food: a tin of bully beef, a tin of cheese, rice and biscuits – certainly not enough to sustain a man over a hike of 350 miles. Before he left to lead his group of sixty soldiers west, he gave them a pep talk:

I estimated that it would take 28 days, that we had next to no food, and admitted that I hadn't the vaguest notion where any more would come from. I also made it quite clear that my main job was to get the main party to India and that if anyone fell out through sickness or any other reason, he would be left. I could not stay with him neither would I allow anyone else to do so. This may have sounded hard but we had to beat the monsoon before it rendered the tracks impassable and speed was essential, waste of precious hours meant more food to be consumed too.

CAPTAIN JOHN PERKINS PAPERS, IWM

Stragglers hiked out with any group they could latch on to, and in many cases were welcomed. Seabury Edwards, a retired taxman, began the trek with his wife, grown-up stepdaughter, 8-year-old son Evan and 10-year-old daughter Yolande. A private who called himself 'Ginger' walked most of the way with them, and they welcomed him partly because he was armed. They suspected that Ginger was a deserter, but in the context of such a journey this was of no importance to them. Desperation walked with the refugees and could propel fellow trekkers into violence, so Ginger and his gun were a deterrent, a comfort and a possible source of food if any game crossed their path.

Madras Sapper, Eric Yarrow brought up the rear as troops retreated over the Chindwin River, through the mountains to the Kabaw Valley, and east to Tamu on the Indian border. He knew that he must ditch all but essential items, as he wrote in his diary:

It was sad having to set fire to my few articles of spare clothing, but it was more distressing to say goodbye to such things as family photos, letters and camera. We had to prepare for a long and possibly hasty walk, and it was quite useless to attempt to overload yourself. In addition to what I was wearing, all I carried

Fred Tizzard and Angus MacLean travelled along this road through Indaw.

was my ground sheet, diary, water container, Rosalynde's whisky flask, towel, biscuits, compass, maps and wallet.

SIR ERIC YARROW PAPERS, IWM

Angus MacLean, setting out from Indaw, cut down his kit with what he calls a 'Spartan disregard for comfort and sentiment'. Food and water were top of the list of essentials. Each of his group carried a small bag of food tied round their waists filled with dhal (dried lentils) and rice. As they drew closer to India, the terrain grew more gruelling, walkers were weaker and packs got lighter:

> Problems finding coolies so offloaded more stuff. My shot gun I consigned in pieces to deep pools, a tweed jacket, spare spectacles, shell dressings, Lewis field glasses which had travelled with me from the gun-pits of France and Flanders were laid aside. My Rolliflex camera had been left at Indaw. All very regrettable but if the load were to bear heavily later on it would be better to have a pair of stout boots than some luxury.

Fred Tizzard discovered when he disembarked at Katha, that the canvas shoes which he had saved for the long walk to India had been stolen. Losses like these could not be replaced as villages were either too small for such luxuries, or shopkeepers had vanished into the jungle along with the rest of the villagers. Not that they were unwilling to help refugees, but many of those on the road were soldiers, and to the Burmese soldiers, whatever their nationality, meant trouble.

Among the soldiers passing through was General Stilwell who travelled in a mixed party which included British officers, a mission doctor, Gordon Seagrave and a group of Burmese nurses. Seagrave had been in Burma for two decades, but the May heat was still a problem:

> We set out on foot. I find my feet don't hurt much if the ground is fairly smooth and I can set my feet down squarely. It is this ghastly heat. After four miles I was exhausted and lay down for half an hour under a mango tree and soothed my parched tongue with green mangoes. There is no shade but at least we did not have to climb mountains.

Three days after they left the Chindwin, Stilwell called a pre-dawn conference after a run-in with yet another of the flimsy bridges they encountered:

> The General got us all together round him and made us a speech. All the different groups were to turn in their food supplies into a pool, then abandon everything they had except what they felt they would be able to carry themselves. I got the nurses together after that, and told them that the Chin Hills and Naga Hills which our trail would cross were famous for their steepness, and therefore they

certainly could not carry so much stuff as to make them lag on the march. We must vindicate ourselves by covering the ground as fast and as far as the long legged Americans. Furthermore we would certainly be called on to care for the sick en route; so each girl must take a little first aid kit, with the drugs for malaria, dysentery, headaches etc. My speech was very effective, for tonight I find the silly girls threw away their blankets, and have only enough for one to every group of three. They even threw away their silk longyis and kept one extra cotton outfit each.

A Burma Surgeon by Dr Gordon Seagrave (1944)

Eighteen-year-old Alwyn Sepping was the son of the Superintendent Engineer of Burma Railways, and he and his family were keen hunters:

We were adequately armed to take on any marauders, my father and uncle with 12-bore shot guns and ample cartridges, me with my Colt 45 and my mother with a light 410-bore. The final essentials of our kit were chunks of saltpetre to replenish the salt content of the body lost through perspiration; few people are aware of the danger of heat exhaustion caused by the dehydration of the body which, if very advanced, can be fatal.

Alwyn Sepping papers, British Library

One constant complaint in the diaries of refugees is the lack of salt among their rations. Some improvised. Soldier George Vellacott was also on the road from Katha: 'An intake of salt was so important that some of us learnt to scrape and eat the salt from the dried sweat on our arms, a habit which in better circumstances we found hard to break.'

Once they had offloaded unnecessary belongings, few of the walkers had any idea how to survive in the jungle. Alastair Tainsh, one of the kingpins in the refugee organisation in Assam, had acquired intimate jungle knowledge. His kit list would have been the envy of any refugee who scrambled through the jungle-clad hills. As any soldier knows, footwear is paramount:

Socks, short puttees and well-studded ammunition boots[61], as many pairs of spare laces as days' marching to be done. The Bata canvas hockey boots are equally good, and for fast silent marches, are better than the heavy army boot. They however last only a week, and sometimes less in bad conditions.

Centre of South Asian Studies, University of Cambridge

---

61 Ammunition boots were standard issue in the army until 1958. They were made of leather with steel heel and toe caps and studs.

Mr Shortis of the Burma Sugar Co., walked out through the Hukawng Valley:

> Shoe leather became one of our major problems and repairs and adjustments
> to foot gear was one of our chief employments when in camp. Two pairs of my
> own shoes had worn out and I should have been in a bad way, but for a pair
> given me by Mr Cunningham. He himself had carried on for quite a while
> with two left footed ones, and Mr Shakespeare had the painful experience of
> having to walk a considerable distance barefooted owing to shoe trouble. Mr
> Dickinson, although in possession of a pair of heavily nailed ammunition boots,
> the right kind for this work had to contend with a painful sore in the sole
> of one foot which required careful and skilled dressing every morning and it
> speaks highly of his pluck and endurance that he weathered through to the end
> on his own flat feet.
>
> CENTRE OF SOUTH ASIAN STUDIES, UNIVERSITY OF CAMBRIDGE

Numerous refugees arrived in India having walked most of the way barefoot,
among them Gerry Halpin and Yolande Edwards. A short-lived solution was
to tie leaves round the feet which provided a modicum of protection for a
limited period. Even those who were properly shod, endured blisters, swollen
and bleeding feet. At Sandhurst, officer cadets like Eric Yarrow had been trained
to inspect their soldier's feet. He recorded in his diary on 14 May a few days into
the trek:

> Everybody including myself was becoming footsore I had a foot inspection in
> the afternoon and got through almost an entire roll of elastoplasts. It took us
> all our time to keep everybody on the move. Our chief difficulties during the
> march were firstly to keep warm at night for we had nothing other than what
> was in our haversacks, secondly food was scarce and we had few utensils to eat it
> with. Fortunately the monsoon had not broken but the heat was intense.

Yarrow and his men had been engaged in a fighting retreat for 3 months, and
none had been trained for jungle warfare. The knowledge gleaned from this
defeat would be utilised in the subsequent campaign and given in lectures by
men like Alastair Tainsh:

> The way to keep fit in the jungle is exactly the same as anywhere else. All one
> needs is sound sleep, clean water, a reasonable diet and a liberal use of soap and
> water. One must learn to make oneself comfortable in the worst of conditions.
> It is not being tough or clever to sit in the open all night when one can make

a shelter and build a chung[62] in a couple of hours with a kukri. If one has to spend the night out and away from camp it is best to start thinking about the matter several hours before sunset. First there is dry wood to be collected, and this in the middle of the monsoon is not easy to find. However usually in bamboo clumps there are a few bamboos which have died and with a little encouragement can be lighted. Then there is water to be boiled and food to be cooked. Once these domestic matters have been started, it is best to lose no time in cutting bamboos or saplings to build a hut.

Tainsh recommends using bamboos to form a structure similar to a football goal, but 8–9ft wide. More bamboos are leant against the cross bar, then the structure is roofed with leaves from the banana or another large-leafed tree. For comfort and protection against leeches, a sleeping platform needs building underneath. Tainsh gives detailed instructions for its construction:

> The easiest way to do this is to place on the ground two logs about six feet apart, on top of these are laid at right angles a dozen or so poles, all about three inches in diameter. These are tied to the logs with creepers, rattan cane or bamboo strips. Now a number of absolutely straight bamboos must be selected for the

---

62   A chung is a sleeping platform.

Temporary shelter used by fishermen on the Irrawaddy River similar to that described by Tainsh.

flooring. These are cut to the required lengths and then split at the nodes. By continuing these processes down one side, the bamboo can be flattened out like a board. These bamboo boards are now laid across the poles and tied down, thus completing a dry and fairly comfortable shelter.

Alastair Tainsh estimated that a shelter like this would take 2 hours to build and house four people for the night. But he did advise that: 'This work should be practised constantly before men are sent to the jungle.'

There lay the difficulty. Even those refugees who knew they would have to set off for a trek to India, had not had the foresight or opportunity to learn such techniques. Even the party which included Tizzard, MacLean and Vorley, hadn't the skills to hand to build such a structure, despite Jack Vorley's career in the forestry service. Skill is required to fell trees and to cut bamboo, as are tools. Undernourished refugees, most of who were surviving on a handful of rice a day, did not have the necessary skills, tools or energy to build such shelters. Fred Tizzard recorded in his diary the precautions that Helen Vorley took when the group settled down to sleep every night:

> Mrs Vorley raises a laugh by the thorough way she sweeps away the leaves from her 'bed' instead of leaving them to cushion the ground. The laugh will be on the other side if one of these nights one of us shares his couch with a snake or scorpion.

Janet Lindop, who had gone out on tour with her district commissioner husband, was another who knew how to rough it in the jungle. She routinely found a clean flat stretch of ground, scooped out a hollow for her hip and settled the dogs at her feet. As a speaker of Burmese she was a definite asset to the group, and like Helen Vorley she had nerves of steel. Janet's husband was the senior civil servant at Magwe:

> It had been important to stop panic as much as possible ahead of the retreating army so that supplies would be waiting for them. Each morning the native postmaster rang me up to see if I was still there, and I think he felt as long as I answered, things had not got desperate.
>
> JANET LINDOP PAPERS, IWM

Even the practical Mrs Lindop reveals a touch of sentiment in her choice of personal items. Secreted on her person were some 'tiny bits of jewellery'. Sometimes *objets trouvés* were too much to resist during endless days of walking:

> Sometimes we came on things abandoned by people ahead like an alarm clock that I fancied and carried for some days, and then in my turn laid it down again.

Bamboo footbridges are still vital in rural areas.

After some time, I noticed that George's [sweeper - cleaner] bundle on his head was swelling visibly. When I asked him to show me what he had inside I found he'd been picking up all I threw away and he confessed that the Thakinma [mistress] could not be allowed to lose such things. He said he was perfectly willing to carry them.

Available statistics show that most casualties were young men. Janet Lindop came across two soldiers who had rice but no idea how they should cook it, and this may well be part of the explanation. There were many young men travelling alone without the culinary skills to cater for themselves with the rations available. Some had sent families on ahead, others were soldiers, and others were Indian migrant workers too young to have a family or they had left them behind in their homeland. Few of the trekkers were aware of the versatility of the ubiquitous bamboo. It is used for building, flooring, roofing, scaffolding and water pipes in

Burma today, and larger species can grow up to 150ft high. The stems become hollow and the nodes effectively seal each section. The Chinese used these as water carriers and mobile rice cookers, a technique which some of the British Army adopted during the retreat. Alastair Tainsh describes how to construct an improvised kettle from bamboo:

> The outer skin of the bamboo is peeled off until only about an eighth of an inch of wood remains. The bamboo is now filled with water and a few leaves are stuffed in the top. The base of the bamboo is now placed near the fire at an angle of forty-five degrees, and held in position by a forked stick or some similar arrangement. The water in bamboo keeps the wood from burning.

During their monsoon walk, trekkers became mud-encrusted, but Tainsh warns of the importance of keeping clean in the jungle:

> One must wash in the jungle, and most important are one's feet and legs. There are some people who think once they are away from so-called civilisation, it is tough not to wash. Nothing could be more foolish. Washing is not only refreshing after a hard day's work, but it is essential to get the mud and dirt out of the scratches and leech bites that one collects during the day.

A clean water supply was the biggest problem for all refugees, and so they invariably bedded down for the night close to streams. Inevitably little distinction was made between water supply and latrine, and the water became polluted as did these improvised campsites. Those washing in the streams also stirred up mud and silt, which gathered in receptacles used to fetch water. Tainsh warns:

> The water in the jungle is often muddy; this mud contains mica and there are few things which can irritate the intestines more than mica. Therefore it is worthwhile straining the water through a folded handkerchief if one has nothing better. One very simple and quick way of making water safe to drink, is the colloidal silver method. All one requires are two Victoria silver rupees soldered on to two copper rods about ten inches long. These are the electrodes, wires connect them up to three flat torch batteries arranged in series. By stirring a bucket of water with these silver electrodes, the water becomes safe to drink in thirty seconds. If the water is very muddy it is best to double this time. However, this does not get rid of the mica.

Although some refugees had torches, and therefore probably dead batteries, the chances of them knowing this technique must be slim. Tribes who live in the remote jungle areas on the Indo-Burmese border drink the water in which vegetables are cooked. And as they cannot be dependent on food drops by plane,

naturally they also forage for free food. The Burmese nurses accompanying Dr
Gordon Seagrave and General Stilwell were mostly from the Shan States, another
wild and mountainous region. Wild greens, raspberries and gooseberries were
among the treasures they found to supplement the diet of their party. To the
initiated like Alastair Tainsh the list is even longer:

> The jungle does provide certain edible plants, such as the inner stem of the
> banana tree, bamboo shoots, growing tips and roots of the wild ginger, the tips
> of young bracken ferns. In some places the yam and wild tomato are found. It is
> advisable to learn to recognise these plants before trying to eat them.

Advisable too because shoots of the yellow-stemmed bamboo are poisonous. For
most the main danger was malaria, the borderlands they were escaping through
are still notoriously malarial. Many of the British had stocks of quinine; soldiers
were routinely issued with an anti-malaria drug, atebrine; most did without drugs.
But Alwyn Sepping's family bought insect repellent in the market: 'It was a locally
made, unpleasant smelling ointment but very effective against mosquitoes.'[63]

---

63   Centre of South Asian Studies, University of Cambridge.

11

Walking the Line

The last days of Rangoon were described by eyewitnesses as chaos, but that was nothing compared with the last days of April 1942 in northern Burma. The single track railway line heading to the northern town of Myitkyina was the focus of this chaos. The railway line still sits on an embankment a few feet above the surrounding plain, just as it did in 1942. Perhaps four trains a day run on the track laid by the British, and it is frequented more by pedestrians than rolling stock. Straight as a Roman road it heads relentlessly north. In April 1942, a bird's eye view would have revealed an assortment of steam trains on the line. Some pulled carriages overflowing with refugees; others were stationary, unable to get up steam thanks to a lack of coal or water; at least one had been derailed after an overloaded engine had failed to reach the necessary torque to mount an incline.

The single track railway line running north to Myitkyina.

In the blazing sun of late April, men used buckets to replenish the trains' water tanks from nearby streams, and when the coal ran out, soldiers foraged for wood to fill the hungry firebox. Chinese and British soldiers may have been allies, but in their desire to outrun the Japanese they almost came to blows over which train took precedence on the track.

Captain John Perkins was one of the few heading south in search of food supplies, which weren't reaching the north because the line was jammed:

> It was a tiresome journey with endless waits allowing hospital trains to pass full of wounded and dying. Carriages crammed to capacity with fellows sitting on the roofs. Hundreds of evacuees, Indian and Anglo. I spoke to several doctors I knew, and they were nearly crazy. No sleep, no food, no punkahs[64], indescribable filth. Men were dying of the heat and in between while evacuee women produced babies just to add to the general confusion.
>
> CAPTAIN PERKINS PAPERS, IWM

Like a scene from the 'Wild West' the train was attacked by a band of pro-Japanese Burmans. After the shootout, the driver ran off into the night, and Perkins and some fellow officers achieved that boyhood dream of driving a steam engine. He wrote in his memoirs a few weeks later: 'We took no notice of signals and had to stop at all points just in case they were against us. How we never ran into anything in the dark, I really wouldn't be knowing.'

Perkins was attached to army headquarters, but communications were in such a parlous state that neither he nor anyone he encountered seemed to know their whereabouts. He had also lost both men and belongings. Hearing that troops were now in retreat across the Chindwin, but army records were heading north to be flown out, Perkins did an about turn and headed north again.

Among those also travelling up the line in these dog days, was Reginald Dorman-Smith and his wife, destined for the new headquarters of the Government of Burma in Myitkyina. The army was hastily requisitioning premises in this pretty town on the banks of the upper reaches of the Irrawaddy, and a new headquarters building was under construction. Trains had been commandeered to carry the wounded, whom it was hoped would be flown out from the field used as an airstrip on the outskirts of the town. Medical personnel squeezed along these packed trains to offer morphine injections to those in greatest need, and when that ran out, a syringe of distilled water was used in the hope it would act as a placebo. Headquarters personnel were transporting crates of documents destined to be airlifted to India, including the casualty lists. Officials from Rangoon University were carrying suitcases of documents listing

---

64   A large fan made of palm leaves, usually waved by a servant called a *punkah wallah*.

An old teak house in Myitkyina.

the names of staff, bank statements, cheque books and details of the endowment funds. Women, children, the elderly and sick were all vying for a seat however precarious on any of the trains going north.

Against the flow of the railway moved small groups of soldiers, among them some men from the Glosters, survivors of the campaign with no idea where the remainder of their units were. General Alexander had decided on 28 April that the army was to withdraw via the Chindwin River which lay to the south and west, and the stragglers knew that the Japanese were closing in. During the retreat from Lower Burma, a lorry load of maps left Rangoon and vanished.[65] Any hope of communication was stymied by a complete lack of radio sets, although the army did employ the ancient trick of using sun and mirrors to produce signals in Morse code. This was known as the heliograph, and had been popular in the Boer War on the vast plains of South Africa, but its origins date back to 405BC when the ancient Greeks used their highly polished shields to signal by reflecting the sun.

In the first week of April, Langham-Carter took the train to Myitkyina to recce the airfield prior to switching evacuation flights from Shwebo to the north.

---

65   On 22 January a lorry was loaded with maps on the orders of General Hutton, it left Rangoon and appears to have been ambushed or abandoned.

Law and order was starting to break down. Petrol was at such a premium, that the bicycle which he had taken with him was stolen from the train. The landing field at Myitkyina was 3 miles outside the town, and today lies beneath a dead straight, broad road, running past the university buildings. Carter saw that this out-of-town location would pose more logistical problems than Shwebo, as more lorries or buses would be required to carry refugees, and there was already a transport

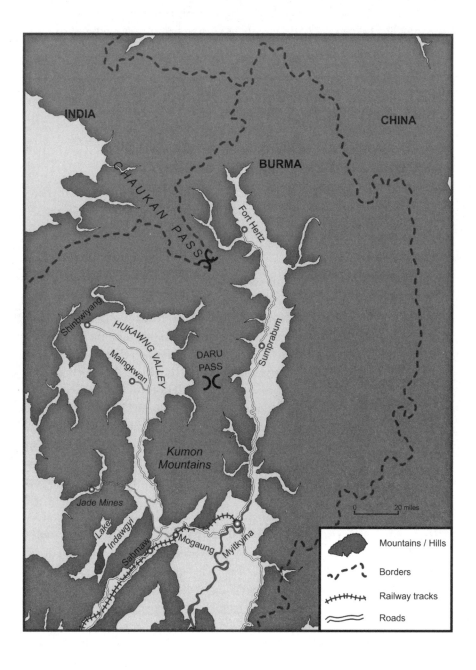

shortage in Myitkyina. Additionally, there was another element to frustrate an efficient system, by this time there was no telephone service connecting them with the south, and telegrams were taking weeks to arrive. The only sure means of communication was to have a message physically carried by messenger.

Undaunted, within 4 days the first refugee plane rose high over the Kumon Mountains and headed south for Chittagong. Carter had organised a bamboo and thatch transit camp for refugees at the American Baptist Mission School on the river bank just south of town, and bought supplies from the bazaar to feed the thousands. The following day, 9 April, there was the first shower of the season. The monsoon was on its way.

While this new air evacuation scheme swung into action, no government orders filtered through from the south. Myitkyina existed in a vacuum, punctured only by news from the wireless saying that the 'military situation is in hand'. Orders had still not been given to evacuate Burma, but as he tried to prioritise the needs of the disparate groups of refugees, Reginald Langham-Carter remarked in his diary on 15 April:

> I now notice that a number of able-bodied youngish men are getting out who could help in the war effort. They claim that they must escort their families and it's certainly true of many Indian women that they can't cope by themselves.
>
> REGINALD LANGHAM-CARTER DIARY, BRITISH LIBRARY

Sceptical but compassionate, he allowed one male escort to fly with each family. But he noticed that there were other men, who put their families on the plane and returned to duty, or left for India on foot. Many helped out by driving lorries, or working in the kitchens in exchange for board and lodging until their departure. From the comfortable armchair of hindsight it is obvious that there was a lack of leadership and clear orders about what these men should be doing. Those who had found seats for their families on planes could set off on foot knowing their dependents were safe. Surprisingly, room was found for four British officials carrying suitcases of Rangoon University records. However, air evacuation was to be cut short. By 16 April pilots were finding that banks of cloud and mist building up over the hills were making landing at Myitkyina impossible. Some American planes arrived to boost the numbers, then one of the pilots brought a message from India:

> Message from officer in charge of camp at Dibrugarh to which evacuees are driven from Dinjan, says his camp is too full, he can take no more today and only limited numbers hereafter. I sent him an urgent message by the pilot that the Burma situation is now critical, thousands of refugees are reaching us, we ourselves are greatly overcrowded but still manage to find somewhere for everyone, and that people would prefer bad or even no accommodation in Dibrugarh to remaining in Burma with the Japs.

On the following day Reginald Langham-Carter learnt that the military situation was getting out of hand, despite reassurances from the radio to the contrary. It was 22 April and he decided to let all officials over the age of forty-five fly out. It was frequently expressed by Carter and his contemporaries that anyone over forty-five was not considered young and fit, and was therefore unable to walk to India. Meanwhile younger men started to prepare to walk over the mountains to Assam in north-east India. At this point the British still held Mandalay, several hundred miles further south, and the army had not retreated across the Irrawaddy. In fact army chiefs had not even announced the decision to retreat to India, although the wounded were now being given priority when planes did land at Myitkyina. Second in priority were essential military personnel, and finally civilian evacuees. In fact even a ton of army records which arrived from Maymyo by truck, was given precedence over the women, children and elderly people waiting patiently for evacuation to India. Later there were more allegations of racism, as newspapers claimed that the ruling white minority were given preference on the last planes to fly out of Myitkyina.

Among those stumbling along the railway line to Myitkyina, in the searing heat of late April 1942, was Cherie Walmsley. Her home town was Yenangyaung where her father had been a stenographer for Burmah Oil, but after his death the family had moved to Rangoon. Cherie and her brother Alan left the capital as

Looking west to India from the outskirts of Myitkyina.

part of a Red Cross convoy but when it was attacked by the Japanese, they hid in a brothel in a jungle village. The family were reunited in Maymyo where Cherie's grandfather was headmaster of the government High School. At the end of April they left only to find that the Ava Bridge had been blown up by the retreating British. Sixteen-year-old Cherie, her mother Enid, brother Alan and sister Sylvia took shelter in a silk weaving factory, where they cocooned themselves in rolls of silk using the looms as improvised beds. Next morning they joined an overloaded boat carrying refugees to the only remaining refuge: the north:

> When we got to Katha the villagers were shouting not to go further because they'd heard the Japanese were there, so without warning the boat was scuttled. People were jumping off and swimming to the shore, by the time our turn came and we stepped off we were ankle and knee deep in water. Walked to the railway station and the railway people amongst us said that they would try to get a train together of sorts. Eventually got a few carriages and an engine and some coal from the sidings. Got a couple of seats on the last carriage. When we were on the boat we met a soldier, who said he had become separated from his unit, his name was John Forsythe from the Cameron Highlanders. When we got on the train it was John who secured the seats for us.
>
> CHERIE WALMSLEY PAPERS, BRITISH LIBRARY

Although her account doesn't specify the place, the Walmsley family probably boarded the train at Naba Junction, a tiny but key station on the north–south line. As the train started to chug along there was a surge of Chinese soldiers from the jungle who climbed on top. When fighter planes machine gunned the train, her mother told her to hide under the seat. When the train restarted it struggled on for a few miles before it ran out of steam:

> So we all got off, no platform – so when we jumped, we landed on dead bodies, which by now were in a state of decay – the stench was awful. We walked along railway lines for a couple of miles, now out of range of the stench and almost dying of thirst, we stopped and dug holes till we reached water. It was all muddy but tasted like nectar.

The one hope of this crowd of 3,500 was to head north to Myitkyina from where, they had been told, planes were flying to safety in India. It is still a tough journey today, and those who make it are more likely to be heading for the jade mines nearby. Few villages lie alongside the line, the jungle has been replaced by paddy fields, and the land is bordered on both sides by steep hills. To the west the Mangin Taung runs for 150 miles from north to south, to the east the Gangaw Taung. On the second day of their journey to Myitkyina, they came across a derailed train that had been heading south to pick up refugees. The contents had spilled onto the line, and the 3,000-strong group became looters: 'We found large bottles of Horlicks, sugar, butter, packets of flour. Mum made toffee out of Horlicks and with the flour we made Chappattis and rolled it on our thighs.'

Cameronian soldier John Forsythe had become the man of the Walmsley family, carrying what food the family had. Everyone carried what little they possessed in a pillowcase, which could double up as a pillow at night. Among the other refugees was a large group of Anglo-Burmese who worked for Burma Railways. Cherie nicknamed them, the railway boys:

> The railway boys tried to extricate one of the wagons and placed all the old and the sick and little children in it and pushed it up the line. Someone asked if anyone had anything red they could use as a flag in front of the wagon. I reluctantly gave them my swimming costume (I used it to bathe in the streams). By now lots of people were getting sick, malaria, dysentery, typhoid, no medicines were available it was bad. As usual our family was last in the line of trekkers, I think it was me. I was always a dawdler, even at school I always used to say somebody has to come last, and so it was on the trek. To hurry me along they would say, 'If the Japanese come up from behind, you'd be the first they would kill.'

The Japanese were coming up from behind, but Cherie and her companions stumbled on to Myitkyina, discarding clothes and anything else they felt they could live without. In this capital of Kachin State, 800 miles north of Rangoon, the air is a few degrees cooler but by May the difference in temperature is negligible. With thousands of others, Cherie and her family made their way to the airfield, although the term airfield was something of a misnomer. It served its purpose but was in fact a landing strip cleared in the jungle, which clustered thickly at the edges. There was no traffic control tower, and the plane from India identified the spot using the sparkle from the nearby Irrawaddy River, and the range of mountains to the northwest of the town.

Among the crowds was the Halpin family who had arrived from Mandalay by paddle steamer. The head of the family, William Halpin, had taught at Maymyo English High School, and in the family party was his mother-in-law, wife, an aunt and the four children, aged 4 to 17. By 6 May they had been queuing hopefully at the airfield for 3 days, returning each night to the refugee camp on the southerly outskirts of the town, where missionaries from the Baptist Church fed and watered them. Everyone in the crowd was aware that the rainy season would soon cut off this escape route. The vast white pillows of monsoon cloud would make take off and landing too dangerous, and obscure the mountains between Burma and India.

Some of these refugees had evacuated first to Mandalay, then moved gradually further and further north as the Japanese advanced. Many had said farewell to husbands who had set off to walk to India, while their families travelled north to fly out. Despite the extreme heat, many women wore several layers. Luggage was limited to one suitcase, and they were loath to abandon favourite dresses which they could not cram inside the suitcase. The crowd included older men and women as well as children, all of whom it was considered would be unable to make a long trek to India. Most of them had never flown before and there was an air of excitement. When the two transport planes landed, room was made for wounded soldiers, and the rest were packed in until the aircraft was at capacity.

As families waited in groups, small children and babies whingeing in the heat, sharp ears detected another sound. It was familiar to Cherie Walmsley and her family who had heard it on the railway line to Myitkyina: the engine of a Japanese Zero, 'After the pushing and shoving, the door was closed leaving one little girl behind, her family already on the plane, she was screaming for her mother.'[66]

As it swooped in to take a closer look, would-be passengers looked on terrified, and started to run for the jungle round the perimeter of the field. The events took only seconds. The first plane flew three times round the airfield only a hundred feet above the ground. Some interpreted this later as a warning pass. Then three Zeros swung in even closer. As four or five people attempted to scramble out of one plane, it was strafed with bullets from nose to tail. The roar of the Zeros' engines was echoed by the scream of passengers, then silenced by the staccato burst of bullets. As the Japanese fighters turned for a second pass there were only moans from inside the fuselage, before it was hit for a second time and any survivors finished off. The fighters vanished into the sky as quickly as they had arrived. On the ground lay a tangle of suitcases. The carcass of the last transport plane due to fly out of Myitkyina was a sarcophagus. Traumatised civilians crept from the shady fringe of the jungle to do what they could. The little airstrip was littered with bundles and bodies. Ex-forestry worker Jack Barnard was a member of the Burma Rifles and dashed to help:

> I went over and offered my assistance, but it soon became obvious that there was nothing I could do. There was nothing anybody could do for the torn blood-splashed corpses littering the body of the plane save give them a decent burial.
>
> CENTRE OF SOUTH ASIAN STUDIES, UNIVERSITY OF CAMBRIDGE

The remaining refugees were trapped in a bottleneck. Either they could wait to be captured by the Japanese, or they could start the trek to India. Dressed in sandals and cotton frocks they were not prepared for the journey ahead. Cherie Walmsley and her family had already travelled hundreds of miles from Rangoon and were undernourished and ill-equipped for a trek over the mountains to India:

---

66   Cherie Walmsley papers, British Library.

In a state of terror hungry and thirsty we fled down the line again, the way we had come in the first place. By now we had no shoes, worn out with walking, and the sleepers were hot, feet were cut and bleeding. We finally came to a village called Sahmaw, it had a little sugar factory which had been sabotaged and there was a mountain of sugar which was slowly melting with the heat of the sun.

She was just one of a terrified crowd of refugees who were all starving. In the heat haze rising from the plain, a cow appeared and was spotted by the mob:

Someone shot it in the head whose aim was not very good, people were turning into animals themselves, With their knives they went in, taking away lumps of meat. Within a matter of minutes it was almost a carcass.

Cherie's mother had assumed her children had taken part in this frenzy, and when she discovered they had not, she despatched Cherie and her brother to see if the animal's tongue was still there:

I was feeling very weak, I sat astride it, like on horseback, and held the horns back while Alan pulled from the front and then cut it. Mum cooked it that evening while Sylvia and I went in search of a stream. We had a good soak, swimming about and when I got out, I just sat on the bank and wept my heart out – I couldn't believe that I could find such peace in the midst of a bloody war.

The exact whereabouts of the Japanese was uncertain so, hearing a train, Cherie and her family thought rescue was on its way:

In the distance skirting the horizon was a thin wisp of smoke, which was moving towards us. We all gathered our bags and started to make our way to the station. All the other people were in the same mind. It was fortunate that we were not on the front line so to speak. As it got into the station Japanese soldiers who must have been hiding under the seats, swarmed out and started firing machine guns, and we turned and ran back to our hut and just waited there for the worst to happen.

Cherie Walmsley and her family were captured. John Forsythe, who had stuck with the Walmsley family through so much, tried to convince the Japanese that he was a civilian working for the timber firm Steel Brothers. But he was separated from them, and they never saw him again.

Among the corpses on the airfield that day was Gemma Wardleworth. She and her aunt Emma Childers had boarded the plane and it was about to take off. As

Sahmaw station scene of dreadful events as refugees tried to escape.

the fighters zeroed in on the Dakota and began to machine gun the plane, the pilot Captain Holmes threw his body across Emma Childers whom he knew. His heroic instinct saved her life but left her with four bullets in her back. Gemma was killed instantly, shot in the head. Unknown hands carried Emma Childers to hospital where she awoke 2 days later:

> I was in a sort of maze and heard heavy footsteps coming up the stairs, and supposed it was stretcher cases arriving. The tread stopped at my bedside however and I opened my eyes to find five fearful and ferocious looking Jap soldiers with fixed bayonets and grizzly beards standing round my bed glaring at me, I was certain my number was up.
>
> ANGUS MacLEAN PAPERS, CENTRE OF SOUTH ASIAN STUDIES,
> UNIVERSITY OF CAMBRIDGE

It was 8 May and the Japanese had captured Myitkyina. Emma Childers was evidently not considered a security risk, and eventually went to live in a goods wagon in a convent in Mandalay where she spent the next 3 months until she was arrested:

> I was thrown into the town lock up, a common jail with iron bars at which people could come and stare at us, and a cement floor and filthy latrine. One

evening soon after I got there a drunken Gestapo officer came along and did all sorts of things to me. He struck me savagely on each side of the head so that I saw stars, repeatedly tripped me up so that I had to fall on the cement floor and each time I was down he either kicked me or beat me with his sword. He made me kneel and say England was very bad and Japan was very good, in Burmese. I know little Burmese and was afraid of getting it the wrong way round. He pretended that he was going to thrust his sword into my stomach and into my throat and I had to kneel for decapitation.

Emma Childers spent two and a half years at a prison camp at Tavoy in Burma's tail, where the invasion had all begun. She had let slip that she was the widow of an army officer and endured more torture and solitary confinement, but a smuggled copy of the complete works of Shakespeare kept her sane. She resolutely refused to allow Japanese doctors to remove the bullet near her spine, saying she would wait until the end of the war, which she did.

It is believed that as many as 300 people died on 6 May 1942, nearly all of them civilians. There is no known grave, no memory of the tragedy among the people of modern Myitkyina, and no one was ever prosecuted for this war crime when peace came in 1945. A large reclining Buddha and surrounding temple were built in 1990, paid for by a Japanese businessman and his wife. In the grounds is a memorial to over 6,000 Japanese soldiers who died at Myitkyina in subsequent battles. It also commemorates those Burmese who were killed there during the Second World War. The site of the former airfield is unmarked, discovered only with the help of a knowledgeable guide.

Bodies are buried beside this line near Sahmaw.

12

Monsoon Mud in the Hukawng Valley

As mid-May approached, and the temperatures soared, vast banks of cloud filled the sky, messengers of the monsoon. They jostled for space on the horizon over several days. The overture of lightning and thunder was followed by giant blobs of rain which spattered the dust like bullets. Then came gusts of wind and finally the rain proper: giant sheets of water roaring down from the sky turning single storey buildings into drums, drowning out conversation. The rainy season had begun. The inevitable arrival of the monsoon had been anticipated and dreaded by every refugee. From every puddle and drain emerged frogs with their guttural cries. Raindrops battered down foliage and gathered in pools on jungle palms, bending them down until the water gushed groundwards, soaking hapless refugees beneath. Every ditch, dip and drain filled within minutes. Streams swelled and surged across the dry ground, transformed into rivers. Rivers filled like overflowing guttering; banks burst unable to contain the volume of water. Dusty paths soon became muddy bogs, dry valleys were reborn as swamps, and travelling across country was beset with danger. To the farmer in the East, the monsoon is an exuberant confirmation of life, filling the paddy fields with water; irrigating the flood plains of the Irrawaddy and Chindwin, and the other myriad rivers of Burma. Fish flourish in these muddy swirling waters, vital protein for the villages squatting alongside, between jungle rim and riverbank.

When the Japanese invaders advanced from south and east, they were propelled by knowledge of the monsoon. Driven by this imperative, their target was to capture Burma before the rainy season began. However, in 1942 the monsoon was early and unexpectedly heavy. In 1941 it had arrived on 21 May so, when the retreat sounded in the first week of May, British generals believed troops would still have time to reach India. By 8 May, British and Japanese armies were racing for the Chindwin knowing that the monsoon was imminent. The route ran through dense and almost uninhabited forests which are crossed and re-crossed by dry sandy river beds. These were rivers-in-waiting, masking a trickle of water, and

It cuts three hours off the journey by motorbike, but this flimsy bridge has to be taken down before every monsoon.

even quicksand, but when the monsoon rains thundered down, they would be revived. Even in the dry zone of central Burma, floodwaters rushing down from the north can turn an innocent dry river bed into a grave for man or truck. A wall of water transforms sand into liquid cement, to encase and suffocate victims caught in its path.

As the highly motorised British Army headed through this territory, time forced them to abandon trucks and jeeps when they got stuck in the sand.

They knew the broken road surface would become more treacherous when the monsoon arrived. Army engineers laid corduroy tracks, much like the rolled paths sold for gardeners today, to improve passage across these dry river beds. Still there was one part of Burma where no one ventured in the rainy season. Even the abundant wildlife which inhabited the Hukawng Valley in the north, moved out during the monsoon.

The Hukawng Valley today is a nature reserve, a sanctuary to some of the world's dwindling population of tigers. Tiny streams rise in this unspoilt wilderness, joining together to form the headwaters of the Chindwin River, the largest tributary of the Irrawaddy. Some of the world's rarest species of flora and fauna live in the vast forests lining the valley. Orchids, duck and deer are among them. In the dry season the trek through the valley is a strenuous but not impossible journey of 300 miles. In the monsoon rains of 1942, the valley became a graveyard for thousands, and also earned the name Valley of Death.

The valley had been identified as a potential escape route long before thousands of refugees were forced to use it. A forestry officer from the logging company Steel Brothers had recced the route and reported it was 'impracticable'. He calculated that a hundred fit able-bodied men a day might be able to travel through the sparsely inhabited valley, but no more, because of the lack of inhabitants and therefore supplies. Instead Steel Brothers chartered a ship to take their staff from

A river bed in the dry season.

Rangoon on 19 February.[67] The last 100 miles of the valley route was through almost uncharted territory where there were even fewer villages to supply travellers with food. This was the land of the Naga tribe, renowned as headhunters who decorated their houses with desiccated human heads. British political officers believed they had successfully dissuaded the Nagas from this ancient custom after an expedition in 1937, but the tribes were so remote that no one was quite sure.

As central Burma was overrun by the Imperial Japanese Army, so troops and refugees fled towards the apex of Burma. Here they were effectively trapped by mountains. North of Myitkyina lies the Kumon range, and beyond that the Himalayas; east are the vast uninhabited mountains of China; and south lies the Gangaw range. Myitkyina is at the base of what is still known today as 'The Triangle', crossed by a few opium trails and ancient mule tracks between India and China. Into this inhospitable wilderness stepped thousands of terrified refugees, many of whom had witnessed the massacre at Myitkyina airfield and knew that the Japanese were close behind them. The majority were women, children, the elderly and those who were not considered fit enough to set off on a 300-mile walk to India. The choice was to remain and be captured by the enemy, or to walk.

Civil servants were also among those caught in Myitkyina, but their first concern was to destroy secret documents, burn thousands of rupees in the safe, and demolish any machinery or buildings which might be of use to the Japanese once they arrived, which they did on Friday 8 May. One vital piece of equipment for such a trek was a map, yet this was the one omission in nearly all cases. It is on record that the assistant district commissioner at Myitkyina burnt all the maps in the local office to avoid their capture by the Japanese. Many refugees had travelled up to Myitkyina by train, and had no local knowledge. Verbal directions seem to have filtered through to some, but from what source is uncertain. Piecemeal preparations had been made. Food had been dumped at a building in Maingkwan some 30 miles along the valley; civil servants had flown to India to ask whether any arrangements had been made on that side of the border; and a narrow path had been cut through mountains northwest of Myitkyina to provide a route into the Hukawng Valley. This was the path taken by Colonel Stoker, an army medical officer who had arrived in Myitkyina with wounded men after 5 months on the frontline:

Well there we were in Myitkyina, none of us very fit, no hope of flying. We tried to obtain as much information about the route to India as possible. What we did get was fairly reassuring. First we were told we had 102 miles along a

---

67   The company's 2,500 Indian staff had left in an organised convoy via the Taungup Pass on 1 March. Camps and provisions were prepared for them in advance.

good road. Then we would take a brand new path cut for the occasion through the jungle of the Kumon Mountains to the Daru Pass nearly 5,000 feet high. After crossing the pass we would descend into the Hukawng Valley and 70 miles from the beginning of the path we would reach Maingkwan. Here ample food stores of an Indian nature awaited us. Up to that point we would have to carry all our own food, although it was probable that rice would be dumped along the way. After Maingkwan there would be organised huts and supplies en route from India perhaps.

COLONEL STOKER PAPERS, IWM

Maingkwan was the main village in the Hukawng Valley at the time. Seven decades later it has been overtaken by other settlements in the area, which is still sparsely populated and has come under strict military control. Under colonial rule, British officials showed their faces once a year accompanied by a substantial military escort. From Maingkwan, Stoker was told the route grew more gruelling, with a hundred mile slog through the valley before reaching the mountains straddling the border with India.

Stoker and his companions set off on the narrow track running north towards Fort Hertz. For part of the journey they had transport, but most refugees who took this route were on foot, although a few drove bullock carts to transport food and possessions. The Halpin family had also been among the crowd at the airfield. Like many Anglo-Burmese families their allegiances lay more closely with the British. The eldest of the family was their Burmese maternal grandmother in her mid-sixties, and the youngest 4-year-old Peter. Much later, Gerry Halpin, the eldest of the four Halpin siblings wrote an account of the trek. In a curious technique, he distanced himself from the events by referring to himself and the family in the third person:

They started this trek to Fort Hertz on a metalled road, carrying their own food, clothing, cooking utensils, ground cover, bedding and normal footwear, shoes for the English speaking part of the family and open toed slippers for Grandmother and Aunt Mia Thoung. Having no thought as to how tortuous the journey was going to be, they were ill clothed and totally ill prepared in provisions carried to meet the terrain to be crossed and inclement jungle rain and cold conditions they were destined to encounter.

HALPIN FAMILY PAPERS

This was a common experience. Refugees had packed a suitcase believing they were to be evacuated by plane to India, not to walk 300 miles in driving rain, over some of the most inhospitable terrain in the world. The governor's official report after the exodus stated bluntly:

Few of the evacuees were in any way prepared for the conditions which they would have to face; they had no supplies of food and the European and Anglo-Indian women were in many cases clad in flimsy cotton frocks and high-heeled shoes.

GOVERNOR'S REPORT ON CIVIL EVACUATION, BRITISH LIBRARY, P.75.

As the refugees streamed north, rumour passed them on the road: stories of Japanese atrocities against women, and the names of those wanted by the invaders, broadcast on Radio Tokyo. These included William Halpin, although there was no logical reason for this. Occasionally an army truck passed, or groups of Chinese troops, and when an aeroplane was heard, the crowd dived into the bushes for cover.

Five days after leaving Myitkyina the refugee column was stopped by soldiers. The governor had flown to India a week before, most of the bureaucrats had abandoned their desks, and administration and communications were non-existent. The army was the only body with any authority, and they informed the refugees that they were not to take the road to Fort Hertz, but instead detour via a jungle track over the mountains to Maingkwan. This was the route taken by Stoker, although it would seem unlikely that the Halpins had managed to travel 102 miles in 5 days with an elderly grandmother and a 4-year-old in tow.

Ironically their original destination, Fort Hertz, was never captured by the Japanese and later was used as a base by the Chindits. Planes landed and took off from there, although whether this small mountain outpost could have supported a refugee population is a moot point. However, the route from Fort Hertz to India was over the Chaukan Pass, which had been deemed too difficult for any but the fittest. Standing at 15,000ft, the pass is surrounded by uninhabited and challenging terrain on both sides of the border. Even groups of the famously rugged Gurkhas who attempted this route, suffered casualties.

Fort Hertz was reputedly another 15 or 20 days' walk along a proper road, whereas the route through the Hukawng Valley was of unknown duration and hardship. Nevertheless, faced with diversion from the road into the jungle, the Halpins and others complied. The diversion coincided with the beginning of the monsoon.

People were stunned but no compassion was shown to any person. The Halpin family problems started here, as they did for hundreds and thousands of others who were also diverted. The route or track they followed was through thick jungle, very hilly, with no camps or cover and on mud tracks. Some parts had been used by trucks and these were left abandoned where they had broken down due to mechanical failure, fuel shortage or bogged down up to axle depth in soft slimy mud. The Halpins, like others, walked as conditions permitted for about 7 hours a day but barely covered 5–6 miles some days, less when it was very hilly and when they were drenched by the rain. Every evening before dark, the family stopped walking for the day, and built an improvised shelter with leaves, if found, for a roof:

Gerry and Mike collected firewood, father collected water and the three ladies
prepared a meal (mainly soup of a sort) of boiled rice and any root vegetables
they could find during the day. While cooking was taking place father, Gerry
and Mike built a shelter as best they could on the higher land for the night.
The rice was collected when we left Myitkyina by the Grandmother and Ma
Thoung and this was carried by the ladies, a chore they shared (even when they
were slipping and falling about because of muddy footpaths, they insisted on
doing this work or they threatened to remain behind). Gerry's mother in the
meantime looked after Peter and washed any change of clothes until we were
left in clothes that we stood in.

HALPIN FAMILY PAPERS

Four-year-old Peter in fact, had to be carried most of the way to India by his
father or elder brother. Colonel Stoker had always intended to take this route
over the Kumon Mountains, but found it no less difficult:

At once after stepping off the road we plunged into the thickest of jungles,
clothing a slope steeper than any ordinary staircase. Ankle deep in mud slipping
and sliding with rain coming down in torrents at the end of an hour we had
only just reached the foot of the slope. We crossed a small stream in spate and
immediately began to ascend just such another hillside. Up and up we went
grasping trees, roots, creepers, we thought we would never get to the top. When
we did it was only to find that the whole process had to be done over again. At
the end of a very tiring day we had covered only six or seven miles.

COLONEL STOKER PAPERS, IWM

Dark and impenetrable, the jungle is crowded with dense thickets of bamboo
interspersed with scrub, which host a cornucopia of thorny plants from creepers
to shrubs. The jungle floor is invisible beneath a litter of detritus: bent and broken
bamboo, roots and leaves. Inhabiting this base layer are legions of ants, like the
centimetre-long chestnut ants with a ferocious bite, said by mountain tribes to
be extremely tasty. Then there are fabled 'tarantulas', bird spiders, which hide in
holes, emerging to sink fangs into their prey. In the evening snakes emerge to
feed, although they are usually wary of contact with humans. Bamboo vipers
loiter in holes, while muscular pythons are camouflaged up in the tree branches.
Foliage is dense, and paths can be tricky to follow, particularly in the rain:

We had some difficulty in lighting a fire owing to the rain that had fallen in the
night, but eventually made a start. We were still groaning through the Kumon
mountains which in places rise to 8,000 feet. There was plenty of rain and this
turned the path into mud which sadly interfered with our progress up the very

A 'path' through bamboo jungle near Myitsone.

steep hillsides. Climb, climb, climb, for seeming miles at a stretch and attainment of the summit would only mean having to descend a slope just as difficult. To make matters worse my old trouble the dysentery now came on so badly that I found I could hardly walk and carry my pack.

A friend who had managed to hire some coolies, 'lent' one to Stoker, and the sick colonel staggered on without the weight of his pack to add to his troubles:

That night we slept at the bottom of a ravine near a fast mountain torrent. The water was snow water and marvellously fresh for washing. Thick jungle surrounded us. The scene was like one from a film of a trek to the west in the early days of American pioneering. Hundreds of camp fires, families and soldiers of a dozen different nations, bullocks, horses, mules, ponies being watered and fed, and throughout the whole mass a constant going and coming which gave the atmosphere a sense of tense excitement as though great deeds were on the move.

Of the 40,000 people who left Myitkyina to walk out through the Hukawng Valley, some began their journey by taking the road west to Mogaung, rather than heading north towards Fort Hertz. Mogaung is a hot, dusty little town today but the road is well used by a stream of motorbikes, their passengers two-up and almost invariably helmetless. They are following a dream of riches to be found in the jade mines at Hpakant. Like most roads in rural Burma, the route seesaws between a bog deep enough to ensnare a lorry in the wet season, and fine dust which penetrates every orifice in the dry season. Once they have successfully negotiated the road, thousands spend their days clawing and scraping the mountainsides in the search for hidden wealth. Each stone or boulder is closely examined as it is dug out. What outwardly looks like a potato may on the inside be the most sought after jade in the world: imperial jade beloved by the world's jade connoisseurs, the Chinese. These jade mines were worked under colonial rule, and the route was of a similar standard. Still to the few men who knew the Hukawng Valley, a route via the jade mines was infinitely preferable. Forestry officers made a vain attempt to persuade refugees to go that way. Once they had reached Hpakant in the mountains they should follow the Uyu River to its confluence with the Chindwin, and then to Homalin. Here an elephant track opposite the town would take them through the hills to Tamu where camps and supplies were being organised. Most refugees were suspicious of the motive for this diversion, believing they were being sent into the arms of the Japanese. Nobody was quite sure where the Japanese were, and the Chindwin River was

Indawgyi Lake near the jade mines, the route avoided by so many refugees.

an obvious route for patrols to take as they headed north to cut off the escape to India. Doggedly, refugees headed west, bypassing the route to the jade mines and entering the notorious Hukawng Valley.

The valley is so flat that there is practically no drainage. The road surface is either loose soil or clay crumbled into thick dust by motor or cart traffic. The rains turned it into quagmire, cars could not move, carts got stuck and evacuees on foot could only progress by shuffling along the edges, clinging to the jungle at the sides and floundering in soupy mud from ankle to thigh deep. The Hukawng Valley became a swamp, the favourite habitat of leeches, bane of the Forgotten Army. Leeches are not poisonous but when they sink their teeth into human flesh, infection can result if the wound is not properly treated. Even Colonel Stoker had little of his medical kit left by the time he encountered the leeches of the Hukawng Valley:

> Sleep was disturbed by our first experience of leeches. I had hardly lain down than I felt something soft at the back of my neck, not realising what it was I put up a hand and found a horrid slimy thing clinging to the skin. Reynolds removed it with the aid of a match and we saw what it was, all bloated with blood and resembling a piece of black jelly.

A lighted match or cigarette is one way to dislodge a leech once it has clamped its jaws into the victim, but moist tobacco mixed with red pepper is another remedy, as is alcohol or salt. All these were in short supply among refugees. What leeches love above all is to reach the mucous membranes, and to do that they enter the rectum or penis. Forestry man Ritchie Gardiner found one halfway up his urethra, he managed to catch it in time, although in his diary he doesn't mention which method he used to remove it! Urination usually detaches the leech from the penis, but medical help is needed to detach them from the rectum, although defecation may also do the job. Most people are unaware that they have attracted a leech until they spot it hanging from their body, although they cause itching in the genital area. Tropical ulcers, which are also known as jungle sores, can result from a leech bite and these are the danger, as they may become infected.

By the time trek survivors reached India, most if not all had leech bites, but hunger and thirst were their main considerations on the journey. The Halpin family were lucky. In rural areas the Burmese eat wild plants in their daily diet as a matter of course, and Aunt Mia Thoung and their grandmother foraged in the jungle to make soup every day. But once their rice supply ran out, soup could not provide the calories necessary for climbing mountains on difficult paths:

> Very occasionally we passed a village barn with rice left in it, surprisingly. Here many decomposed corpses were seen lying by the stack of rice, presumably where they laid down to rest.

All those who set out on the trek in May found bodies along their path. Some refugees had been on the road for weeks, held up by air attack, weakened by cholera and frustrated by transport shortages. In the mountains, walkers could at least take some pleasure from the scenery. Despite his dysentery Colonel Stoker did:

> We started the next day with a rickety bridge across the river and immediately came to the longest climb yet. Up and up zigzag fashion the muddy path wound on and on. All day it went on. I thought we would never reach the summit. Sometimes the gradient flattened but only to take fresh heart and ascend once more. We were in the bamboo forest and the humidity was oppressive. At last, at three in the afternoon we could go no further and made camp in a Kachin[68] village a little way off the main track. Under different circumstances the journey would have been very enjoyable. Every now and then as the forest opened out we would get lovely views across wonderful hills, trees grew to incredible heights, birds of all colours and the butterflies defied description.

After 6 days Stoker and his companions reached the Daru Pass. From here they would drop down into the Hukawng Valley. After the steamy confined jungle paths the ridge brought fresh air and a view of where they were heading:

> It was a wonderful sensation to find ourselves marching along a very narrow ridge with a steep precipice on each side and get glimpses every now and then of the plains strung out blue and hazy in the distance. From this ridge down to the floor of the valley was one long continuous steep slope lasting for ten miles or so. That night we slept in a Kachin Village, our first in the Hukawng Valley. It was deserted.

As so many refugees found, a party of soldiers had preceded them, in this case Stoker reports they were Sikhs. Armed Allied soldiers are often reported to have terrorised villagers as they marched out to India, the Chinese in particular were notorious. Erstwhile friendly villagers vanished into the jungle when they heard refugees were expected, a tactic that was used by village women throughout the four-year Japanese occupation. Villagers were extremely scared of the Chinese too, who moved at great speed and had enormous stamina. They were lightly equipped, and by this stage in the retreat their bamboo shoes had worn out and they were virtually barefoot. Many of the British who had dealings with Chinese soldiers, expressed admiration for them as soldiers, but found their behaviour unconscionable, as did Colonel Stoker:

---

68   The Kachin tribe is the main tribal group living in the mountains north of Myitkyina.

Passed by a large Chinese force. We noticed that many of these troops were carrying tinned milk, sardines, bully beef, all stores that are not normally carried by Chinese armies. Later we passed along where the main body of Chinese had already passed and found the earth littered with empty tins. One of their liaison officers told us that there was plenty more to be had in Maingkwan, but on arrival there we found that these stores, collected for refugees from Burma, had all been looted by the Chinese. The officer in charge of the stores had apparently looked the other way when the Chinese arrived.

Stoker and his companions managed to 'find a small amount of rice' and left for Maingkwan. The entire Hukawng Valley is embroidered with streams and they soon approached their first substantial river. This early in the rainy season, it was only 50 yards wide and the water level reached halfway up their thighs. Nevertheless, the current was strong and made foothold precarious:

We realised from the size of the river bed which was 300 yards wide, and the thirty foot banks, that when the monsoon came, this would be an insuperable barrier. At the other side of the river we plunged into a muddy swamp along which we made our way with difficult haste. Haste, because a rumour came flashing along the line of evacuees that the Japanese forces were approaching Maingkwan. From plain thick jungle we now began to come across an occasional paddy field and at long last in the late afternoon... a small paddy plain and there in the distance was the large village of Maingkwan into which we trudged after altogether 11 days marching instead of the promised seven and after about a hundred miles instead of the promised seventy. A thirty mile difference seems very little, but in our circumstances it was a great deal, the extra four days of disappointment when we failed to reach Maingkwan, the low state to which our rations were reduced, all affected us both physically and mentally.

There was little to cheer them in Maingkwan, a small colonial outpost with a few rows of huts and a mission house. Sergeant 'Bunny' Katz had taken the train from Myitkyina to Mogaung before setting out on foot to Maingkwan. At the Mission House he found the height of luxury, to a soldier who has been on the road for 4 months: a bed. He wrote in a letter home, posted when he reached Assam:

We can't get any information of what really lies ahead, only rumours, very nasty ones. Refugees were dropping by the roadside exhausted, dead bodies could be seen at every little jungle shelter, semi-disintegrated bodies, some with the bones of the skull showing, the stench was unbearable, the scene frightening. I began to understand the real meaning of 'refugee'. An Indian, an old man was sitting in the mud, the dead body of a youngster naked by his side, but what struck me most was the peaceful expression on this boy's face, how different from the horrible frightening looks on the other faces. The old man showed no signs of grief, a least no outward signs.

CENTRE OF SOUTH ASIAN STUDIES, UNIVERSITY OF CAMBRIDGE

The road west was a 'fair weather' road. These still exist in many regions of modern Burma, but are nothing more than compacted dust, unblemished by the addition of rocks. Their existence is not usually marked on maps, nor are there many signposts. Regular stops at hamlets and villages are necessary to ask directions, and these are not always reliable, as many villagers don't travel far from home. Although you need to wear a dust mask to travel on them, 'fair weather' roads often give a smoother ride. When the rains begin in May, and throughout the rainy season they become unusable, more suited to mud wrestling than travelling. The Chinese Army had abandoned trucks and jeeps along the fair weather road out of Maingkwan, because after only a week of rain the route was impassable: the mud was already 2ft or 3ft deep.

The Inuit people are said to have forty different words for snow, because it is a ubiquitous feature of their landscape. In the same fashion, the tribes which inhabit this part of the world ought to have forty different words for mud. Throughout the diaries and letters left by refugees who made the trek, there are descriptions of the mud. In some places it was swamp-mud: wet, slimy, with a high water content, often covered by a layer of swamp water which would bathe the walker's foot as it was pulled free. In others the mud is described as like Vaseline, glutinous, glossy and slippery as ice. In others like plasticine: turgid with enormous craters formed by those who had gone before. In many places the mud clung limpet-like to refugees' feet, sucking off boots and shoes. For 50 miles from Maingkwan to Shinbwiyang, undernourished refugees were forced to clamber through mud. Every few miles there would be yet another river to cross. Conditions would have taxed men from the SAS who train for such eventualities and are fit and well fed. As well as the four children in the Halpin family, they were accompanied by their grandmother and aunt, diminutive Burmese women wearing the longyi, a tube of material tied at the waist, much-worn by both men and women in Burma because of its versatility. It can be worn short or long, used as an improvised sleeping bag, and teenaged boys even convert the longyi into shorts to play football. Gerry Halpin and his father had adopted European dress:

As days rolled on they found the streams they had to ford were like torrents and became extremely difficult to get across especially for the ladies with the dresses. Gerry and Dad would provide a crossing patrol, using their staves and a rope tied across the stream as a guide. Many distressed folk were helped across by the pair and were fortunate not to have any accidents, although some folk were nearly carried away with the strong flood water.

HALPIN FAMILY PAPERS

Occasional huts had been built along the route a few weeks earlier by the Chinese Army. These were viewed with hope and relief. Inside there might be an opportunity to light a fire and cook a meagre hot meal or at least brew a hot cup of tea. At the bare minimum these huts offered a night's sleep sheltering from the rain, which might not have fallen by day, but inevitably deluged them at night depriving them of rest. Almost without exception the huts would be occupied; and almost without exception the occupants were dead or dying. Those with strength and the courage to tackle corpses very probably infected with cholera, tried to remove the bodies. Most gave the bloated bodies a wide berth. If they hadn't died of cholera, then there were other potential killers: typhus, typhoid and blackwater fever (so called because the urine turns black). The biggest risk in the Hukawng Valley was malaria. A prison was built in the valley some years ago, and detention there is said to be a death sentence thanks to the malarial nature of the area. While many of the Europeans who set out to walk to India were equipped with anti-malarial pills such as atebrine and quinine, the Indians, Anglo-Indians and Anglo-Burmese were less fortunate, unless they knew what to forage for.

The British escaped along this narrow track on the far side of the Chindwin River at Homalin.

Wild plants are still used as traditional anti-malarials by many of the Burmese, including a delicate leaf with an unpleasant bitter taste, known in Burmese as 'pann khah'.

Either side of the track along the Hukawng Valley dense jungle stretched for miles; it formed walls either side of the path. Moving down this dark tunnel it was impossible for refugees to see the next camp or any landmarks in the distance. Colonel Stoker and many others found it oppressive:

> The jungle was bamboo and gave no shelter from the rain, we cut a few sticks as supports, spread on them two groundsheets and a gas cape with one groundsheet on the ground and into this inefficient shelter seven of us tried to sleep like pigs in a sty.

At the end of a long day's walk, making a shelter drained the last few ounces of energy. On fine evenings it was tempting to do without and save the calories to expend the next day:

> The evening was beautifully fine and we neglected to build any sort of shelter with the horrid result that when the very heavy rain came down at midnight unexpectedly, we got drenched in less time than it takes to tell. It rained all night and showed no sign of stopping at daybreak.

Some refugees carried mosquito nets, but the fine mesh was soon transformed into lattice work as the nets tore when stretched between bamboos. Mosquitoes carry the danger of malaria, but the most irritating pest of the rainy season was sand flies, so small that even a pristine mosquito net was no protection:

> These dreadful pests came out in such numbers that the air was filled with them. So small as to be invisible they bite any and every bit of exposed skin they can find. The bite itches not only as soon as it is inflicted, and through the rest of the night as soon as the bite is warm. Do what we could, we could not escape their attentions, and nobody slept that night.

In 1942 the monsoon rainfall was said to be exceptional, but there are no records of the actual amount:

> With the rain that had already fallen and which was now showing monsoon-like characteristics, the land was a swamp. Sometimes for stretches of several miles we would be pushing through mud up to the thighs. It was never less than ankle deep. The jungle on each side was dank and rotten. We were now on the more popular route and every two or three hundred feet was a corpse. Occasionally already eaten by the ants to a gleaming white skeleton, more

often than not it would be a putrid stinking mass of bloated flesh covered with a seething blanket of maggots. Scores of animals, mostly horses and bullocks lay dead or dying. There was no one disease predominating, but every condition could be seen. Malaria, cholera, dysentery, old age but each case was complicated by extreme exhaustion.

Most of the corpses were Indians. Around them lay the treasured belongings which they had carried hundreds of miles: blankets, clothing, a brass tray. Beyond the corpses churned more streams, widening and deepening rapidly with the monsoon. Too deep to ford and too dangerous to swim, refugees had to beg, borrow or build rafts and canoes. On the bank, Colonel Stoker's party found a group of women and children who were elbowed aside by the crowd every time they reached the head of the queue. It was reminiscent of another great trek west:

It was more dramatic than anything Hollywood has produced. One irresistibly thought of the 'Covered Wagon' on looking at it. Imagine a wide sweep of water running round a sandy beach. Dark brown peaty water curling smoothly by. On this side, a flat stretch of sand and on the other a steep bank with dense dark jungle right up to the water's edge. A great crowd of people in little groups, all colours, tribes and nations covered the near bank. At a little distance from the water were all the abandoned bullock carts left here because of the impossibility of getting them over, or even if over, getting them along the narrowing track. Scattered here and there were the fires of families cooking their evening meal. Upstream the bullock drivers were engaged in swimming their cattle across the water. Some animals entered the river and swum across with little trouble, some refused and had to be driven with sticks and stones and curses. Plying to and fro were several bamboo rafts, looking as they lay low in the water, perilously overcrowded with huddled refugees clutching their belongings and praying for a safe crossing.

The hero of the Hukawng Valley route was the local political officer, Cornelius North, who had organised what supplies he could. As Burma fell town by town to the Japanese, and power stations and telegraph offices were blown up to prevent them falling into Japanese hands, North had to rely on food from the immediate area. While there were paddy fields in the lower section of the valley, most inhabitants were small groups of Nagas and Kachins who lived by subsistence farming and hunting. Neil North[69] had managed to build small storehouses, and some huts along the track, but he was one man trying to help a flood of refugees. On 15 May the authorities in India were told by telegram that 500 Europeans and

---

69   Cornelius North was also known as Neil.

9,500 Indians were walking to India. Accurate numbers are impossible to gauge, but it's known that 40,000 people set off from Myitkyina after the bombing of the airstrip. Despite the hundreds of civil servants working in Burma at the onset of the Pacific War, few of them stopped to help the thousands of refugees attempting to escape to India. Neil North was an exception, as was the man who risked his own life to save thousands of others, 23-year-old Liverpudlian, Bunny Katz, a sergeant in the British Army. They became the heroes of Shinbwiyang.

For many of those who survived the trek from Burma, the story of the demise of the children of the Bishop Strachan's Home was the most poignant. These were the so-called 'orphans' with mixed-race parents, who had been abandoned to the care of the Church of England. Their journey had begun hundreds of miles away in Rangoon, but by 6 May they were among the thousands who witnessed the bombing of the airfield at Myitkyina. The doughty headmistress Lillian Bald had scooped up waifs and strays from other schools along the journey. Staff and pupils from St Matthew's School Moulmein, St Michael's Maymyo and St John's Toungoo were in the group. On 7 May they joined the stream of people heading north until they reached Milestone 102, where officials were diverting refugees west into the mountains. Here, Lillian Bald appealed for a military escort to help the adults and older children to walk out through the Hukawng Valley. The under-twelves and staff from the school who were aged and infirm, were taken to Sumprabum by jeep and lorry, and the army gave them food and money. Two soldiers, Captain Young and Sergeant Shaw, volunteered to escort the others to India. Five weeks later they had not even reached Shinbwiyang, but had spent a month walking through the rains. From the village of Tai-Hpa, Miss Bald sent a letter asking for help:

> This is an SOS message to do all that lies in your power to help us as best you can. Captain Young has earned our deep gratitude, for the responsibility he has undertaken is most nerve-wracking. He has shown indomitable courage, and very often he forgoes sleep and rest in search of food for us, when we have come to the end of our supply, and nothing but starvation looked ahead.
>
> ANGUS MacLEAN PAPERS, CENTRE FOR SOUTH ASIAN STUDIES,
> UNIVERSITY OF CAMBRIDGE

The captain had with him a year's army rations, which the group had been living on. After 205 miles of walking, this supply had almost run out. There was still a hundred miles to go until they reached the railhead at Ledo in India:

> More often than not we live on one meal a day. There were days when we thought we would starve and then would strike a village where we've had rice. We usually live on watery rice as this is the only way we can make the supply go far. Needless to say 60% of us have tummy trouble, sores, bad colds and fevers.

Seven of our girls have malaria, ninety per cent feel and know that it would be fatal to carry on. So we are staying put in this village and Captain Young and Sergeant Shaw are going ahead for help in the way of food and transport.

I wish a sea plane or planes would come for us, as this is a river village, a very swollen river at present. We have had a very hard and dangerous journey so far, steep precipitous mountain climbing in the pouring rain through dense tropical jungle infested with wild animals. Captain Young met a leopard. Across dangerous rapids, walking through paddy fields and nullahs[70] waist deep in water and ploughing through the jungle path in slush often thigh deep. On an average we do six miles per day, but there have been days when we have accomplished 14 to 17 miles. We have slept in the jungle without shelter. We have slept with highly decayed corpses around us. It was a common sight to see dead and dying people all the way.

The refugee rumour mill had warned the group that there were 300 Chinese bandits on the way, although before this story was passed on from the refugee officer's in-tray, this slur against the Chinese allies had been crossed out. The bandits were just one reason to stay put:

Most of us feel we cannot walk on any more. We are all on the verge of physical collapse. I feel you will do your very best for us to get us to India by sea planes or sending us food by planes till the rains are over, when motor transport could be sent for us. Believe me we cannot do any more rapids or rivers or hills in the state of health most of us are at present. Most of the children are sans blankets, sans shoes, sans change of clothing. Trusting you will remember us in your prayers and thanking you very much and with love from the children and our best wishes.

Captain Young got as far as Shinbwiyang with Lillian Bald's SOS message. The official report says that he died 2 days later, which would make his death in the latter part of June. The casualty list gives a date of death for Captain Young as 29 August 1942 at Shinbwiyang. Sergeant Shaw who accompanied him is not on the casualty register, but official reports give his death as occurring just before that of Captain Young. The exact dates of death of the rest of the school party are uncertain. On 1 September four girls and one boy were still alive out of the twenty children who had set out from Milestone 102. None of the adults survived. Lillian Bald, her 65-year-old brother, a niece, and two young nephews died at some point before 21 August, the date their bodies were found at the village of Yawbang.

---

70   An Indian word meaning stream or drain.

The tragedy wiped out the Bald family. Miss Bald's two sisters, Mary and Becky, had accompanied the other group to Sumprabum where they came under the wing of the fighting padre Father James Stuart. Father Stuart was a neutral Irishman, and like all the priests from the St Columban's Mission had opted to remain in Burma to help where they could. He had answered an SOS message from a British Army colonel, who found himself in Sumprabum with forty-nine refugees on his hands. This was the group of young children and their carers. Father Stuart spoke good Kachin and was just the man to help the group. However, while he was out in the villages recruiting coolies to carry the children to safety, Chinese troops arrived. The soldiers stole rice, clothes and fired a pistol through the bathroom door when the children refused to unlock it. The plucky matron of the Bishop's Strachan Home, Mrs David, managed to hide a little rice

This river will become a deadly torrent with the advent of the rains, rising up the sides of the ravine.

from the soldiers, but it looked as if this group too would starve to death. When the priest returned with the coolies, he was arrested by the Chinese. The situation escalated, with Kachin tribesmen squaring off against the Chinese, shots were fired and the soldiers beat a retreat. Just as the refugees thought they were safe, the Japanese arrived. Father Stuart used a combination of play-acting and humour to calm any fears that he was a spy, but it was the enemy who saved them. The Japanese officer in charge had been to a Baptist school before the war and was a Christian. He allowed the refugees to sit out the monsoon in Sumprabum, and allowed Father Stuart and a fellow priest to forage in the villages for supplies. On 2 October 1942, a cavalcade of elephants and coolies took the children on the last leg of their journey to safety. Fort Hertz, or Putao as it is now known, was the only place in Burma which was never occupied by the Japanese. From here the British Army airlifted the refugees to safety. Lillian Bald's two sisters, Becky and Mary were not among them. They had died at Sumprabum on 13 August, on or around the same day that their sister had succumbed in the Hukawng Valley. Father Stuart and his fellow priest Father McAlindon, joined the top secret Office of Strategic Services (OSS), the forerunner of the CIA, working as spies in occupied Burma.

Casualty figures for those who died in the Hukawng Valley are inaccurate. Recorded deaths stand at fewer than 5,000, but bodies sank in the mud and lay unburied until the jungle grew over them. European deaths were more likely to be known and recorded, largely by other Europeans who passed their bodies, and informed the authorities on arrival in India. But the Indian death toll will never be known, although the British Library does hold a register of those who arrived safely in Calcutta and sought help. Those on the trek record frequent Indian corpses, often by food stores. As people trudged through mud 3ft or 4ft deep, they would stumble over roots, rocks and what at first sight appeared to be sand bags: these too were the bodies of the dead.

13

The Heroes of Shinbwiyang

Twenty-three-year-old Liverpudlian, Bunny Katz displayed the humanity that most on the trek abandoned as they cast aside their belongings. As he walked up the Hukawng Valley, the young sergeant was horrified to see pregnant women attempting the same journey. Precious seats on planes evacuating women and children from Myitkyina airfield, had all too often been filled by able-bodied men who could have set off on foot. On 12 May Bunny Katz and two mates reached the refugee camp at Shinbwiyang to find there was an outbreak of cholera:

The view northwest from Myitkyina towards the Hukawng Valley.

As far as I could see, no medical help of any sort was available, although a number of doctors had passed through, none would stay over to help, not even for a couple of days. I learnt that the man in charge was C.W. North of the Burma Frontier Service [Force]. It seems to me that this fellow was the only one to stay at his post.

CENTRE OF SOUTH ASIAN STUDIES, UNIVERSITY OF CAMBRIDGE

A typical village clearing.

The camp had been a village of four Naga huts in a small jungle clearing, until the first refugees arrived. Cornelius North had organised the building of long dormitory huts constructed from bamboo and palm. Soon they were providing shelter to thousands. Before beginning the trek up into the hills, Bunny Katz and fellow soldiers queued for rations, as he wrote to a friend, Ted:

> There was a huge crowd outside the go-down[71], we helped force them into a queue. The blighters would come two or three times for rations without being detected. Now Ted this is the strangest part of the story, something I cannot explain but I feel sure you will understand even though others are certain to discredit it. You know how things are between Brenda and me. Well perhaps it really was telepathy, I seemed to hear her voice, 'You are staying Bunny aren't you? You can help here, *really* help.' And somehow the cholera epidemic didn't seem so frightening, I felt that I would never get malaria – how could dysentery touch me if I take care of myself – and so on. I must point out here that everyone, North included, thought the evacuation would be finished in a week or less, the Japs would by now have closed the last door to India, the stream of refugees would soon dry up, the monsoon would make the rivers unfordable.

Katz and his two fellow soldiers volunteered and soon, armed with their Tommy guns were guarding the ration store from dawn till late at night:

> The male refugees never once considered the women and kids, we had to use force to get the females at the front of the queue but on the whole it wasn't too hard a job keeping them all in line. The military were the worst. Officers came barging up the steps of the go-down with no consideration for anybody else. One, I think he was a colonel, was too demanding and even insulting, I kicked him down the steps, what else could I do, this was no ordinary situation. Another party of officers demanded to be allowed entrance to help themselves ignoring the fact that we only had a limited supply, we kicked them out too. Refugees were dying of cholera, dysentery, malaria or exhaustion. As there were no volunteers to do the burying, men for this job were chosen at the point of a gun, North certainly went the right way about things.

Neil North and Bunny Katz made a formidable team, sharing the responsibility of running the camp, and nursing each other when inevitably they both succumbed to disease. Hearing that a backlog of refugees was building up at a river on the forward route, the two men left Shinbwiyang to try to establish a

---

71 A word used in the Far East for warehouse

ferry service with Kachin tribesmen. Returning 2 weeks later, Katz found the camp had deteriorated:

Shinbwiyang had an atmosphere of death about it, the stench, which greeted me, it almost bowled me over. The whole village had been used as a latrine, the disintegrated bodies did not relieve the situation either. The refugees here had that hopeless look in their eyes. I felt near to tears at this pitiful scene. Meanwhile the food position was becoming more critical and people began calling at the bungalow for food. As none in the bungalow appeared to take much notice I took on the job of rationing, but there was insufficient food to go round, how people survived at this period was a miracle. Women came to the door crying for nourishment for the children. What could I do I felt like crying myself. Most of the officials in the bungalow gave no helping hand at all, contenting themselves with rest before moving off to the next camp.

Trouble was marching their way in the person of 4,000 Chinese soldiers. On 1 June a gadget was rigged up so that the next plane could pick up an urgent letter addressed to the government in Assam. Planes had a hook fixed on the wheel axle with which they picked up a message written on a piece of paper and strung on a piece of string between two bamboos. The camp asked for medical

A Kachin chief's hut. The Kachin helped bring in sacks of supplies dropped near the camp.

supplies, food and information about the onward journey from Shinbwiyang to Assam. Hundreds of refugees had already left for the steep climb west, but none knew the names of villages they might pass through or where, if at all, food was to be found. Neil North was still sorting out the ferry several miles to the west. A group of senior civil servants had stopped in Shinbwiyang, but set off on 5 June leaving Bunny Katz and an army medical orderly to deal with the Chinese. Within an hour he had succumbed to a bout of malaria. A few hours later the Chinese stragglers dribbled in and began looting, while Katz tried to hold them off at gunpoint. To his relief a ration plane flew over dropping twelve bags of rice, and he asked the Chinese commander to provide an armed guard in exchange for feeding his troops. The plan worked and the Chinese left the following morning.

There had been so many deaths while he was away, that Katz decided the rudimentary hospital building must be burnt and a new one built. Inside were half a dozen dead bodies. Among the volunteers to help were the Halpin family who had taken 3 weeks to walk from Maingkwan to Shinbwiyang. By this time the family had teamed up with Nellie Baker, a teacher. As the camp was threatened once again by Chinese soldiers Bunny Katz had an inspiration, to fly a Union Jack over the huts and claim that it was a British Army camp. It was Nellie Baker who made the flag out of scraps of material. It proved a deterrent, no more.

Hundreds of refugees were about to starve to death at Shinbwiyang, when one morning supplies rained down thanks to the RAF: sacks of tins, ration biscuits and rice attached to parachutes. To exhausted refugees it was also a low flying hazard, at least one was killed when a sack of rice crashed through the roof of a hut. Another had a close shave when a sack hit the side of the hut and upended the flimsy structure.

This food drop was closely followed by 'orders' to the government officials presumed to be running the camp. The officials should leave and make for India by any possible route, while refugees were commanded to stay put, because conditions in the hills were so atrocious. Bunny Katz, a lowly sergeant was a volunteer, and had been hoping that some officials might be sent to help him. With the help of some of the refugees[72] he quelled the fights over rations and moved and stored the food.

During this enforced break in their trek, William Halpin realised that his 67-year-old mother was not going to manage a hundred mile journey over the Patkoi Mountains to Assam. Gerry was sent ahead to see whether he could find coolies to carry his grandmother over the hills. After 2 days he reached an unfordable river, and was forced to return. Immediately he went down with malaria and one by one the family succumbed to illness. On 20 June their

---

72   Bunny Katz names Mr and Mrs Halpin and Gerry Halpin, Baxter, Wakefield, Miss Baker, and Mr and Mrs Doran.

THE HEROES OF SHINBWIYANG   193

grandmother died, followed 3 days later by Aunt Mia Thoung. They were the first members of the Halpin family to be buried at Shinbwiyang.

Neil North returned in the third week of June, and between bouts of malaria and dysentery he and Bunny Katz continued to run the camp. The monsoon appeared to have deterred the Japanese from patrolling the Hukawng Valley, but Allied planes managed to supply the camp throughout the rainy season. An extraordinary feat when oppressive mist hung over Shinbwiyang on most days, so that the inmates could not even see the tops of the trees. About a thousand refugees remained there. Occasionally newcomers arrived, some helped most did not. Kachin tribesmen, who had vanished into the jungle when Chinese soldiers attempted to rape their women, reappeared and helped to collect rations dropped by plane. To the refugees this was a blessing as at times 90 per cent of the camp population was ill. An RAF pilot who helped drop supplies throughout the monsoon described Shinbwiyang as 'a charnel house'. He knew there were many European and Anglo-Indian children there, and suggested the RAF buy some teddy bears and woolly monkeys from Calcutta to cheer them up. This was done and two sacks filled with soft toys were included in the next planeload. But on the day the flight left, bad cloud prevented anything being dropped at Shinbwiyang. On the return flight the crew saw a pathetic notice at another village and dropped the soft toys there instead.

Some medical help did reach the camp from India. Two doctors were parachuted in, but this was a sticking plaster solution. Refugees were dying from lack of proper nutrition, and the diseases brought about by their location in this notoriously malarial valley. Mrs Halpin fell ill and on the night of 13 September died in her sleep. Her eldest son wrote afterwards:

> She slept on the floor next to Gerry and he was the first to notice she was very still and shook her to wake her up in the early morning light, found her cold and still and saw ants going in and out of her nose and mouth.
>
> HALPIN FAMILY PAPERS

With his father also ill, it was 17-year-old Gerry who had to arrange his mother's burial, just as he had for his aunt and grandmother.

> Everybody was devastated and no more so than father with the sudden loss. He started openly blaming the disaster on his patriotic stubbornness that Britain would not let us down and force us to abandon everything and leave Burma. Father got weaker taking less and less food, no matter how the family pleaded with him to think of the younger ones. He had without anyone knowing asked Miss Baker to look after the children when he died and even told her that his being alive was hampering the rest moving on towards India.

Two weeks to the day after his wife died, William Halpin took a turn for the worse in the afternoon, humming a hymn. Within an hour the children were orphans, and Gerry buried the fourth member of their family at Shinbwiyang. On 29 September, the children led by Gerry Halpin and Nellie Baker, began to climb into the mountains on the final stretch of their journey to India. Neil North and Bunny Katz remained at the camp until 19 September when a Royal Army Medical Corps doctor and soldiers arrived to take over from them. There were still 200 sick refugees at Shinbwiyang, and both men had doubted whether they would ever leave the Hukawng Valley. Exhausted and malnourished they too left to walk through the mountains to India. They counted twenty-five skeletons a mile for the first 26 miles. After 20 days of climbing and sliding, they arrived in Margherita and were admitted to hospital.

Today Shinbwiyang has grown into a small town. It stands beside the Ledo Road, which follows the route along which so many refugees struggled to reach safety in India. There is no memorial to the sad part Shinbwiyang played in the history of Burma, and of the British Empire: for many refugees this was their rubicon.

14

Heading Through the Hills

Hills erupt from the plains of Burma. Not rolling and gentle, but strident and steep. Thrusting slopes that challenge the skill of road engineers and the will of climbers. Green with tangled forest and jungle clinging to outcrops of rock, the hills range in rows, on and on, they rise and fall like a giant corrugated iron roof. Tribes such as the Chins and Nagas who live in Burma's mountainous areas, have footpaths which wind through this apparent wilderness. They hunt the elusive creatures native to the hills and farm the steepness, taming it with terraces. Villages hang precariously over the inclines, linked by empty winding roads. An occasional motorbike or car negotiates the hairpin bends which typify roads

Refugees had to scale hills like these in the borderlands.

built by the British Army during the Second World War. Tribal footpaths over the hills can accommodate four feet or two, but these paths are too precipitous for wheeled transport. In 1942, the road makers had not penetrated into the Patkoi Range or the Chin Hills which separate Burma from India.

As hungry refugees plodded out of Shinbwiyang, they had little idea of what was ahead of them. Crossing the river beyond the village, they met a wall of hills. To the misery of mud, monsoon and malnutrition, they now had to add mountaineering. Missionary Russell was with a group which had set out from Sahmaw. They were lucky enough to have a pony and a mission elephant called Maggie, who had already pulled her weight by towing vehicles out of the mud in the Hukawng Valley. The missionaries left Shinbwiyang 3 days after the first rains. Zig-zagging up the path into the mountains, once again they were enclosed in a tunnel of jungle thick enough to block out the view, but not dense enough to provide any shelter from the rain.

> Rain began to come down in sheets and the clay of the path rapidly became thick mud. It was so slippery that to get round the steepest corners we had to go on hands and knees. We were destined to learn a good deal about mud of different qualities. During the frequent and torrential downpours the path became a rushing cataract of yellow water, each great footprint left by an elephant, a deep puddle. On the slopes, it was difficult to stand; one looked desperately for any projecting root or stump, against which to place the foot, or for any overhanging branch or bamboo, by which to haul oneself up. The short and level area at the bottom of a dip was an unspeakable slough, round which one picked a precarious way, if at all possible. When the weather was fine the mud rapidly became a clay of a most remarkable glutinous kind. One learnt to sympathise heartily with a fly on flypaper! Every few steps, the shoes were dragged off our heels, until in desperation we tied them on with string or webbing cut from our haversacks. The continual drag on the shoes soon caused its disintegration. When I reached the end of the trek, both heels had gone long before, and the soles of my shoes were only retained in places by such ligatures.
>
> RUSSELL PAPERS, BRITISH LIBRARY

Many refugees, like the surviving members of the Halpin family, had already lost their shoes in the swamps of the Hukawng Valley; many Indian refugees were barefoot when they set out; even army ammunition boots were not immune to the power of the mud on this journey. Captain John Perkins led a group of soldiers through to India, by the time they began to climb into the Naga Hills they were in a bad way:

> Several were bare foot – their feet lacerated and torn by sharp stones and the wounds festering. Shirts and shorts were hanging in ribbons and everyone was

looking a bit starry-eyed from lack of food and sleep. Now and again a man would be unable to rise from the ground after a rest and implore to be left to die. After a certain amount of kicks and abuse they would plod on. It was not easy to swear at a man when you knew exactly how he felt, but one could not allow them to give up; as long as they hated the sight of me, and had a grouse to take their mind off the real issue it didn't matter.

CAPTAIN PERKINS PAPERS, IWM

Every 10 or so miles, makeshift camps offered rough palm leaf huts for shelter. Cornelius North was the man responsible for these hasty efforts, but the scale of the refugee crisis had not been foreseen and they were hopelessly crowded. Wherever refugees congregated, the mud multiplied, exacerbated by the problem of raw sewage. Refugee mud connoisseurs noted in their diaries that the mud in the camps was generally 'black and stinking'. Even the fastidious Burmese nurses who travelled with Dr Gordon Seagrave were too exhausted to seek privacy under these conditions, as he wrote in his diary: 'The nurses are so tired now that they have lost all sense of shame and don't even bother to leave the road to answer the call of nature. And nobody cares about it either!'[73]

Dysentery, which afflicted every refugee at some stage in their journey, held hidden dangers as people looked for a place to relieve themselves. Tribal paths through the Naga Hills ran along the tops of ridges. When walkers dashed into the jungle on either side of the track, they often found a sheer drop on one side and a steep bank on the other. It all added to the misery. As refugees used the last dregs of their energy to climb through the mountains on the Indian side of the border, many did not bother to leave huts or shelters to relieve themselves, fouling them for later inhabitants.

None of the refugees recorded harvesting rainwater to sustain them on their journey, they relied on the streams and rivers which were plentiful. But every water source was surrounded by refugees, camping and fouling the ground and the water. As the monsoon engulfed the highlands, these streams rose to impassable barriers. There are many extraordinary accounts of attempts to cross the rivers. Some were crossed using makeshift rafts, constructed from bamboo poles roped together. Whole families drowned in these attempts. Starving refugees who had been held up for days without food, fought for places and swamped the overloaded rafts. One of those who attempted to swim a river swollen by monsoon rain was Captain John Perkins:

It was probably one of the most foolish things I have ever done. However leaving my pack, with my boots round my neck I swam across. There was one

---

73 From *A Burma Surgeon* by Dr Gordon Seagrave.

There is no road to
this remote mountain
village.

nasty moment in some fast current when I went under but I won through
and gasped on the other bank. The exhibition helped others and one or two
prepared to swim also, but two horses followed next and the poor brutes got
into trouble and drowned, so no one attempted it after me.

Deep in the Naga Hills, the missionaries from Sahmaw had Maggie the elephant with
them, who was a lifesaver for many. As Padre Russell and his companions trudged
along, they had heard evil stories of the power of the Namyung River. Nearby, lay
the village of Tagap Ga and the eponymous refugee camp, where soldier's wife Lillian
Mellalieu and her sister Irene became stranded. Corralled in a narrow valley the
Namyung had been swollen by storms in the hills, rising from ankle to shoulder deep
in a matter of hours. The missionaries were stuck there for 4 days, even the amiable
Maggie could not attempt to cross that. Padre Russell wrote in his diary:

> The night before we attempted the crossing was spent in a group of shelters,
> which rose like an island from a sea of unusually black and stinking mud. It
> seemed really a waste of time to go down to the edge of the river and endeavour
> to wash off the worst of the day's dirt, one was sure to be plentiful befouled
> again returning to the camp! But to remove, in the rushing water the pounds
> of clay that transformed shoes and socks into unrecognisable masses, did at least
> make for ease in putting them on again next morning. One of the outstanding
> horrors of a march such as ours was the loathsome business daily repeated, of
> dragging on wet footwear in the cold light of dawn. Many a pair of socks came
> to an untimely end by fire, because the owner hung them up to dry at night
> over the camp fire and forgot them until the morning. But by this stage in any
> case, few of our socks boasted toes or heels; they were literally anklet socks.

RUSSELL PAPERS, BRITISH LIBRARY

They used the time well, making a rope from split bamboo which would help to provide a handhold as refugees crossed from one side to the other. On 23 May water levels had dropped a little and the river was only waist high, about 4ft deep:

So strong was the current and so rough the [river] bed that no woman and few men could stand against it unaided. This was to prove Maggie's finest hour. Loaded with women, with kit, with men too, she strode through the rushing waters, ever returning with another burden. With her aid we stretched the cane rope from bank to bank, but it was not as much use as had been hoped. On our side the bank was high and there was no convenient tree by the water's edge to which to make it fast. As a result those who sought to cross by its aid could not reach it until well out in the current. But in spite of that it was instrumental in saving lives. An Indian wading the stream higher up, lost his footing and was swept down. Clutching the rope despairingly as he passed, he hung on, the water dashing over his head and shoulders. Rushton and another waded out and tried to get him to turn upstream, and to drop the heavy waterlogged bundle to which he clung.

The Indian survived to continue the trek. But there were thousands more waiting on the bank, and it was Maggie the mission elephant who was the heroine of the day:

Maggie too did her bit of lifesaving. A group of people, including several women were in difficulties in mid-stream, and were at the point of exhaustion. The mahout[74] seeing their plight, with great presence of mind brought the elephant alongside them, and using her great bulk as a backwater, [they] were able to struggle to safety.

Russell attempted the crossing on foot gripping an 8ft long bamboo. But the current was so strong, bludgeoning his body, and he slipped in mid-stream. Spinning round he was pulled underwater, but managed to cling to his bamboo cane, struggle to his feet, and drag himself into the overhanging bushes.

The grossly swollen rivers had another use. Fast currents quickly and efficiently disposed of the dead. Concomitant with the number of rivers, was the steep hill before and after each torrent. Range after range of densely wooded hills greeted the walkers as they climbed to each summit, sometimes the hills were 6,000ft high, and the slopes were 1:1. Here and there a small Naga village stood on a hilltop, or hung onto a steep slope. Parents urged their children to keep walking; missionaries whistled and sang hymns; Fred Tizzard thought of his baby daughter kicking her legs in her excitement at seeing him again, and numbly viewed the scenery:

---

74 Elephant handler, the Indian equivalent of oozie.

Except in Switzerland, I had not been before so in the heart of the mountains. The view from the ridge beat most in Switzerland, yet it roused no response. The Swiss mountains are friendly. But the green valleys I looked deep into today and the peaks ranged one behind the other into hyacinth distance, called no invitation. They are unpeopled, for the traveller there is no welcome there and few paths to guide him. After a casual glance I tramped on, eyes fixed as usual on the path ahead.

Up and down. Down and Up. Mostly upwards, occasionally in sunlight above the clouds, but generally tramping through drizzle. I wore my oilskin gas cape above my pack, but still was cold. If the man who contracted for my army pack had to carry his worldly wealth in it he too would learn that it is absorbent instead of waterproof. Hills and valleys were hidden, only the closer trees showed through the rain. They were shrouded in rank moss, ragged moss streamers swung from the branches, instead of grass moss grows beside the path, and noisome fantastic fungi sprouted from rotting wood. It is a country Arthur Rackham would delight to draw, whose people must naturally be animists, worshipping tree spirits, most of them malign.

FRED TIZZARD PAPERS, IWM

Captain John Perkins and his soldiers did not eat for 3 days as they climbed through the Naga Hills hoping to come across one of the infrequent ration camps: 'Oddly the lack of food did not worry me much, except for occasional visions of multi-course dinners which I could actually smell.'[75]

The missionaries all had food fantasies: the ideal breakfast in bed with the newspapers, or a slap-up tea at the best tea shop in Calcutta. One craved tinned pears, another cream pastries and Russell fantasised about sirloin steak. Few conversations are recorded, and most remember walking in silence, certainly by this stage in the journey. For many Britons their thoughts turned to home. Captain Perkins walked with Sergeant Kirkland:

I myself was often reliving scenes that occurred when I was a kid. Occasionally he [Sgt Kirkland] would speak of Ireland and his home and he was particularly interesting on his stories of service in the East, Hongkong, Singapore and Shanghai. After a time you become numb to your difficulties and just plod on taking little notice, or so it appeared to me.

Despite the latitude, the journey through the Naga Hills was cold, and the rain felt ice cold as soon as they stopped walking. Nights were also cold, and many recall throwing themselves down beside the path to sleep rather than using

---

75   Captain John Perkins papers, IWM.

A British Army road climbing a typically steep hill.

precious energy to build a shelter. Sleep was often difficult as refugees passed them all night long splashing their way through the mud, and soldiers fired rifles and tommy guns until the noise sounded like a miniature battle. Once he was over the border into India, Fred Tizzard was filled with renewed energy:

Each morning, although it is some time since I had a real sleep, I feel fresh and strong when we start, and eager for the march. My weight is down a couple of stone since Marjorie left Burma, and now the thickest part of my leg is a comical knobbly knee. But I never feel really tired, and each dawn am impatient to hurry on towards Marjorie and Rosemary Ann.

As we tramp along I imagine my arrival. They live in a house on a hill. Sometimes Marjorie sees me coming and runs down the drive to meet me. Sometimes a servant will not let me in, so grubby a tramp, until Marjorie is sent for to recognise me. And the room differs. Sometimes when I go into it I see our silver, and in the wardrobe my suits and shirts, all pressed ready for me to arrive. Other times a glance round the room shows me that nothing my crew took from Sagaing has got through, and we have nothing left but what was in Marjorie's cushion cover and is on my back. But always in her cot there is Rosemary Ann, ready with a radiant smile to greet me and her blue bear.

15

Tea to the Rescue

Tea, that doyenne of English beverages is grown in abundance in the highlands of Assam on the Burma–India border. Colonial tea planters' bungalows still stand in this lush green landscape which is watered by up to 12in. of rain a day in the monsoon. Tranquil hills are covered with contoured terraces of tea bushes, interrupted here and there by grey tree trunks. These trees give shade to the tea pickers as their hands dart above the greenery, whipping off the young top leaves. At the outbreak of the Pacific War, the men who ran these plantations were largely British, with a workforce of hundreds at their command. It was only natural that when the British Army needed labour they should look to the tea

A traditional dah hanging in a palm leaf hut.

gardens of Assam. Thousands of tea garden labourers were requisitioned by the army to build the roads towards Burma, roads which would serve the retreating army, but would also aid the civilian refugees. What they were constructing was not roads in the sense that we understand them, but earth tracks winding up and down the hills. In some places they followed the line of an existing mule track which was widened to accommodate wheeled transport, in others jungle was hacked aside with dah[76] and kukri. Many of the road-builders were from hill tribes, and even they succumbed to the diseases prevalent in the highlands between the two countries.

The army began to push a road through from Assam in March 1942, General Wood was in charge of the Herculean efforts this required, through border country which he described as:

A desert varying from 100 to 200 or more miles broad, and extending south to north some 400 miles, that separated the two settled areas of India and Burma. This desert was not only almost devoid of land communications and transport in any degree commensurate with the evacuation burden it was called upon to sustain, but food supplies therein were little more than sufficient to sustain the meagre population at their normal low level of subsistence.

GENERAL WOODS REPORT, INDIA OFFICE RECORDS, BRITISH LIBRARY

General Woods' orders were to build the road, but he was also put in charge of the refugee problem from the Indian side of the border. Modern refugee emergencies are supplied from the air, but in 1942 battle duties had to come first:

Providing relief was prevented until motorable roads had been driven over the hill barrier as a road was needed to transfer substantial tonnages. A porter carrying 50lbs must consume a minimum of 2lbs a day of his load, with a 12 day march each way, 24 days without a rest day. Therefore only 2 lbs of supplies are left from each load. Mud got so bad in the north that a porter could not carry a load more than three miles and that took ten to 12 hours.

Rumours of the new road had reached those walking to India. It was said that an army was travelling along it, an army that would expel the Japanese from Burma. The rumour was somewhat premature. Although two roads were beginning to snake their way through the borderlands, it quickly became apparent that army road-making efforts might be scuppered by thousands of refugees, who brought with them unwelcome tropical diseases. The British Army still goes to great lengths to maintain the health of its troops, keeping them on a diet familiar to their stomachs,

---

76   A dah is the versatile Burmese tool still used by farmers.

importing army staples such as bully beef to foreign locations to avoid travellers' diarrhoea. Hygiene is enforced by officers, as one of their principal jobs is to look after the health and welfare of their men. As hundreds and then thousands of refugees streamed through the hills, army headquarters became alarmed that retreating troops would be infected with typhus, typhoid and other diseases; once they reached Imphal, these exhausted men were expected to defend India against the Japanese Imperial Army. Their other concern was that 75,000 Indians working on the roads through the hills would be infected. In fact when one group of Indian labourers heard that cholera was on the march with the refugees, they downed picks and decided to return to their villages. The rudimentary road which had provided some relief to the exhausted refugees was closed to them.

Refugees had begun to trickle across the border in January, and as the numbers swelled, the men and women from the tea gardens had built small refugee camps and provided food. As soon as General Woods was appointed he had ordered the camps to be enlarged and properly provisioned. Still the main problem was beyond his control:

> When the refugees reached the hands of the Indian authorities they were invariably in a poor condition at a stage of the journey when the greatest of their physical trials had yet to be faced; and crossing of the 5–8,000 feet hill barrier that, varying with the locality, involved anything from 5–15 days of most strenuous physical effort. Before reaching the Indian authorities, refugees had been sustained on little more than a handful of rice.

In his report he voiced a criticism which was to ricochet off the walls of Burma Government Offices for many months to come: why had so few Burma civil servants stayed to help the refugees?

> A point difficult of comprehension is why, when the advance of the enemy progressively released so many government officials, so few were spared for service in the Burma portion of the desert.

It was the Indian tea planters who stepped in to save the lives of thousands of men, women and children who fled Burma. They left their comfortable bungalows in the hills of Assam to live under the same conditions as the refugees. Some even gave their lives. Colonel Stoker was one of the many who benefitted:

> We walked out of the jungle into a small clearing. Here was an area surrounded by a railing. Inside the railing could be seen kitchens, stores, first aid posts and a stack of arms. At one point we got hot tea, at another marvellous stew cooked under the expert eye of the doctor.

COLONEL STOKER PAPERS, IWM

It was not just the physical needs of refugees which were sustained by the tea planters' service, their help gave exhausted and malnourished refugees the will to continue on the final leg of their journey. Among the many tea planters who gave their services was D.S. Hodson who was based at the northern end of the border, near Dapha:

> It was worth a great deal to see today's refugees arrive 150 in number, to witness the help given, the swollen feet and legs washed and dressed, the sores and ulcers treated and bandaged on one who had walked in with the whole of his feet completely raw, the children and others fed with milk and sago, men given a hot cooked meal of curry and rice, how grateful they all were, the way the parents thought of their children first, the joy when the babies lapped up the milk and went to sleep, the laughter of boys and girls when they were served with a hot meal; and shown a dry place in which to sleep, and the thankful relief when we told people that they would from now on be carried on a stretcher whilst the children would also not walk until they were fit.

The voluntary efforts of the tea planters were reinforced by men sent to help by the Indian government. Alastair Tainsh was among them. After the event Alastair Tainsh used his diary as the basis for a report which gives some idea of the men's initiation as aid workers. He started in May when it was believed there were only 9,500 Indians trudging over the hills and an estimated 500 Europeans. Margherita is the little town down in the valley below the tea estates, and the Europeans based there had given up their golf course and polo ground as the site for refugee reception camps. Transporting food supplies over the mountain was still a problem. Porters saw British officials running for their lives and refused to work, others had been looted by soldiers at gunpoint. Tainsh came up with the idea of driving a herd of goats up to the camps to provide fresh meat, but in practise the goats found the conditions heavy going and few survived. The monsoon had set in by this time and he described the route as like a 'buffalo wallow' in some places and akin to 'Vaseline' in others. Soon he encountered refugees. The first European refugee he met was the wife of Cornelius North, hero of Shinbwiyang. She had made the journey on horseback with a string of porters. As Tainsh continued along the trail, he discovered that Burma Frontier Force cavalry had looted porters carrying supplies to refugees, so food was not available at subsequent camps. Camp commandants later routinely disarmed soldiers as they came through, preventing further looting and allowing refugees to make the final stages of the trek in comparative peace and safety. Many had spent the entire journey nervously listening to the crackle of gunfire. There were some remarkable survival stories, among them a missionary couple, Revd and Mrs Darlington who had made the trek with their 6-week-old baby. At one of the rivers he found several corpses so he tied rattan cane to their legs, pulled them

Sketch map of one route taken by refugees through the Naga Hills showing camps set up by the tea planters.

	CAMP.	CAMP.	MILES	TOTAL
1.	LEKHAPANI	TIPONG	3	3
2.	TIPONG	N. TIRAP	4½ -	7½
3.	N. TIRAP	KUMLAO	6	13½
4.	KUMLAO	BUFFALO	6	19½
5.	BUFFALO	NAMCHICK	4	23½
6.	NAMCHICK	NAMGOI	8½	32
7	NAMGOI	NAMPONG	3	35
8.	NAMPONG	SHAMLUNG	9½	44½
9.	SHAMLUNG	NAWNGYANG HKA	6	50½
10.	NAWNGYANG HKA	TAGUNG HKA	9	59½
11.	TAGUNG HKA	NGALANG GA.	8	67½
12.	NGALANG GA.	NAMLIP	10	77½

to the river and threw them in. When he arrived at his allotted camp, Tainsh raised the Burmese flag, hoping that the peacock would give approaching refugees a psychological boost as they glimpsed it from the path. On arrival they talked of starvation, cruelly the banana trees so abundant in the jungle were not in fruit, but some cut the trees down and ate the central core of the stem. Few supplies had been dropped in the hills, and refugees were dependent on the goodwill of villagers who had little enough of their own. Alastair Tainsh was in a similar situation and had little food with him, but he commandeered some cattle which had been used as pack animals, and were being abandoned because they had sore backs and couldn't carry their loads.

On 25 May, soon after he arrived, he recorded helping an exhausted elderly man to a seat and administering hot sweet tea and rum:

> We still possessed ideals rather than common sense, and we gave rum and tea to a man, who if he ever reached the next camp, would certainly never have reached India. At this stage it was necessary to differentiate between people who were beyond our aid, and those who might respond to treatment. There was so much to do, and such shortage of supplies, that any wastage on hopeless cases would be to the detriment of those who still stood a chance of recovery. It took time and many heart-rending moments before we could harden ourselves to adopt this obviously sound, but seemingly uncharitable attitude.
>
> TAINSH REPORT, BRITISH LIBRARY

Inevitably as the tsunami of refugees continued, Tainsh and the other men running these camps became inured to the dreadful sights they witnessed on a daily basis. Many refugees had lost the will to live, some made little crosses out of pieces of wood or bamboo and planted them in the ground by their heads before lying down by the path to wait for death. Children who struggled to keep up with their families were regularly abandoned to an uncertain fate. In some cases it was the children who outlived their families. Occasionally other trekkers would rescue these stray children, but hundreds of orphans are recorded as arriving in India. At one refugee camp a British soldier took charge of a Tamil baby. He persuaded the villagers to make it a cot, and made an improvised feeding bottle from an empty aspirin bottle and a condom. There are also records of childless couples 'adopting' children who survived the trek.

Fred Tizzard encountered many of his old colleagues from the Irrawaddy Flotilla Company on his journey. One in particular haunted him:

> 'Is there any food to be had on the way?' he questioned urgently. 'No idea', I said, 'Probably no more than we've found so far'. 'Then we can't make it' he muttered, 'We're all in.' He looked it. Eyes deep sunken and dull. His boots were worn out. We pass like that, men who have shared cheerful evenings in one anothers' cabins

these many years, I looked back several times to see which way they were going,
until they were lost in the winding column behind, and wondered whether we
would all meet again. A man has still a deep reserve of vitality to draw on when
he begins to feel all in. One unexpected good meal restores his confidence. Or,
when alone he would give up, he keeps on because he is one of the column.
Many of the English and most of the Indians are like that. They seldom walked
much before, they started unfit for the journey, but they tramp, single file, in
parties. Each one, however weary, moves along automatically as a package on a
mechanical conveyor, drawn by the movement of the next man ahead. While the
leader had confidence and strength, all keep going.

There is nothing one can do to help old friends met on the way, unless alone
and too sick to carry on, they need someone to stay with them. Suggesting that
they join our party would not be welcome. This party is already too large, and
includes four women and two unfit men. The smaller the party the better, now
that for all but rice we must depend on what we find on the way. The occasional
chicken is a boon to a party of three, but does not go far in a meal for a dozen.

FRED TIZZARD PAPERS, IWM

Altruism was not a quality found among many survivors.

When refugees arrived at a camp, the tea planters found that few of them
wanted to leave. The mantra of the men who ran the camps became 'Keep them
hungry, keep them moving', so that people didn't lose the will to get out of the
jungle as soon as possible. The flow of people started at dawn and never seemed
to stop, at its peak there were 1,000 refugees a day passing through each camp.
Many had the telltale signs of malnutrition, little white flakes in the corners of
the eyes and the edges of their tongues red and sore. On arrival everyone was
searched because people were taking too many stores from the limited number
of RAF supply dumps in the jungle. Searches were profitable and the finds were
added to the camp larders to find their way into the daily 'stew' served at 8.30
every morning. As Alastair Tainsh wrote in his report after the event:

We had to be absolutely ruthless in order to maintain control of a hunger-
maddened crowd. Before that there were no organised feeding arrangements
and it had been survival of the fittest and the best armed. Many free fights in
the crowd and we didn't hesitate to use our canes on men, women and children
alike. Anyone who tried to push forward, or made a noise was taken out of
the queue, beaten, and put at the end. Some came up for food a second time.
We told them 'If you are taking more than your share you will die. You will
never reach the top of the next hill.' This was truer than we had anticipated, for
over-eating killed 17 people in the next few days. Often they did not bother to
cook the extra rice (which they were given), but ate it raw, with the result that
it scoured their intestines. It had the effect of having bad dysentery, and after

passing large quantities of blood they would sit down on a wet place and add a chill or pneumonia to their troubles. When we heard of the deaths on the road we all became adamant and cut down the dry rations and tried to issue only cooked food.

After this breakfast, staff walked round the camp to tell people to move on. The wise got away before dawn, and could get the next march done, before reaching a ferry across the swollen Nawngyang River by 1pm. The camp doctor went round doling out sick notes to those whose physical condition was so desperate that they were unable to move out. The rule was 'to get as many people alive to India as possible'. Alastair Tainsh wrote:

> If they did not get out by the specified time we drove them out. This was done in all the camps; it was the only way to get tired and demoralised people to safety. We allowed no one who came in to camp before mid day to stay. After that hour we didn't encourage them to go on as they would be unable to reach the springs near the top of the hill before nightfall. We reckoned that few refugees could move at a pace of more than one mile per hour.

Every day Alastair Tainsh had the grim task of dealing with the corpses:

> The fresh corpses were quite easy to carry, but some of the old ones required several trips before we had collected up all the bits and pieces. The head and ribs always gave the most trouble.

Rain was falling steadily but he managed to set fire to some by piling dry grass and wood on top during dry periods. Many corpses were found with their lower half exposed, and there were many instances of gold teeth torn from the mouth of the dead and their belongings rifled. Corpses were most common on steep hills, and as camps were sited close to water, there was often a steep hill afterwards. Colonel Stoker counted a corpse every 20 or 30 yards. There was an even more remarkable phenomenon:

> Around corpses hundreds of butterflies were dancing.[77] Many of these were people who had stayed till the end, and families had gone before so that they were travelling alone and did not know how to cook and what was safe to eat. Many were found lying on their backs with their legs drawn up and their buttocks bare.

> COLONEL STOKER PAPERS, IWM

---

77   It was said that the butterflies drank the sweat.

Tainsh ran the camp at Shamlung, a narrow valley with hills on either side so steep that he described them as cliffs. Beside the river on both sides there were level strips of ground covered with tall reeds, banana trees and scrub:

> The climb from Tagung Hka was very difficult, the track very muddy. Refugees fell face down often and after falling a few times people gave up trying altogether and lay where they fell waiting for death to end their misery. Steel Company elephants had caused huge holes. In one place I found a soldier-clerk named Cherryman who had died, having stepped into a mud hole three feet deep from which he was unable to get out. There was no doubt that these elephants caused more deaths than the lives they saved.

Tainsh was not immune to the knee-high mud. He got so wet that every night he took off his wet clothes, and put on dry ones in order to catch a few hours sleep. In the morning he put his wet clothes back on.

Once they had passed out of Tainsh's hands, refugees on this route through the borderlands headed for the Pangsau Pass which was the highest point on the border. India had been their goal for hundreds of miles, but they still had fifty more to walk before reaching the railway line which would carry them to Margherita. The last part of the journey included the notorious Golden Stair, where the path dropped hundreds of feet in a flight of rough steps made from branches laid across the muddy path. Coolies abandoned several stretchers at the top, and in at least one instance a sick man was tipped off into the jungle by coolies and left to die.

For those who reached Margherita there was a hospital. Europeans were treated to food served on a china plate, a hot bath in a bucket of water and a change of clothes. Accommodation was strictly segregated into civilian and military, with Europeans and Anglo-Indians together, and Burmans and Indians. Many refugees got no further than the hospitals, dying there. Nearly all those who completed the trek spent some time in hospital recovering from the effects. A major destination for refugees was Imphal, a name which became familiar to many veterans as an important army base in the ensuing war. Ten large refugee camps sprang up around the town, but on 10 May before the monsoon had begun, the Japanese bombed Imphal, killing thirty people. Six days later there was another raid. Many Indian truck drivers who had been meeting refugees on the new military road and bringing them on the last stage of the journey, headed home, as did many camp staff. The compassionate General Woods who had done so much to help the refugees watched as the drivers compounded their desertion:

> In order to ensure that the desertion would not be followed by forceful action to bring them back to their duty, these local drivers ran their lorries off the road down steep embankments, and in many cases not only turned over their

lorries or burnt them to cut the tyres to ribbons. At a time when the weather was deteriorating and a general slump in the health of refugees was taking place, and when so little transport could yet be spared to the refugees from the army, this action was most bitterly cruel and unquestionably caused the death of hundreds. It was however a painful and heart rending experience to witness these unfortunate refugees, among whom exhaustion was growing apace, and for whom we could do little except feed them and give them medical help. Their crying need was for transport. It was the golden key for resolving all difficulties.

GENERAL WOODS REPORT, BRITISH LIBRARY

Once again it was the tea planters who stepped in to help, providing twenty-five lorries and drivers to bring up supplies to feed the camps, but they could not cope with the flood of people on the road. Other routes along the 900-mile border were equally muddy and disease-ridden. And what of the fearful headhunting Nagas? On the contrary, accounts are full of the kindness of Nagas, who fed and housed refugees passing through their villages. Fred Tizzard, Angus MacLean and the rest of their party were treated hospitably in many Naga villages, and even slept in a Naga chief's hut:

Even the children of this unwashed people have a dignity, the Nagas are masters of their own wild hills. When at dusk soldiers and refugees lay sleeping under every hut I thought of the compliment the Nagas show us. Whenever British troops had come before they came as enemies, and strong. This time we come as the remnants of a beaten army. But there is none of the contempt and hostility we met from the Burmans. The Nagas are themselves a warrior people, they have known defeat, and tonight a beaten foe sleeps without fear around their home.

FRED TIZZARD PAPERS, IWM

When Fred emerged from the mountains, through breaks in the showers he saw the plains of Manipur State illuminated by sunlight. He burst into song:

The track still led down steeply and still though the rain. No more mountains. I found myself singing 'I'll walk beside you'[78] as I marched in the rain. And when the gradient was easier I ran to gain time. Near the foot of the hills a wide torrent, knee deep, had to be forded half a dozen times. Foolishly I would not delay to take off my suede shoes each time, it did not matter so near the end of the journey, so soaked them thoroughly.

---

78   A popular song from the first half of the twentieth century.

In no time it seemed I was on the level and out of the rain. Looking back, the mountains steep behind me were blurred by driving squalls. Somewhere right on the peak was the village, where we spent last night and I hoped never to see mountains again. Impossibly remote it seemed, here in the sunshine.

Squelching through the bog at the foot of the mountains, Fred emerged onto the Manipur Plain. His pipe and tobacco pouch had been abandoned in the jungle between the Irrawaddy and Chindwin Rivers:

At a Manipur farmhouse I asked to buy milk. They had none but offered ten Capstan Cigarettes for a rupee, five times their legal price. I bought them at once. How wonderful the first tasted. And a little farther on I bought 18 small bananas for five annas, and ate them all. On the outskirts of a village I bought natural milk in a tin so grimey that I hesitated, but drank all the same.

Outside his garden gate in the village sat an old Indian, with a basket of polished rice moulded into balls with palm sugar. He stopped each refugee who passed along, the Indians and the British soldiers too. My turn came and he held out a ball of the sweet rice. Please accept my help, he said. I did, and I wish he could know how good it tasted, that first sugar since the Chindwin.

As the government tried to piece together the facts of the great exodus from Burma, the censor was put on alert for information. A file in the India Office Records contains the results of their efforts, recounting how whole families were wiped out. The Wilby family was one example, they had set out from Myitkyina after the airfield was bombed:

Mrs Wilby left with her baby of 2 ½ and a son of 12, also her two daughters, two nieces, and Fred Thompson a friend, also a Mr Davidson were in one party. After a week or ten days trekking Thomson sat down and passed away. Davidson who was nearly all in, saw his friend die like that and went off his head, rushed into the forest to perish. Mrs Wilby and the others trekked on and on, finally she had to leave her baby by the roadside for it had died from starvation. A few days later her son died and they had to leave him. Full of sorrow she and the four girls trekked on until she dropped and died from starvation and exhaustion. Trekkers came along and found the four girls dying beside the body of Mrs Wilby. They tried to induce the girls to go on with them but they were too weak and exhausted to move. They told the men to go on their way and save themselves, which they could not do if they were with them. When they realised the girls could not move, they had to leave them and go on their way.

INDIA OFFICE RECORDS, BRITISH LIBRARY

Like many husbands and fathers, Mr Wilby had set off to walk to India believing his family would be flown out from the airfield at Myitkyina. The account continues:

> Somewhere in Assam they met Mr Wilby who was on his way to Burma so as to find his family. He asked the trekkers if they knew where his family was. This gentleman told him how they had passed his family one by one along the road, and how they had pleaded with the girls to try and come along with them, but they were dying and could not move. Mr Wilby with a few villagers went to the place where the trekkers had left the girls. When they reached the place no signs of the bodies could be found.

16

Through the Chaukan Pass

Wild elephants are known to have used the Chaukan Pass as an ancient migration route linking populations in Assam and Burma. The giant footprints of the pachyderm are still more likely to be spotted in streamside mud than those of homo sapiens. This is one of the areas of the world in the twenty-first century, which can claim to be largely unexplored. As one of those who survived the desperate journey of 1942 wrote afterwards:

> Now we know why this stretch of country is uninhabited for 100 miles. Not only is there not a trace of men, but mammal and even bird life is conspicuous by its absence: truly a forgotten world, where solitude reigns supreme.
>
> DIARY OF MILLAR IOR/M/3/1180

There *are* animals hiding in this forgotten world: takins, tigers, samburs and elephants, but they shy away from human contact. This is the mountainous apex of Burma where it meets India and China, their borders looking as if they were drawn by a cartographer with no control over the pencil. Hkakabo, the highest peak in Burma, stands where the three borders connect. A little to the south is Diphu Pass, where an old trade route crosses into India and then north to China. Two of Burma's great rivers rise in this region, the Salween, and the two streams which join at Myitsone to become the Irrawaddy. A handful of Europeans have explored this remote region, most notably in 1895 Prince Henri of Orleans took an expedition overland from Hanoi to Calcutta, to search for the sources of the Irrawaddy River. Even in the twenty-first century, 'new' tribes have been discovered, such is the nature of the terrain.

In May 1942, as the Japanese were knocking at the gates of the northern tip of Burma, a Dutch surveyor named Moses claimed that he had travelled over the Chaukan Pass to India and knew the route. His claims led to a nightmare trek in one of the most inhospitable environments in the world. Refugees who attempted the route did so in the monsoon and without proper equipment. Their disastrous story led to a rescue attempt in which several men were killed; three planes crashed looking for them; and at a time of scarcity, supplies for 2½ years

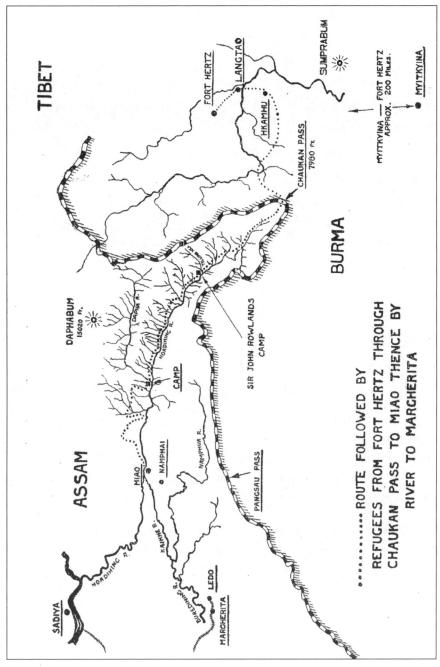

Without elephants Mackrell would have been unable to rescue those who got stuck near the Chaukan Pass.

Myitsone, the beginning of the Irrawaddy River soon to be flooded for a hydroelectric
scheme.

were dropped to them and most were never recovered. Their survival was a
miracle, and was thanks to two men and their elephants. Among the survivors,
was a pregnant woman and her 8-month-old baby.

News was slow to reach the triangle at the top of Burma. After witnessing the
burning ruins of Mandalay, Frank Kingdon Ward, arrived in Fort Hertz in early
May. He told the local official Eddie Rossiter, 'an early collapse was not imminent'
and left for Tibet. This was the first war news that Rossiter had received since 7
April, as he had no wireless transmitter, and he prepared for a trek. His Shan[79] wife
was 5 months pregnant and the couple had a baby son John; although his family are
not mentioned at all in the letter he wrote home to his mother in Ireland:

> The road to China was comparatively easy, and from various places in China I
> could have flown to India. There was no route at all to India, there was it is true
> a path marked on maps, but this was through deep jungle and at the very best
> of times required 6 weeks and no villages at all existed, this means no food was
> obtainable en route, all would have to be carried by coolies and foods for the
> coolies would have to be carried also, and so on.
>
> INDIA OFFICE RECORDS, BRITISH LIBRARY

On 9 May a runner arrived from John Leyden, Rossiter's opposite number in
Sumprabum, 8 days march to the south:

---

79   The Shan tribe found predominantly in the northeast.

Myitkyina had been entered by the Japanese, all the Myitkyina officials had cleared away (by another route) and that he was coming to meet us, and we both had been ordered by government to proceed to India. He said India had promised to send a party to meet us at the Chaukan Pass (the boundary) and were sending up food supplies. It was only because of this assurance that I agreed to go at all, I had prepared to disregard the orders and go to China as starvation along the India route seemed more than probable.

Rossiter assumed, wrongly as it transpired, that the remains of the Burma government had been in contact with officials in India, and therefore the risk of taking the Chaukan Pass was considerably reduced. As the Imperial Japanese Army advanced north, desperate radio messages were sent by the British, but many did not get through. Mandalay had been a crucial link in the chain of communication, and it was in enemy hands, and surviving military radio equipment had been destroyed after troops crossed the Chindwin River. Leyden had personally prevented 500 refugees from taking the northernmost route on the same day he sent a message to Rossiter. Notices were now posted in the town to deter others taking this route.

Rossiter set off 2 days later with his family and a tea planter, named Millar who had accompanied Kingdon Ward but was due back at his job on an Assam tea garden. They rendezvoused with Leyden on 13 May. With food for 26 days and 300 porters[80] to carry it all, the expedition was off to a propitious start. By now the group included Sir John Rowland, an energetic man in his 60s who throughout April had kept Burma Railways operating while acting as the driving force behind the Burma Road. He had been allocated a seat on a plane from Myitkyina but, despite his age, gallantly refused the place and said that as his staff could not fly out, he would walk with them. With him were his office staff and their families, in all about eighty people.

Scotsman Ritchie Gardiner, a forestry man, now serving with the Royal Engineers was another on the route to the Chaukan Pass. He had looted a few maps from Myitkyina before he left:

On one of the maps was a cartographers track traced across a map where the significant word 'unsurveyed' appears on more than one place, and where the contouring is so fine as to make it evident that the gent deputed to fill it in had no intention of committing himself too deeply.

RITCHIE GARDINER'S DIARY, BRITISH LIBRARY

---

80   Millar's account gives the figure of 120 porters.

He too had his doubts about Moses, whose stories had influenced the choice of route to which the group were now committed. John Leyden concurred:

> [He] asserted that he had travelled through the Chaukan Pass 18 months previously, and said that in the course of the journey he had slept only one night out of a village, and had done the complete journey in ten days.

Leyden was obviously sceptical of these claims, and wrote in his diary for 14 May:

> Talked to Moses. I find myself puzzled, his plausible talk and easy assurances nearly convince me that he has crossed the Chaukan though his information is contrary to all local information. Moses maintains that an advance party should get through in 12 days.

This was the new plan, to send two of the fittest men, with sufficient food, to make contact with the rescue party which was believed to be on its way. John Leyden and Millar the tea planter volunteered. With them went porters, a cook and a skilled elephant tracker. Leyden and Millar walked and slept in continuous heavy rain for the next 9 days and nights. As Millar wrote:

> We followed the course of the Nam Yak River up to the pass, crossing it 18 times on the day of reaching the Pass, which was the 19th. The going was extremely difficult, the river being fordable only with difficulty at several crossings. We therefore left a note on the Pass for Rossiter when he should arrive, advising him to conserve rations. The weaker members and women and children would have to make shorter marches. In truth from that time onwards I had grave fears as to whether any but the strongest members would be able to proceed more than 2 or 3 miles a day. It was therefore important that as few as possible be left behind to require rations over a longer period.
>
> DIARY OF MILLAR, INDIA OFFICE RECORDS, BRITISH LIBRARY

However, there was trouble ahead for the main party led by Sir John Rowland. After 10 days of walking in the pouring rain, they too reached the 8,000ft high Chaukan Pass, and the coolies refused to cross into India. Without them the walkers could not carry food for the larger section of the journey, which would take them through the mountains and down to the railway station at Ledo. In his diary Sir John wrote: 'Doubts now arose as to whether we were in the real Chaukan Pass as there was another saddle further south which seemed to be a mountain pass.'[81]

---

81   Diary of Sir John Rowland, British Library.

Ritchie Gardiner became addicted to his diary, and from this emerges a fantastical picture of the Chaukan Pass, which he described as a 'weird' place:

Heavily afforested by trees which are gnarled and look very old. They are frequently hollow at the base and their trunks and branches heavily festooned with moss which gives them an unearthly and depressing appearance, reminiscent of the forest in the Wizard of Oz. Huge rhododendron trees, not bushes, trees resembling elders and chestnuts, undergrowth mostly ferns and bracken: some orchids of which I hope to collect a few. What a relief to be here – we are actually in India by a few hundred feet. Party due from there tomorrow and will be very welcome as rations are dangerously low.

Although they had crossed the border the worst part of their journey lay ahead. The much slower group, including Rossiter and his wife and baby, arrived the next day. Despite the rain and cold they unfolded a white bed sheet, and tied it as a flag to the tallest tree, to mark their whereabouts to the rescue party which they believed was imminent. Another sheet was stretched out horizontally between bamboos. In the jungle ahead, Millar and Leyden were aware that they carried the responsibility for the lives of those behind them. The priority was to reach civilisation quickly. Millar described the magnitude of their burden:

Their survival appeared to me for the first moment to hang on our success or failure. It is not as though they were on a route – they were a party of men, women and children advancing through almost impenetrable country along a trail marked by us by scarring trees. An army of searchers might go out to meet them, but unless they could find our trail, it would be like searching for a needle in a haystack. Their compass course might well be a parallel route many miles away from our line decided on.

From the Chaukan Pass westwards the two men had to cut their way through thick bamboo jungle, along an 8,000ft high contour. The incessant rain had turned maps to mush and ruined cameras, binoculars and other equipment. Anything which they felt they could do without was jettisoned as they hacked their way through the wilderness, Millar wrote:

It was on occasion impossible to get a fire going to cook over, let alone to dry clothes. Of the leeches, blister flies and sand flies I cannot give adequate description, sufficient it is to say that we were getting into a mess. Leyden had a bad fall crossing the Langat River and required assistance over the stretches of difficult climbing which kept on occurring.

John Leyden doesn't mention this fall in his diary, which despite the rain he managed to preserve throughout the trek. The boulders they were forced to climb, were the size of the giant stones at Stonehenge, great cliffs of stone rising from the swollen rivers. The 26 May 1942 was one of the worst days for the two men on whom so much depended:

> Terrible time, bad feet from leech bites and our shoes have given out under the strain of so much rock climbing and water. The people behind must be having a dreadful time as many were inadequately shod. Shoes must be sent for them as soon as we get in. A tiger walked in front of us for some distance before swimming the Diyun [River], Sambhur let us come within 25 yards of them before moving away in a leisurely manner.

These reclusive deer were unaware of the danger posed by humans, and when the elephant tracker managed to shoot one of the herd, the rest did not honk their distinctive alarm call, and showed no fear while the men butchered the kill. Their Nung porters ate the meat raw, a sensible option as fires were so difficult to light. Misa, John Leyden's spaniel also fed well that day, before hurtling into a gorge.

The next day, the obstacles grew worse as did the men's physical health. Food was almost gone and they had not reached the Dapha River, which was the key to finding a route down to the plains. Leyden was suffering from a fever. Millar wrote:

> Progress down the side of the Dehing [River] was tortuous. A maze of large boulders some 15 feet in height average, with deep pools between, and in places where the gorge rose sheer it became work for trained climbers, and our fears for the porters carrying loads were not without cause. Our shoes were now all beyond use, and we daily carried strings of cane wound round our middles as a supply for our feet en route. Without this cane bound round our feet we should have been unable to proceed.

To the east they could see the Dapha Bum[82], a mountain 15,000ft high covered with fresh snow. According to the 2in. maps which they had been using, the Dapha River should be in front of them, but the river reputed to be a sizeable torrent, eluded them. On 31 June the men ate their last rice. In the middle of the afternoon they found the elusive Dapha River: it was indeed a torrent, with no apparent crossing point. Dejected they slumped by a rock without food or hope.

The group behind them were in equally bad shape, but had more food. Ritchie Gardiner wrote on 28 May: 'Can't keep warm. I used to like rice; now I loathe

---

82   Bum is the Burmese word for mountain

the sight of it. I have never eaten bamboo shoots until a week ago but can't say I relish them either.'[83]

With the lingering uncertainty that this really was the Chaukan Pass, they hung on for 5 days, until a group of Indian soldiers arrived and joined forces. As Eddie Rossiter wrote to his mother:

> They agreed to accompany us on – we estimated it was 20 days on to the nearest village. Anyway we started off – no road or even a path, we had to cut the jungle down as we progressed. We continued around mountain spurs crossing many small mountain torrents and all the time in pouring rain. After two days we reached a large river which we had been searching for as we had to have some landmark to find our way and to follow – else we should have penetrated into mountains and probably reached nowhere. The route along the river was awful, at times we were up to our chests in deep fast water, at times rocks stopped us – huge boulders – and we had to climb up the banks and over the rocks, at times we would go up 500 or more feet to get to the other side of the rock – down the same height to the water again. At times huge landslides caused us to make wide detours. Anyway on 11 June we arrived at a place where on account of a river further progress became impossible.
>
> EDDIE ROSSITER TO HIS MOTHER, INDIA OFFICE RECORDS, BRITISH LIBRARY

There they waited, forced to survive on 'skilly soup' a concoction of their pooled rations. A teacup of soup at midday and a teacup at night kept them alive, but for how long? Ritchie Gardiner was one of those who decided to explore the possibility of crossing the river. He described 12 June as 'definitely our worst day so far':

> After a very wet and uncomfortable night we were all inclined just to lie as the river was still up. Attempted to fell a tree, men went off in pairs one up and one down stream. Dangerous crossing found lower down in which several of them had fallen. We decide to attempt it at once and set off at 4 o'clock. Boyt, McCrindle, Howe and I were able to do it without serious trouble. Jardine was frightened to make it and Pratt fell in twice and had a narrow shave from being washed away. Then Fraser fell in and got wedged by a very strong current between a log and a rock. Only his head was above water and he was being badly battered. Sawyer apparently could do nothing to help so I took off my pack and went back, but even with Sawyer failed to release him. Sawyer himself was rather shaken by this time so I told him to go on and make the crossing. He was practically over when he went in and was very rapidly carried down out

---

83   Diary of Ritchie Gardiner, British Library.

of control. I was more occupied with Fraser and none of the others on the far
bank could do anything. He disappeared round a corner in a few seconds. Fraser
by this time had no strength at all and I had practically none left, but I released
his pack and for some reason or other the log wedging his legs shifted slightly,
just sufficient for our joint efforts to release him. Neither of us could face the
crossing again so made our way back to the bank, like a couple of drunken men
both absolutely numb with cold and weak as kittens. We were lucky to find the
fire still in and wood to build it up, so stripped to the nude and got half dry and
warm which served to bring us round.

Sawyer's body was never found, although one sock was found further downstream,
thought to be his. Despite the loss of their companion, Ritchie Gardiner was
frantic to retrieve the rucksack which was wedged halfway across the river:

> There were ten tins of rice in the pack and the river threatening to rise again.
> Fired a shot which summoned Boyt and McCrindle to the other bank but
> they indicated that none of the party would risk coming back to get my kit. I
> made the crossing again, picked up my kit and arrived safely to learn no trace
> of Sawyer. The loss of his pack put us back very seriously in the rations line, as
> he had a tin of cheese, some butter, marmite and all the salt. We had also lost
> Fraser's pack with 6 packets biscuits, a tin of cheese, a tin of butter, a bottle of
> marmite and some ghee. The position is we have ten people now (including
> servants) with enough food for about seven days allowing ½ cigarette tin of
> mouldy rice and one biscuit (also very mouldy), one very weak cup of marmite
> and about ½ ounce cheese per man per day, also very little milk and tea.

The survivors' named their camp after their dead companion. It was the most
inhospitable site so far, little more than a swamp. Fraser was still on the far side
of the river, but crossed safely the following day, and as a bonus shot a python so
snake cutlets livened up their diet.

The group who had stayed put with Sir John Rowland were conserving their
energy as their supplies ran out. Planes passed overhead but the monsoon cloud
and rain made visibility poor. Sir John wrote in his diary, 'Planes don't appear
to respond to signals'. On the afternoon of 25 June the Dehing River rose even
higher, flooding their campsite. In torrential rain they moved their saturated
belongings, salvaged remnants of shelters and regrouped on higher ground.
For 5 miserable days they watched the skies, and prayed to their various gods.
On 1 July a plane rained manna from the skies, but the stranded group were
so weak that retrieving the sacks of food was slow and painful. That evening
four Gurkhas arrived, the vanguard of the relief party. Leyden and Millar had
got through and help was on the way, although there was still a lot of jungle
between them and civilisation.

Assam tea planter Gyles Mackrell was checking rations as they were unloaded at his jungle camp at 5pm on 4 June. Two runners arrived carrying an SOS message from Leyden and Millar who had got as far as what the British called Simon, more properly Saw Am. Grabbing a bottle of whisky, Mackrell left and reached them 2½ hours later. The whisky must have been the best they had ever tasted. Both men were very weak and tired, but had kept notes of their route in their diaries. Mackrell, who knew the area, immediately saw a quicker way to take his rescue party, but first he had to send out for elephants, traditionally resting at this time of year. It took him 2 days to gather a team of twenty elephants and set off. With him was Millar's faithful tracker, Gohain Apana, who had done the journey once, but agreed to return to rescue the others. By now the rivers were so high that even elephants found them a challenge, and one was washed downstream landing on the far bank. Although the region is uninhabited, Mackrell encountered some Mishmi fishermen who agreed to lead him via wild elephant tracks to the main landmark, the Dapha River. Above them rose trees 150ft high. On the third day of the rescue mission, Mackrell wrote in his diary:

All this time it was pouring with rain, bush and bamboo overhead had to be cut away to allow the loads to pass under. The elephants were slipping and sliding down slopes of red clay soil, and scrambling up the other side, loads were constantly shifting as all were overloaded, and the pads merely haulage pads and not strong enough for big loads. By 8pm when it was almost dark we had not reached a place where we could possibly camp. The whole ground was swarming with leeches and there was no water for our number of elephants. Wild elephant tracks and bison tracks everywhere and more leeches than ever if that were possible. When it became totally dark we lit what few hurricane lamps we had and carried on with the grass cutters walking in front, or rather climbing in front of their elephants and the leading mahout using my torch. Gohain Apana and I walked behind the Mishmi guide and stopped every 15 minutes to take off leeches which usually numbered 40-50 by that time. I found later that the best way to deal with them was to carry a pair of nail scissors and snip them off. One had heard that leeches were not active at night and these certainly were although not so bad as they are in the day. At night one only seems to get the ground level leech while by day the incredible plant leeches, green and brown stick out from the scrub about waist high and get in ones' sleeves and down one's neck.

MACKRELL COLLECTION, CENTRE OF SOUTH ASIAN STUDIES,
UNIVERSITY OF CAMBRIDGE

When they found a stream with sufficient water for the elephants, they wrapped themselves in tarpaulins and attempted to sleep.

On 17 June Mackrell and his rescue party reached the formidable Dapha River to find sixty-eight other refugees stranded on a small island in mid-stream. The water level was rising with every hour, and they had been marooned there without food for a week. Mackrell wrote in his diary:

> I made several attempts to get over but it was utterly impossible as the river was flowing at a really terrific rate, being swollen with snow water and rain combined, and the force of the water had washed all the shingle out, leaving no binding between the boulders which were loose and moving on the bottom. The thunder of the water made speech impossible.

After several abortive attempts to bridge the river with trees, Mackrell gave up and set up camp. At 2am he was woken up by 'a different tune in the roar of the water'. The levels were falling. By midday all sixty-eight men had been carried across the river by Mackrell's elephants. Survivors told Mackrell of a European with two daughters aged 12 and 14 and a son aged 10, who were also making their way down from the Chaukan Pass.

Unaware that rescue was a few days away, Ritchie Gardiner and others woke up on 19 June to a dry day and a clear sky with a single large star shining in the east:

> We have never seen a sign like it yet and it served to cheer me up, though we have been disappointed before. Met some Mishmis with news of Mackrell and party at Dapha Wa only 2 days away. I can hardly look at these men without wanting to shake hands, it is such an indescribable relief to know (or hope) that out chief worries are over, even though we may have a couple of nasty days ahead yet. Put up a prayer of thanks.

Gyles Mackrell stubbornly ignored orders that he should give up the search for refugees who had attempted the foolish route via the Chaukan Pass. Eddie Rossiter and his family were rescued on 5 September, and Sir John Rowland and his group, later that month. Rossiter's wife, Nang Hmat, gave birth to a daughter Eileen on 12 December 1942 in India.

Ritchie Gardiner was awarded the Gallantry Medal for risking his life in the attempt to save Sawyer, and tea planter Gyles Mackrell was awarded the George Medal. Another of the group, Kendall, died in hospital in India having survived the journey, and out of the eighty-five Indians who were rescued, fifteen died later. Approximately 300 people are believed to have attempted the journey over the Chaukan Pass. It is not known how many of them survived.

17

The Lost Chinese

In June 1942 a young Englishman, Eric Lambert, mounted an expedition to find the remnants of the Chinese Fifth Army lost in the jungles of Burma. These were men who had fought alongside the British during the precipitous retreat, but as the Japanese invaders swept up to Bhamo and then Myitkyina, they found the way home blocked. Like thousands of civilians the Chinese soldiers had no maps and no food. Unable to take a route northeast from Myitkyina to the Chinese border, they were forced to go northwest, along the plains, then over the mountains into the dreaded Hukawng Valley. The 2,500 Chinese were posted as missing somewhere in the regions' dense jungles.

Jungle in the hills near the Hukawng Valley.

The Chinese had a radio transmitter but thanks to the deep valleys and steep shoulders of the hills around them, only a few weak signals had been picked up by fellow Chinese at Kunming. So concerned about their fate was Nationalist leader Chiang Kai Shek, that he sent his cousin to India to coordinate the search. At the beginning of June, 2 weeks after the opening of the rainy season, they were located on the Upper Chindwin near Dalu. This was 32-year-old Eric Lambert's pre-war stamping ground. As a police officer he had been given the job of surveying the densely forested area between the Upper Chindwin River and Assam, as part of a plan to stamp out the Naga tribal practice of headhunting. His network of local contacts and his knowledge of the terrain would save the Chinese from almost certain death. By mid-June an alternative plan was mooted. The Chinese should hunker down in the forests, and supplies would be air-dropped to them until the monsoon was over and they could travel more easily. There were several cogent grounds to reject this idea, the most pressing was the shortage of planes to supply them. Plus pilots had to contend with low cloud, heavy mists and the resulting poor visibility to fly such missions. The alternative was to launch a rescue attempt.

So keen were the Allies to find the Chinese that Lambert was given a pilot and a plane, at a time when aircraft were in short supply. It was one of the few occasions when the proverb 'looking for a needle in a haystack' really did apply. They skimmed over thousands of square miles of jungle, where trees stood up to 150ft tall, weaving a dense canopy over the ground below. Eric Lambert wrote later:

> The chap with whom I did all the aerial recces within this connection, and the attempt to find the poor devils, was Group Captain Roberts. He is very glad not to be doing another monsoon in eastern India he says. Roberts has lots of guts too, and we had some pretty risky flying over those hills. The most exciting thing was swooping down in a plane with a hook on the wheel axle trying to pick up a message written on a piece of paper and strung on a piece of string between two bamboos. I forget how many runs we made over the target before we finally got the message but the trouble was that there were high bamboos which obstructed our flight in both directions and it was very difficult to get down in the angle between and get up again without stalling the engine. I shall never forget when on the 12th run we picked up a bit of bamboo on the hook instead of the letter and later on a bit of grass.
>
> CENTRE OF SOUTH ASIAN STUDIES, UNIVERSITY OF CAMBRIDGE

This ingenious device was also used by refugee camps such as Shinbwiyang to exchange messages with the air force when they made airdrops. As he scouted the area Lambert discovered the whereabouts of the Chinese, but the next problem was how to extricate them from the jungle without upsetting the local tribes. He drew maps of a route from their temporary camp at Dalu to Shinbwiyang, the tiny Naga settlement which had grown into a refugee camp and today is a town on the Ledo Road. These were air-dropped to the Chinese and the tattered remnants of the Fifth Army started their long march.

However, Lambert was apprehensive about the impact 2,500 soldiers would have when they arrived in tiny tribal villages in this border country. The Burmese peoples have had a long and complex relationship with their Chinese neighbours. The long mutual border has led to an influx of Chinese immigrants over the centuries. The 'old Chinese,' as the Burmese refer to this section of the population, are not numerous, and are woven into the fabric of modern Burma. The so-called 'new Chinese' are buying up plots of land and building distinctive houses of ceramic and chrome in a style alien to the wood, brick and plaster homes of their hosts. In 1942, the Chinese were volunteered by Nationalist leader Chiang Kai Shek, to reinforce British and Burmese troops after the Japanese invasion. Most extraordinary of all, the 'Generalissimo', as he was known, agreed that the American General Joe Stilwell, would command these Chinese forces.

Like their Japanese counterparts, the Chinese had no medical or supply teams and lived off the land. Examples of looting by Chinese soldiers are quoted in many contemporary accounts of the withdrawal and evacuation, and Eric Lambert was aware that this could cause friction, and make Naga villagers uncooperative in his rescue mission, and in future operations against the enemy. Naga chiefs were not the only ones wary of a large body of armed Chinese descending on their patch. The Indian Tea Planter's Association, to whom so many refugees owed their lives, were also reluctant to have their camps exposed to this 'dangerous armed rabble'. His solution was what he refers to as 'the desperate expedient' of using a much more difficult route which he had pioneered 7 years earlier. It meant bridging several rivers in spate, and cutting steps in mountain paths to take the troops over two high passes. Any villages close to the route would have to be protected from the Chinese by bamboo palisades put up round their perimeter. With a team of porters from various tribes, plus interpreters, some Chinese and Indian troops, and two British radio operators, Lambert left base on 24 June.

The rainy season had started 5 weeks earlier, and paths were slippery. At night the expedition camped in villages en route, but Lambert still had to warn the inhabitants to evacuate in case the Chinese who accompanied him misbehaved, normally while they were hunting for alcohol. A day after starting out, ten of the porters were sick, and six of the Indian soldiers had gone down with malaria. After 2 days, there were further problems as other porters vanished back into the jungle to protect their families from the impending return of the rescued Chinese. Without enough porters, Lambert was forced to leave behind vital supplies, and efforts to spread out white sheets to show aircrews where to drop supplies, had so far failed. After 4 days, the party had experienced half an hour of dry weather. Their rice was beginning to grow mould as there were few waterproof bags, and the original team of porters was down from 145 to

105, thanks to desertions and illness. The one glimmer of hope was receipt of a message asking for a dropping zone to be cut on a nearby peak, Okhutchap. But Lambert knew this was fruitless. The mountain was surrounded by particularly dense jungle and it would take several days to clear a patch of solid jungle large enough to be visible from the air.

Five days after setting out, Lambert's expedition was over the top of the 4,000ft high Patkoi mountains, and in Burma. At a tiny hamlet they heard that two Europeans and twenty soldiers had been seen approaching, but still no sign of the Chinese. Supplies were running out and there had been no sign of any planes despite a break in the rain. On 2 July, 9 days after leaving base, a United States plane dropped supplies and they managed to retrieve 108 bags from the jungle. In his diary Lambert confided that there was not enough rice, no cooking oil, salt, sugar and most important of all that British and Asian staple of daily life, tea. The following day a message got through that once they found the lost Chinese, a supply line had been laid for them to enable rescuers and the rescued to reach safety across the border. Another wire from headquarters suggested that if they had not managed to track down the Chinese by 5 July, Lambert should return and leave the rescue to the Chinese who had accompanied him. The next day Lambert went down with a raging fever.

Still unwell but with a couple of days rest, Lambert continued and on 13 July found the lost Chinese, but he still had to get them safely out of the Naga Hills. On the outward journey he had asked village headmen to shore up rickety bridges and warned them to build stockades and camps for 2,500 men on the return journey. This was dependent on the cooperation of the Chinese as well as villagers. To his horror, as he led them via this new and dangerous route, he found the undisciplined Chinese made camp adjacent to the villages rather than at designated camp sites built for them. Although Lambert's 1935 expedition had surveyed the area, its ostensible purpose was to eliminate the headhunting practice. He wrote in his diary on 4 July after a conversation with two tribal chiefs:

> They say all is quiet their way and they haven't taken or lost a head for two years. The Donghi-Lumnu[84] struggle still continues. Last January Hapon made a pact with Lumnu and together they laid an ambush in Donghi's fields close to Kachu, the Rangpang 'Garden of Eden' and took one head. Last month two Hapon men went to Donghi to purchase grain. They were seized by the village, and handed over to the womenfolk of the Donghi men killed in January, and duly sacrificed.

---

84   Two local tribes.

Interlopers in Naga territory were right to be wary! As the expedition hacked its way through the jungle, built six bamboo suspension bridges and climbed steep mountains, the condition of many of the Chinese soldiers deteriorated. Those who died were buried in the jungle. The remainder tramped on, many barefoot as Chinese Army footwear was not as robust as the ammunition boots favoured by the British. At each village they passed, sentries were posted to prevent an influx of Chinese looking for food. Only one incident of bloodshed occurred throughout the trek, and that was due to the language barrier. Interpreters travelled with Lambert and there was a Chinese liaison officer who spoke English, however without them the incident happened in minutes. As had become routine along the route, Chinese sentries were posted in a village cornfield. The village headman misunderstood their presence, and thinking they were planning to camp among the corn stalks, he lost his temper. Drawing his sword and shouting, he gesticulated at the sentry, who stepped away, stumbled and his rifle went off. The bullet ricocheted off the headman's sword and wounded him slightly in the shoulder. Compensation was negotiated by an interpreter and no headhunting resulted.

After 3 weeks, the exhausted Chinese and their rescuers arrived at base. Eric Lambert's forty-three day expedition was a triumph. He was feted as a hero and flown to China where he received the Chinese Army Medal First Class, a rare honour for an Englishman.

Epilogue

The Burmese term for those who die an unexpected or violent death is 'green ghosts' and they are said to remain on earth as malevolent spirits. Burma is a land where every rock and tree is imbued with a spirit, and talking to ghosts is as natural as saying your prayers. In the borderlands between India and Burma, the whispers of thousands of green ghosts mingle with the calls of birds and insects, but the sound will be heard by few as the vast area is still largely uninhabited. Foreigners are prohibited in the mountainous border country which is under military control as is the Hukawng Valley, final resting place of so many.

In hindsight it is all too easy to view the hurried exodus from Burma as a tragedy of errors; to criticise the governor for failing to evacuate non-essential personnel by sea before the fall of Rangoon; to marvel at the hubris which encouraged the British belief that Upper Burma would be held; and to be horrified by the casual racism evinced by so many in this story. However, events in the Burma of 1942 moved so swiftly, and the country is so vast, that it is doubtful the outcome could have been very different. Those who died paid for the mistakes of those in charge, as refugees still do today, except now we have a name for it, collateral damage.

The death toll of civilian refugees trying to escape from the Japanese will never be fully known, even the exact number who completed the journey is uncertain. A report to the British War Cabinet in August 1942 estimated that half a million people were successfully evacuated. But rescue parties were still discovering refugees bedraggled but alive in the mountains in November that year.[85] As survivors regrouped in India, Angus MacLean became the Evacuee Welfare Officer and received letters from those trying to trace the fate of friends and relatives, as well as looking after the welfare of those in the camps. Among his papers is one story that justifies the hasty flight of thousands, and condemns the lack of leadership from the government in ordering the evacuation of women. Some seventy to ninety refugees, stuck in an unnamed camp near the Burma border, fell into the hands of

---

85   1,127 refugees were brought in during September, October and November 1942. Governor's Report on the Evacuation of Burma, British Library.

the Japanese. The correspondent was trying to discover what happened to her sister, Gwen, and had been told by a survivor, Mrs Henderson, that:

> The Japs started their beastliness towards the women. Six young women, among them ... Gwen resisted all Jap advances. They were horribly mistreated, disfigured, hair cut off, and slashed but evidently not killed outright. She does not know what happened to Gwen whether she died or was taken away, but she was in a bad condition. (I pray she died). Her daughter was still alive when the British came in and drove the Japs out. About 30 people left were brought into India. Mrs Henderson's daughter died in hospital in India.
>
> ANGUS MacLEAN PAPERS, CENTRE OF SOUTH ASIAN STUDIES,
> UNIVERSITY OF CAMBRIDGE

There are a handful of accounts of the mistreatment of refugees on the road. Japanese soldiers were more likely to rob them of clothing, food and valuables than to maim or kill, although undoubtedly such robbery would have contributed to deaths along the route as food was so scarce. Compassion on the road was another scarce commodity during the scramble to escape, but there are exceptions. As a survivor himself, Angus MacLean recorded one example of a Burmese woman and her children who had trekked out along the same route as himself and Fred Tizzard. A few days from Imphal she came across two British soldiers who were extremely sick and had decided they couldn't walk any further. Nevertheless she stopped and set up camp nearby, cooked some rice gruel and persuaded them to share the food. This unnamed Burmese woman was risking the lives of her children and herself by such an unselfish action, but after a couple of days, the soldiers and their saviour restarted the journey. All survived.

The number of refugees who completed the journey is based largely on those who sought help from the Indian government. The Evacuees Reception Committee in Calcutta looked after 297,000 who made the journey overland. Another 67,000 travelled by boat from Rangoon to Calcutta in the early stages of the invasion,[86] but there is no record of passenger numbers before tickets were issued in an orderly fashion. Those who did not ask for help from the Indian government were not recorded and therefore not counted. Thousands more died in their attempt to escape. Refugee casualty figures are also muddied by cholera epidemics during the crisis, particularly at Mandalay. The governor's official report estimates that 10,000 people died during the exodus. However, Alastair Tainsh who was in charge of just one route, believed the figure was much higher. He went back along the track between Shinbwiyang and Margherita 6 months later and counted skulls lying on the track. In 96 miles he counted 1,700 corpses. After this

---

86   Governor's Report on the Evacuation of Burma, British Library.

pilgrimage and by questioning hundreds of refugees he was convinced that at least 18,000 men, women and children died on that route alone. This does not include those who died at Shinbwiyang Camp itself or in other places further down the Hukawng Valley. A death toll of such proportions makes sense when 40,000 people are believed to have set out from Myitkyina to walk to India, and it's estimated that 20,000 arrived. Once they reached their goal many succumbed to dysentery, respiratory diseases, exhaustion, heart failure and malaria. At the time army medic Brigadier Shortt summed up the health of those who survived the journey:

> Complete exhaustion, physical and mental, with a disease superimposed is the usual picture... all social sense is lost and they suffer from bad nightmares and their delirium is a babble of crossings, of mud and corpses... emaciation and loss of weight are universal; four stone is a usual figure for a well-built European. Considering what they had endured by way of privation and physical strain, it is nothing short of a miracle that so large a number came through alive.
>
> QUOTED IN GENERAL WOODS REPORT, BRITISH LIBRARY

Those who survived were quick to condemn the lack of communication between military and civilian authorities. Commissioner of Evacuation Jack Vorley gave one salient example, suggesting that 10 days' notice of the army's intention *not* to hold Upper Burma would have enabled him to organise supplies on the routes from Mandalay. Angus MacLean was one of many who condemned the lack of guidance given to civilians in positions of authority about the gravity of the situation. The army was unprepared for, and overwhelmed by, the swift and efficient advance of the Japanese, and once Rangoon was abandoned they lost the means to supply and reinforce. Troops on the retreat were often ill-disciplined and terrorised civilian refugees. Once they arrived in India, they were then expected to defend her eastern border from invasion. Fortunately the monsoon prevented the Imperial Japanese Army from advancing any further than the mountains, and they retired to consolidate their occupation.

Survivors of the trek lost everything when they abandoned the Golden Land, and thousands spent the rest of the war in refugee camps scattered across India, segregated, naturally, by their racial origins, others found temporary homes with friends. Fred Tizzard describes Calcutta as full of refugees as he wrote in his faithful maroon leather diary in December 1942:

> When yesterday, Mrs Havoc of Inya Road passed in the street without seeing me, I did not stop her. Pride maybe – or perhaps one avoids Burma folk because the only topic is what we did at the end.

It was an ignominious end to colonial days in Burma, after which many abandoned life in the East completely and made the dangerous journey home.

One was Mrs Kendall whose husband had survived the perilous walk over the Chaukan Pass, but had died in hospital before the couple could be reunited. On the voyage home her ship was torpedoed by the Japanese, and she and her son spent 13 days in an open lifeboat before they were rescued.

Gerry Halpin and his siblings were among those who spent long weeks in hospital recovering from the trek. Once they did, work was the first priority. Gerry soon found a job in a sawmill and although he returned to Burma after the war, it was in England that he made his life and brought up his family. Like many Burma refugees, the Halpins found themselves transported from a comfortable life with a substantial house and servants, to a council flat in post-war austerity Britain. Forestry men like Geoff Bostock and Jimmie Williams utilised their expertise for the benefit of the army. Jimmie went back into Burma to covertly lead out several hundred elephants which were used by the Royal Engineers to build bridges. Among those bridge-builders was a young subaltern, Stephen Goodall.

Other old Burma hands who spoke the languages and knew the country, were recruited to work behind the lines. Fred Tizzard was attached to Fourteenth Army headquarters and recruited 1,160 Burmese irregulars who served in the campaigns in the Arakan. A few published accounts of their escape in magazines and books, but there were so many war stories of escape and heroism that this predominantly civilian story was largely ignored. With peace in 1945 came the return of troops, prisoners of war, revelations of the holocaust in Germany, and the ordeal of those on the Thai–Burma railway. Wartime rationing in Britain was extended to help feed the continent, and the desire to rebuild lives and forget the privations of conflict was overwhelming. With the anaesthetic of peace, the story of the long walk out of Burma was just one extraordinary tale among thousands. This was no time to dwell on the sadness of the past, but time to plan for the future. For Burma that meant independence and civil war, for Britain loss of empire and its many consequences.

For Fred and Marjorie Tizzard it meant return to England where Fred became an insurance agent in Wales. The couple had planned a future in Burma with their daughter Rosemary Ann. For 300 footslogging miles it was the thought of his baby daughter which had kept Fred going. When he finally arrived in Calcutta and tracked down Marjorie, it was to discover that Rosemary had died 6 weeks earlier, and was buried in a small grave in Tollygunge Cemetery, Calcutta.

There were those who returned to Burma to work on reconstruction in the months after the war, and a few who stayed on as the country claimed independence. Still in the years since, many Burmese have hankered after the 'days of the British' and the ordered society over which they presided. Crossing the border between India and Burma in the great exodus of 1942, there were many who gazed wistfully back and said, 'Poor old Burma'. One mused, 'What did we ever do for Burma? I suppose at least we gave them football.'

Select Bibliography

Fischer, Edward, *Mission in Burma, The Columban Fathers 43 Years in Kachin Country*, The Seabury Press, 1980

Myint U, Thant, *The River of Lost Footsteps*, Faber, 2008

Seagrave, Gordon, *Burma Surgeon*, W.W. Norton and Co., 1943

Slim, Field Marshal Sir William, *Defeat into Victory*, Cassell and Co., 1956

Thompson, Julian, *Forgotten Voices of Burma*, Ebury Press, 2009

Vorley, J. and H., *The Road from Mandalay*, Wilton, 2002

Williams, J.H., *Elephant Bill*, Penguin, 1950

For a military history of the first Burma campaign see, *A Hell of a Licking: The Retreat from Burma 1941–42* by James Lunt, Collins, 1986.

Index

Explore more about Burma during the Second World War

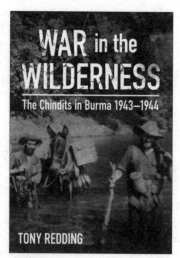

978-0-7524-6078-9
£25.00

978-0-7524-6401-5
£18.99